CONFESSIONS
OF A DANGEROUS MIND

Also by Chuck Barris

You and Me, Babe

CONFESSIONS
OF A DANGEROUS MIND

an unauthorized autobiography by

Chuck Barris

miramax books

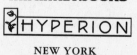

NEW YORK

This book is dedicated to my agent Jennifer Lyons,
to Jonathan Burnham and all the gang at Miramax Books,
to Harvey Weinstein for having the guts to make the film,
to George Clooney for giving the film so much life,
to my sister Riki Wagman for all her help and
to my wife Mary for her never-ending encouragement.
Most of all to Andrew Lazar for never giving up.

There is far too great a disproportion
between what one is and what others
think one is, or at least what they say
they think one is. But one has to
take it all with good humor.
—Albert Einstein

CONFESSIONS
OF A DANGEROUS MIND

Prologue

God, how time has passed.
How can a whole lifetime
pass so quickly with so
little done?
                    —Iris Murdoch

One

It was June 1980, and I was standing in front of a full-length mirror studying my body. What I saw didn't please me. My face was full of deep wrinkles and lines, while the top of my forehead sported hairless patches of skin; vacant and deathly white chunks of scalp that, I realized with a certain amount of terror, could no longer be camouflaged by deft parting and combing. It was very depressing.

"You're a television star," I told myself. "You're a celebrity. They know you all over, nationally and internationally. *Too* many people know you. You rarely have any peace and quiet." I forgot my point. I think I was trying to pep myself up. If that was my purpose, it wasn't working. I was still depressed. Mostly because I looked so awful.

My eyes were crusted with glop, and the hairs in my nostrils were long enough to braid. I saw slabs of flabby meat hanging over the elastic band of my boxer shorts.

I saw liver spots. And warts.

I examined my toes and knuckles, a familiar collection of bulbous and inflamed joints that ached in fair weather as well as foul. I twisted my back and suffered the customary stab of pain in my coccyx, aggravated by sleeping on the soft mattress I was addicted to. The bursitis in my shoulder throbbed. My pot belly was beyond repair; exercising would be a waste of time. The bedraggled prick hanging between my legs was dark and thin and shriveled and dead, like a piece of overcooked bacon. And though I had left the toilet ages ago, the fucker was still dripping urine on the floor.

My fingernails were a disgrace, permanently blackened by my repeatedly stuffing them into the bowl of my pipe, a pipe clenched more often than not between cavity-infested teeth. My asshole itched. My knees hurt. My toenails were brittle and chipped, making them razor-sharp and destructive. My cars were clogged. So were my sinuses.

I was not thrilled.

I walked away from the mirror and stumbled into a table with three small plants arranged neatly at its center. The table collapsed. The plants fell down onto the rug.

"Piss! Fuck! Shit!" I howled. An old fart baying at the moon.

I stared at one of the plants. It was a dainty thing in a little yellow pot. I drop-kicked the little yellow pot neatly through the window that overlooked the courtyard. The broken glass fell conveniently outside. I raised my arms over my head. The extra point was good! I had tied the football game in the last second of play. I jogged back to the bench, head down in false modesty.

Overtime.

Sudden death.

My team moved quickly into field-goal position. I slapped on my helmet and entered the game again. I stood forty-three yards from the goal line, my eyes fixed firmly on my right shoe. The hometown crowd was in a frenzy. Over one hundred thousand beautiful women and handsome men screamed, "CHUC-KEE, CHUC-KEE, CHUC-KEE!" I demanded silence. I needed to hear the signals. There was a hush. The football was snapped back and placed on its mark. I took the customary two and a half steps forward and booted the second little potted plant into the air. It bounced off my typewriter and splashed dirt and roots across my desk. Disgusted, I kicked the third potted plant into the face of my housekeeper, just entering through the open door. She dropped to the floor—her features dented, broken, and battered—and lay on her stomach, mouth open and lips curled back like a guppy. She was gurgling spittle and blood. She was unable to move, or close her eyes, or stop her bowels from emptying into her underwear. I was horrified.

Someone was playing a trombone, and the dreadful blaring bombarded the atelier. I fell to my knees and cradled my housekeeper's head in my arms.

She whispered, "Just wanted to know if there was anything I could do for you."

And then she died.

The trombone continued to honk, beginning to sound more and more like a car horn. It *was* a car horn, blasting repeatedly outside my bedroom window.

* * *

I awoke with a start.

Another nightmare.

I was covered with a cold, clammy layer of sweat. My T-shirt clung to my chest, the sheets to my legs. Would the rest of my nights be filled with nightmares and cold sweat? I had always enjoyed bedtime. Now I dreaded going to sleep. My dreams were like a gang of bad memories riding into my head every night to cause havoc; shoot up the joint; torment me; get even.

For what?

My heart was pounding. My head ached. The morning was beginning like all the others were these days: heart pounding, head aching, body damp and dank, mind confused and slightly frightened. Was I sick? Would I get better? Worse?

Another day.

My birthday.

I picked up the telephone by my bed, placed it on my stomach, and dialed my secretary.

"Hiya!" she said cheerfully.

I muttered good morning.

"Happy birthday!" said my secretary, with spirit.

I thanked her.

"How old are you now?"

"Fifty."

"Wow! That's old," she said, meaning no harm.

I took a moment to rummage through some thoughts.

"Hello?" said my secretary, worried.

"I'm here, I'm here. Hold on." So it's June third, I mused. Time to go. "It's time to go," I said halfheartedly.

"Time to go?" repeated my secretary.

Was I still good? I wondered. I was obviously not as perfect, not as precise as I used to be. Had I become slow and rusty, or, even worse, careless? Burned out, as they liked to say?

"I'm going away," I told my secretary. "I'm going to take a little vacation. Everybody's getting on my nerves. Everything's getting me down. I just want to go somewhere and disappear for a while."

"Am I getting on your nerves?"

"No, you're not getting on my nerves, but everybody else is."

My secretary sighed.

"So," I continued, "just take care of things the way you always do when I go away. I'll let you know when I'm coming back."

"Do you want me to make any travel arrangements for you?"

"No, don't bother. I'll just go to the airport and hop on the first plane that interests me."

"Will you let me know where you are?"

"Maybe."

"Do you feel okay?" inquired my secretary, concerned.

"Why do you ask?"

"Just curious."

I said I was feeling a little depressed.

She said, "Grown-up birthdays are very depressing."

I mentioned that, considering the alternatives, grown-up birthdays aren't so bad.

My secretary said she had never looked at it that way.

Our conversation buzzed along at that extraordinary level for several more minutes. Then we exchanged good-byes, and I hung up.

I flopped back onto my pillows. I wanted to begin loathing the new day in comfort. The fact that I would soon be going out into the real world was acutely distressing. During the past few months I had grown more and more accustomed to staying home, safe and secure, in my apartment; my hobbit-hole, as I called it. I had learned, out of necessity, to entertain myself quite successfully within its confines for hours on end.

It was a small apartment. Four uninspiring rooms and a bath, on Peck Boulevard in Beverly Hills. *The* Beverly Hills. A source of perpetual awe and import to my family back in Philadelphia. ("Chuckie lives in Beverly Hills. You know. *The* Beverly Hills.")

The apartment house was a white stucco affair that reminded me of London. Its name—the Barclay House—sounded English. And the location was perfect. The apartment was four blocks from South Rodeo Drive, and the Beverly Wilshire Hotel. South Rodeo Drive was a wonderful street. It was full of important shops and stores that sold the necessities of life: tobacco, alcohol, literature, and good ice cream sodas. With the proper disguise, I could scurry down the street and around the corner to Dunhill's for a small cigar, or Brentano's bookstore for emergency reading material, or the Pink Turtle Coffee Shop (open until two in the morning) for a bottle of Scotch, a late-night sundae, or a piece of chocolate cake. Whatever else I didn't have, or might desire, others would bring me. My housekeeper brought groceries and tended to my laundry and cleaning. My secretary was responsible for the record albums I requested, the gadgets, the clothes, the making and breaking of occasional dates, the personal mail and business correspondence. My newspapers and magazines were delivered.

And of course there were my possessions, those material things a recluse who has lived too long by himself comes to depend upon and cherish. There were my bed, my pillows, and my comforter, all of which

I had become less and less willing to share. There were my indispensable kitchen utensils, nestled in their appointed places. My cameras and guitars. My phonograph, adjusted to specific levels and never tampered with. And my work area.

The Womb.

It was in the Womb, surrounded by typewriters, dictionaries, synonym finders, and reams of Eaton bond paper, that I spent my happiest hours. It was there that I worked most of the days and half the evenings, attempting to write an autobiography tentatively titled *Confessions of a Dangerous Mind.* The book would hopefully act as a catharsis, exorcising from my mind and body the agonizing frustration, anger, and bitterness that had been brewing there for too long a time. Perhaps, upon completing *Confessions,* I would understand why some of my peers had been nailing me with such fury to the cross for trying to make people laugh, while others had been slipping me medals and presidential citations under the table for . . . well, anyway, as my grandmother would have said, go know.

Such fury. Such fury from critics I had never met and rarely understood. It was these critics—these strangers—who had accused me and my television shows of pandering to evil passions, of flourishing on the embarrassment of others, of orchestrating the emotions of vulnerable human beings to their own detriment, of being a Svengalian symbol of all that was wrong with commercial television, and more.

How did I fare against the never-ending critical lambasting I was subjected to? I became paranoid, that's how I fared. My chronic paranoia had eventually caused me to become a hermit. To wear a disguise in public. Lawrence Durrell wrote: "The sick men, the solitaries, the prophets, are all those who have been wounded." The solitaries. I had become one of them. Introverted, angry, depressed, monastic. Obviously not a very healthy attitude. And if one is not sound of mind, then one should not undertake dangerous assignments. That's why I was going to resign. The main reason, at least. But then what would I do?

Sunshine was creeping across my rug. It was almost seven-thirty. I sat on the edge of my bed, puffed an old cigar butt, and thought about what Bob Boone had said to Tug McGraw.

* * *

It was the World Series. Philadelphia versus Kansas City. Tug McGraw of the Phillies was pitching. It was the fifth game of the series, the bottom of the ninth, with the Kansas City Royals behind four to three. The Royals had the bases loaded with two out. Kansas City had

just won two straight games to tie the series, and now they had a chance
to win a third and go ahead of Philadelphia three games to two. The
game was being played in Kansas City. The ball park was packed. The
crowd of over fifty thousand frantic Kansas City fans were on their feet,
yelling their heads off. It was bedlam. In the middle of all that commo-
tion, Bob Boone, the Phillies' catcher, asked the umpire for a time out
and walked to the pitcher's mound. He said something to McGraw,
turned, and walked back to home plate. You know what he said? He
said, "Isn't this exciting?"

What a wonderful thing to be able to say.

* * *

It was now seven forty-five. I was falling behind schedule. I stood,
stretched, slipped my feet into a pair of oversized slippers, hitched up
my dark blue sweat pants, and shuffled into the kitchen to prepare a
bowl of dog food mixed with kibble for the bastard, Albert. I put the
bowl on the floor and shuffled back to the bedroom. I dressed, choosing
a navy blue sport shirt, jeans, a brown corduroy sport coat, black socks,
and a pair of blue and yellow Brooks sneakers. I went to the bathroom
and glued a mustache and beard to my face. I held the disguise in place
until the glue dried, then tested its strength by making several prepos-
terous grimaces. Satisfied that the beard was secure, I added sunglasses
and a golf hat. The golf hat was bright red with the word *Phillies*
stitched in white across the front. I looked at my face in the mirror
above the sink and smiled.

I left the bathroom, tidied my bedroom, and toured my apartment
to see if everything was properly arranged for my departure. I checked
the electric typewriter to make sure it was turned off. I opened certain
drapes and closed others. Specific lamps were lighted. To discourage
burglars, I increased the volume of my living-room radio. I stepped
outside and picked up the morning *New York Times,* hung a "keep out"
sign on the front door, then closed and locked it.

I returned to the bedroom and found my black leather Hermès
valise. I filled it with a tan summer suit, underwear, socks, two dress
shirts—one white and one blue—and a red-and-blue striped tie. Red
and blue were my school colors. I paused, clasped the tie against my
heart, stood erect, and sang:

> Hurrah, hurrah, Pennsyl-vay-nee-yaah.
> Hurrah for the red and the bluuuuuuue.
> Hurrah, hurrah, hurrah, hurrah.
> Hurrah for the red and the blue.

I always sang a few bars of my university alma mater whenever I donned, or packed, my red-and-blue striped tie.

I added a brown belt to the valise, a pair of brown loafers, and a Walther 9mm automatic and silencer. The gun, silencer, and two spare cartridge clips had already been wrapped in a lightly oiled cloth and stuffed inside a cellophane Baggie. (Actually I preferred a snub-nosed .38-caliber Smith & Wesson police pistol. It was a far more reliable weapon. Pistols didn't jam like automatics. But the Walther's silencer was the best.) I slid the Baggie into the middle of the valise, zipped the valise closed, and returned to the kitchen.

I called Albert.

The dog slunk into the kitchen, moribund and sullen. Albert was a large, shaggy animal, who could have been an attractive dog except for the fact that his head had stopped growing when he was a puppy. Albert's teeny head made him look ridiculous. It had also affected his personality. Albert thought himself an object of ridicule. Consequently, he was surly. I hated Albert, but was stuck with him. And he with me, I suppose. I was bound to the bastard simply because it was either keep him or gas him. (I wasn't the least bit against gassing him, mind you. What I *did* loathe was the paperwork. I despised the thought of taking the cur to the animal shelter and having to fill out all those odious forms.) So Albert lived. They say that a man and his dog ripen into similar appearances and personalities. What a fucking depressing thought.

I told Albert to leave, and opened the back door. Actually, I didn't speak to him, I shouted at him. I yelled, "Outside, you pinheaded son of a bitch!"

I attempted to kick Albert in the ass as he went by, but missed. It seemed that Albert had become an expert at judging his dash out the door and knowing when to tuck his hindquarters in under his belly. His timing had become phenomenal. Lately, I could only make contact with the son of a bitch's ass on an average of three out of every ten attempts, and just one of those three times with enough severity to warrant any personal gratification.

Once outside, Albert threw me a nasty look and disappeared around a corner of the building. I found my book and newspaper, inspected the apartment one last time, and departed. I exited through the back door, locked it, walked across the courtyard, and made my way to Rodeo Drive. I noticed that Albert was following me. I tossed a rock at the cocksucker. He sidestepped the missile, growled, and walked away. I turned to go on, but had a sudden pang of guilt. I had left the dog only enough food for one or two days, and I would be gone indefinitely. But it was all rather academic, since he would be unable to let himself back into the apartment. The pang passed quickly.

I walked up Rodeo toward Wilshire. Taxicabs lined the curb near the Beverly Wilshire Hotel. As I neared the circle of drivers, a cabbie named Little Lewie was saying, "No motherfuckers are playin' baseball in Europe or Africa or Antarctica, are they?" Little Lewie wore a gabardine cap that covered one-sixteenth of his Afro. "And no motherfuckers are playin' baseball in South America or China!"

"So what?" interrupted someone else.

"So why do they keep callin' the World Series, the *World* Series?" persisted Little Lewie.

"Excuse me," I said. "Has anyone seen the Duck?"

"Goin' away, Chuckie baby?" asked a cabbie named Struthers.

"How did you know?"

"You're wearin' your stupid hook-on beard."

All the cabbies cackled.

"Hey, man, I didn't know you was Chuckie baby," said another cabbie. "Shit, you sure had me fooled. I thought you was Kareem Abdul-Jabbar."

All the cabbies whooped and hollered and gave high-fives.

Once again I asked if anyone had seen the Duck.

Someone said he was in the Pink Turtle Coffee Shop.

I walked into the Turtle and met the Duck walking out. He was carrying a large container of black coffee. I said, "Hey, Duck, give me ten minutes to grab some breakfast."

The Duck said, "Yah," without looking up from his coffee.

The Duck was my least favorite cab driver. I disliked everything about him. He was always in a rotten mood, he smelled bad, and he was creepy-looking. His hair was long and stringy, with random chunks of it dyed white blond. His face was long and stringy, like his hair. The Duck's clothes were a combination of fine silk and old government-issue throwaways. His blouse was always unbuttoned to the navel. No one knew whether the Duck was an ugly man or an ugly woman. He could have passed for either. The cabbies would talk about the Duck behind his back. They would say, "What a strange motherfuckin' duck." That's how the Duck got his nickname.

I sat at the Turtle's counter, drank their rotten coffee, and opened my *New York Times*. But almost immediately I heard someone standing behind me say, "Hi! You're Chuck Barris, right?"

I looked up from my newspaper. I had to look farther up than I anticipated. The speaker was an enormously tall female. I said, "How did you know?"

"I could tell. That beard ain't worth dick. I could tell it was you. I said to myself, 'That's Chuck Barris with a dumb fake beard on his face.' " The girl was at least seven feet tall, with a low voice, little feet, and a rather large, festering sore on her upper lip. She said, "You're from Philadelphia, right?"

"Yes, I am," I replied. I *really* disliked being disturbed before I finished my morning coffee.

"I'm from Philadelphia too," the amazon bellowed. "How old do you think I am?"

"Twenty-two," I replied.

"Close. Twenty-three. I'm a hooker. At least I *was* a hooker. I come from a very rich family."

She stopped talking. I imagined I was supposed to say something, so I said, "Good."

"Anyway," she said, a bit breathlessly, "I think you're great. I loved you on television. Want a blow job? I'll give you one. I'm the best there ever was. Got any money on you?"

"No," I lied.

"Then I'll give you a freebie. Want a freebie?"

"I don't think so," I said, eyeing the congestion perched on her upper lip. "Not during breakfast, thank you."

"You don't know what you're passin' up, little fellow. My name's Daffodil Rosner." Her hand shot out to be shaked. I shook it. "But you know what they call me?"

"No. What?"

"The Monumental Suck."

"No kidding." I was beginning to like the tall girl with the low voice.

"Look, here's my room number," she said, writing it down on a paper napkin. "If you want me later tonight, give me a call. I'll meet you someplace and give you the best blow job you ever got in your entire life. Your *entire* life. I shit you not. I'll knock your socks off. Anyway, I think you're terrific. About a year ago I got raped and strangled by a pimp, the fuckhead, and when I was in the hospital, *you* cheered me up every single day. You made me laugh. I think you're terrific, or did I say that already? It doesn't matter. 'Bye. Remember, if you want the best head you ever got in your whole life, call me."

"Good-bye," I said, "and thank you."

As the Monumental Suck departed, she bumped into the Duck walking toward me. "I'm next," he said into my left ear.

I paid my check, walked out of the coffee shop, and entered the Duck's taxi. We drove to the airport.

On the way, the Duck said, "You're goin' to New York."

"Where?"

"New York," he repeated. "American Airlines, Flight Twenty-eight. It leaves at eight-thirty."

"How 'bout that? What am I going to do there?"

"You're gonna kill a wop named Moretti. Mario Moretti."

"Who?"

"What's the matter?" growled the Duck. "Your ears clogged or somethin'? I said you're gonna kill a wop named Mario Moretti. He's staying at the Plaza. Go straight there from the airport. There'll be a message for you at the hotel telling you what to do next. Here's some mugs on the guy."

The Duck held out a small manila envelope over the back of his seat and waved it impatiently.

"There's two pictures in there," said the Duck, "an old one and a new one. The new one is a wop police shot of the dude. He was in a lineup in Rome about a month ago. He's a short bastard—even shorter than you. He's only five feet tall." The Duck paused. "Think you can handle it?" he said. His eyes looked at me through the rearview mirror, then darted away.

"I think so," I said. I really hated the Duck. I never could understand why the Company recruited such filth. "What's this guy's rap?" I asked.

"I don't know, and frankly I don't give a fuck."

"You know something, Duck? You're a world-class asshole."

"Yeah? Well, let me tell *you* somethin'. I worry about you lately. You're not the hotshot gun you used to be. You're gettin' old." Once again he glanced at me through his rearview mirror. "You're a burn-out," he said, "and fuckin' burn-outs fuck up."

"Fuck you, asshole."

"Fuck you, too," said the Duck.

"You know what I'm thinking right now, Duck?" He didn't answer. "I'm thinking that when you stop at the next red light, I'm going to put a nice, fat hollow-point right through the back of your stupid head."

"Yeah, yeah," said the Duck, and then I heard him mumble to himself, "The cat's a fuckin' burn-out."

Christ, I thought to myself, even the low-life Duck hates my guts.

* * *

The airport was jammed with tourists. There seemed to be an inordinate number of cowboy hats, sandals, Hawaiian shirts, Mickey Mouse ears, Bermuda shorts, and stretch pants straining to cover gigantic asses. "A fucking sea of polyester," I muttered to no one in particular, and walked to the check-in counter marked *New York—Kennedy Airport—Departure 8:30 A.M.* There was a line. I dreaded tourists, and I dreaded waiting in lines. What I dreaded most of all was waiting in a line full of tourists. Which is exactly what I was doing.

"You a Phillies fan?" asked a cheery man standing behind me. He was fat, which accounted for his being cheery. He wore a high-school ring, and green-and-black checkered slacks.

I said I wasn't a Phillies fan.

"Then why are you wearing that hat?"

"None of your fucking business."

"Now lookee here, mister . . ."

I turned away from the dork, muttering profanities loud enough for him to hear. I was in a horrendous mood. My beard was itching me to death. And so was my asshole. The Duck had upset me, and now this fat farthead wanted to chat. When it was my turn, I said to the reservations clerk, "I think I have a prepaid ticket to New York waiting for me."

"Your name, sir?"

"Sunny Sixkiller."

Part One

Go out there. Do the
best you can. Then
fuck it.
　　　—Yogi Berra

Two

I guess it all started with the job interview in January 1963.

I hadn't worked for over eight months, and my unemployment was about to run out. My rent was overdue, my telephone disconnected, my wristwatch and guitars hocked. Unfortunately, the situation wasn't new to me. I had been in this sort of dilemma before—many times, as a matter of fact. It was almost becoming a way of life.

It seemed I was unable to hold a job past the month of May. In May I would develop terminal spring fever and immediately find fault with the company that had temporarily employed me. Either the position was too boring, or my boss was an asshole, or I would convince myself there wasn't any chance of advancement, and I'd quit. In the nine years since I'd graduated from college, I had been in six different positions, and God knows how many total months I had been unemployed. In 1963 I was thirty-three years old, a modern-day Willy Loman sauntering aimlessly into oblivion.

"Why do you *always* lose your job in May?" my sister had asked me over the telephone on the last of my many attempts to scrounge from her.

"A glandular reaction to the change of season. Probably genetic," I had answered.

"*I* don't do it. *I* don't quit jobs in May."

"You apparently escaped the curse."

"That's poppycock," she had snapped.

"Easy for *you* to say."

My sister always found time in her busy schedule to remind me of my small disasters and ineptitudes. "You've been out of work for *ages,*" she had said. "It's been eight months now. Doesn't that bother you? Aren't you the least bit concerned?"

"Yes," I had answered, "I'm concerned."

I was more than concerned. I was slightly desperate.

"Well, you're going to have to figure *something* out," my sister had said, making little effort to conceal her anger. "I can't afford to lend you another penny."

It was shortly after that telephone conversation that I saw the help-wanted ad.

COLLEGE GRADUATE: FREE TO TRAVEL

That was the headline on a small advertisement that appeared in *The Washington Square News,* New York University's weekly newspaper. At the bottom of the ad was a telephone number. I called, and a man with a no-nonsense voice answered the telephone. After rechecking my basic credentials—college degree, desire to work abroad, lack of any immediate entanglements—the man agreed to an interview.

He gave me a time and a place: nine o'clock the following morning, at an address on Washington Square South.

The next morning, at exactly eight-fifty, I stepped off a bus at the end of Fifth Avenue and turned onto Washington Square South, my hands jammed deep in my overcoat pockets, my chin tucked down into my scarf. I looked for the address among the identical four-story houses that faced the park. When I finally found the correct one, I noticed that the only difference between it and all the others was a small bronze plaque on its front door that read: *North American Center for the Arts.* The plaque confused me. I couldn't begin to guess what the Center did, or what I could possibly do for the Center.

Another waste of time.

I rang the doorbell, and a large man in his early fifties opened the door. He wore his hair in a brush haircut and stood erect, as if in a constant state of present-arms. The man wore a shirt and a tie, and a tan cardigan sweater instead of a suit coat.

He said, "Barris?"

I nodded.

The man nodded back. I stepped inside, and he shut the door behind me. He took my coat and scarf, placed them on a coat tree, and led me into a living room. The room was dark, gloomy, and crammed with Louis XIV furniture, most of which appeared strikingly uncomfortable. There was a conspicuously out-of-place desk jammed against a far wall. I was shown to a seat by the desk. I sat down and waited while the man in the cardigan sweater organized his papers.

When everything seemed to be in its proper place, he turned to me and said, "I am a recruiter for the Central Intelligence Agency."

"Jesus," I murmured.

"Pardon?" said the man.

"Nothing, sir," I replied, straightening into an erect, quasi-military posture.

"Are you familiar with the responsibilities of the Agency?"

"Yes, sir," I lied.

The CIA were spies, weren't they? I could become a goddamn spy! A secret agent! Fedora, trench coat, pearl-handled revolver. Paris, London, Rome, Singapore, Bangkok; running around Europe fucking one Mata Hari after another. Adventure, intrigue, romance, and God knows what else.

Patriotism! Of course. Patriotism, too. I would be serving my country. I couldn't recall any of my relatives ever serving their country. I'd be the first fucking patriot in the history of my entire family! But I wouldn't be able to tell them. I wouldn't be able to say that I was a spy, so how would my family and friends know? On the other hand, who cared if they knew? *I'd* know, and that would be all that mattered. Besides, I needed a job—any job. I was so excited my heart was pounding through my sport jacket.

"How would you feel about working for the government?" asked the man.

"I would like working for the government very much," I replied, hearing a slight crack in my voice. Then I told my second lie of the morning. "As a matter of fact, I've *always* wanted to work for the government."

The man in the cardigan sweater studied me, adjusting a large, lined notepad on his knee. Without letting his eyes leave my face, he reached across his desk, snapped on a tape recorder, and began the interview. For the rest of the morning, the man in the cardigan sweater asked me reams of questions, and I gave him reams of answers.

"Are your grandparents living?" was the man's first question.

"No. They're all dead."

"Were your grandparents born in America?"

"No. I believe they were all born in Europe."

"Did you get along with your grandparents?"

"Yes. I loved them all very much. Especially my grandmother on my mother's side."

* * *

I had always loved my grandmother, something I couldn't say for the rest of my relatives—and I had a lot of relatives. I was born into a large middle-class Jewish family that lived in a large middle-class Jewish neighborhood in West Philadelphia. My grandfather was a rich immigrant who had lost his fortune in the Wall Street Crash of '29—a year before my birth. That financial twist of fate wreaked considerable havoc with the family's collective psyche; bankruptcy, plus some rather foul play by Mother Nature, combined to produce an assemblage of diverse problems among my relatives. Most everyone suffered from something: severe hypochondria, acute sexual problems, an obsequious admiration of the wealthy, chronically whiny voices, and the longest noses of any Jewish family in America. To be sure, there were moments when my aunts and uncles and cousins were tolerable, but most of the time they gave me a splitting headache. (I understood my grandfather's attitude completely when he entered a room and said, "Hello, some of you.")

But my grandmother was a doll. Not a great looker, but a great lady. And she was a trooper. She loved to travel; she went anywhere without the slightest hesitation, and she was marvelous company. During the summer of 1953, I took my grandmother on a camping trip. We went to the Pocono Mountains of Pennsylvania. Just the two of us. (My grandmother was seventy-five at the time.)

We pitched a tent by Lake Wallenpaupack, not far from the town of Blooming Grove. We roasted weenies for lunch and, in the afternoon, took a long walk by the lake. That evening we had dinner in Blooming Grove and saw an early movie. Later we sat in front of our tent by a crackling fire and chatted for hours. That night my grandmother and I slept in goosedown sleeping bags under a starry sky, and in the morning when I awoke, she was dead.

I sat for hours looking at her. Then, when the sun was full on the lake, I packed our belongings into my Volkswagen. Our bags and camping equipment filled the entire backseat and most of the passenger seat, and I wondered how my grandmother had fit into the car in the first place. In any case, it was better this time if my grandmother lay horizontally. Sitting upright, she tended to slide from one side to the other. So I zipped her body into a sleeping bag, placed the bag on the roof of the Volkswagen, covered the bag with a tarpaulin, and tied everything securely in place with a length of heavy rope.

I drove to Blooming Grove and parked down the street from the police station. I went inside to report the death and to ask if there was a mortuary nearby.

While I was inside the police station, someone stole my car.

* * *

"Are your parents living?" asked the man in the cardigan sweater.

"My father's dead. My mother's living."

"Were your parents born in America?"

"Yes."

"Where?"

"In Philadelphia. They were both born in Philadelphia."

"What was your father's occupation?"

"He was a dentist."

"And your mother?"

"My mother's a housewife."

"Any sisters or brothers?"

"One sister."

"Older or younger?"

"Younger. She's seven years younger than I am."

"She's living, I presume."

"Yes."

"Does your sister have an occupation?"

"She works as a secretary for the head of a Philadelphia advertising agency."

"How do you get along with your sister?"

"Okay. We've always gotten along okay."

Which was a lie. We never got along. I got along better with my sister's friends than I did with my sister. Friends like Tuvia Friedman.

* * *

I was sixteen; my sister was nine. We were living in a row house on Aberdale Street in Philadelphia. It wasn't a great house, and it wasn't a great street, primarily because my father wasn't a great dentist. On that particular afternoon, I was in the bedroom my sister and I had shared since she was born. We slept in twin beds. I wouldn't sleep alone until I left home two years later.

Anyway, my sister was downstairs taking a bass violin lesson, and I was in our bedroom with her friend Tuvia Friedman. Tuvia was older than my sister. Tuvia was thirteen. I was sitting on the edge of the bed, and Tuvia was lying on the floor playing with our dog, Albert the First. (There would be, in time, eleven Alberts, counting Albert the Pinhead.) Albert the First was crouched down on his front paws yapping his head off, his rear end hoisted in the air, his tail wagging furiously. Tuvia was teasing Albert with a pencil. I watched my sister's friend and the dog for a while, then I opened the fly of my trousers and pulled out my prick. I asked Tuvia to give it a lick.

"Why should I?" she asked, tickling the dog's ear with the pencil.

"Because my weewee tastes like a strawberry lollipop. My sister told me that strawberry was your favorite flavor."

"It is, but . . ."

"Honestly, a man's weewee tastes just like a strawberry lollipop. I don't know why, but it does. Here," I said, wagging my prick in her face, "put it in your mouth and see if it doesn't."

Tuvia Friedman stuck my prick in her mouth, gave it a few licks, and quickly made a horrible face. She told me my weewee didn't taste like a strawberry lollipop at all. "Your peenie tastes *awful,*" she said. She was very angry.

"What *does* it taste like?" I asked somewhat curiously, stuffing it back in my pants.

"It doesn't taste like anything good. It just tastes *awful.* I'm going to tell your sister you made me put your peenie in my mouth."

"No you won't."

"Why won't I?" she asked, standing now, her hands on her hips.

"Because if you do, I'll tell your mother you made Albert lick your crack."

"I did *not* make him do that!" sobbed my sister's friend.

"I know," I said. "So what?"

Tuvia Friedman never mentioned the incident to anyone.

* * *

"So, by and large," said the man in the cardigan sweater, "you'd say you had a normal, healthy childhood." He was somewhat annoyed at my lack of attention.

"I'm sorry. Yes. By and large."

"Fine. Let's move on. What college did you attend?"

"The University of Pennsylvania."

"Did you go directly from high school to college?"

"No. No, I didn't. I—ah—worked for a year before going to Penn."

"Where did you work?"

"I worked in a steel mill. I thought the experience would be helpful, you see. It would give me a chance to get a look at the real world. Make me appreciate college, if you know what I mean."

Which was a lie.

I didn't go to Pittsburgh to work in a steel mill because I thought the experience would be helpful. I went because of a cockteaser.

* * *

Her name was Julie Candaleri.

I met Julie in June of 1948, a week after I graduated from high school. Julie was petite, vivacious, cute as a button, and a cockteaser of the first magnitude. (Perhaps she wasn't technically a cockteaser, but then I wasn't sure what a real c.t. was. If, after an evening with a cockteaser, one experienced excruciating pain from the waist down—if that was the test—then Candaleri passed with flying colors.)

Julie was working that summer at a charity camp outside of Philadelphia. I was an apprentice film editor in the city, with no idea of what I wanted to do with my life. But I did know what I wanted to do that summer.

Fuck Julie Candaleri.

The desire to hump Julie started as a pleasant objective and quickly deteriorated into an obsession. Every night I would drive all the way out to that goddamn charity camp and attack her. And she let me. She never let me fuck her—but she *did* lead me to believe it was a definite possibility. And so I persevered.

Rain or shine, I would be down by the lake among the crickets and grasshoppers, or in the empty arts-and-crafts cabin, trying to shove my hand up Julie's incredibly short shorts, or down her carelessly buttoned middy blouse. The shape of my nuts was at the mercy of Candaleri's whims. Many a night I would drive back to the city with nuggets the size of basketballs, and the resulting agony would often force me to pull over to the side of the road and attempt to lift my father's ancient Oldsmobile off the highway by its rear bumper. (I was told that lifting heavy objects helped relieve the pain in a lover's untapped gonads. It never helped me.)

"Dear God," I would pray while hoisting the family Olds, "please let my knees come together again. Just one more time. Do it for me, God, and I'll never bother you again."

But God wasn't listening, or else the subject grossed Him out, or else He didn't give a rusty fuck about the state of my reproductive organs. My nuts remained the size of basketballs.

"Fucking cockteasing bitch!" I would wail at the dark, barren road, and the owls would hoot some bullshit back to me.

But I would always forgive Candaleri for the elephantine agates swinging between my knees; for the pain, for the anguish, for the sleepless nights. Because I loved her.

And then one night Julie Candaleri told me she would be leaving
Philadelphia.

"Leaving! Where're you going?"

"I'm going to Pittsburgh."

"Pittsburgh! Why Pittsburgh?"

"To school, silly. I've been accepted at Carnegie Tech."

I uttered a low, inarticulate sound. "But I thought you wanted to
go to Penn," I whined. "I thought you were going to stay in Philadelphia!"

"Well, I'm not."

"Well, what about *me?*" I asked.

"Well, what *about* you?"

I quit my job in Philadelphia and moved to Pittsburgh. I enrolled at
the university, but rarely saw a classroom. I spent most of my days
across town on the Carnegie Tech campus, sniffing out Julie Candaleri.
At night I'd play my ukulele under her dormitory window.

"Cut it out," Julie said one September evening during the walk
back to her dorm.

"Cut what out?"

"The ukulele playing. It's embarrassing."

"I thought it was romantic."

"Well, it isn't."

"Okay. I won't play my uke."

"It doesn't matter, anyway," Julie said.

"What doesn't matter?"

She sighed, looked at me, and said, "I don't want to see you
anymore."

"*Not see me anymore!*" I hollered, stopping dead in my tracks.

"Will you *please* keep your voice down," hissed Candaleri, looking
this way and that. Other couples were standing in the dormitory en-
tranceway, kissing each other good night, copping little feels, and listening to us.

"Why? Why don't you want to see me anymore?"

"Because you embarrass me with your stupid ukulele playing."

"I said I wouldn't play my uke anymore."

"And you're short."

"I'm *short!* What kind of reason is *that?*"

"It's a good reason," said Candaleri. "I decided that since *I'm*
short, I would be more comfortable if I went with somebody tall."

I couldn't believe my ears. "I came all the way out here to Pitts-burgh—" I snorted, "—and went to all the trouble of matriculating into the goddamn university—just to be with you. And now you tell me you're not going to see me anymore because I'm *short!*"

"I didn't ask you to come to Pittsburgh," said Candaleri calmly.

"I *love* you," I said sadly. (Maybe I did.)

Julie Candaleri took an inordinately deep breath and rolled her eyes up to her forehead. "Honestly," she said. And then, after what seemed like the passing of winter, she added, "Okay, we'll keep seeing each other. But not as much."

It was all over by Christmas. During the holidays, a tall, handsome football star named Al Marinaro offered Julie Candaleri his fraternity pin, and she took it. (Within a year, she and Marinaro would get engaged.) The last time I saw Julie Candaleri was just after she was pinned. She and Marinaro were coming out of a campus movie theater. Neither one of them saw me. (Probably because I was hiding behind an automobile.) Unfortunately, they both appeared very happy. And, I had to admit, they were a great-looking couple. Pretty, petite Julie, and big, tall, handsome Al. They had it all.

* * *

Meanwhile, I was stuck in Pittsburgh.

Just before Christmas of 1948, the registrar's office notified me that I had flunked out of the university. I welcomed the new year broke, directionless, and bitter. I began spending my time in the local taverns. I was always in a bad mood and found myself in more fistfights than I'd like to remember, most of which I lost. In February of that year I was forced to leave the university's dorms, and I moved into a rooming house down the street from the Duquesne Gardens. I never considered returning to Philadelphia, or even going back to college. I'm not sure why I didn't, but I didn't. Maybe it was because Julie Candaleri was the first person I had ever loved, and I lost her. Or maybe it was my anguish running rampant. Like the rat in the electrified box.

THE STUDY OF THE RAT IN THE ELECTRIFIED BOX

Place two rats in an electrified box. Turn on the current and watch them translate their pain into violent combat. Now place one rat in an electrified box and turn on the current. Watch him chew his foot off. The rat, having no one else to destroy, can always destroy himself.

Is chewing one's foot off enough self-punishment? Not always, perhaps, but sometimes it just has to do. So I stayed in Pittsburgh, got a job in the Homestead Steel Mill, and chewed my foot off little by little.

* * *

"So it wasn't a wasted year for you," said the recruiter from the CIA.

"No, not at all. It really made me appreciate college."

"And then," the man said, pausing to turn the tape over, "you returned to Philadelphia and matriculated at the University of Pennsylvania."

"Yes, sir," I replied. (Which wasn't far from the truth.)

"And then what did you do?" asked the man. "After you graduated from college?"

I made the guidette pregnant, is what I did.

* * *

I met her when I moved to New York to find a job. I wanted something in television. It was 1955, and I thought the industry had a definite future. So I became an NBC tour guide at their studios in Rockefeller Plaza. That's where I met Georgia Barclay. She was a tour guidette.

Georgia was from Georgia. (Her parents had thought it cute to name their daughter after the state they lived in.) She was five feet two with naturally blond hair, a saccharine southern accent, and immense eyes, teeth, and breasts. She had been a Georgia University cheerleader, and had retained a cheerleader's personality (which is kind of fun to be around when you're twenty-five, but can very well be grounds for murder by the time you're twenty-six). With her seductive eyes, her sexy sugar accent, and her big, bouncy cats, she had won the job as a tour guidette minutes after she arrived at Rockefeller Plaza. Her next objective was to marry either a rich executive, an up-and-coming Young Turk with enormous potential, or a rich Jew-boy with a pocketful of credit cards. At that moment, I was neither up-and-coming nor rich, and consequently I stood little chance of getting anywhere with Georgia Barclay. She hardly knew I existed, and when I did say hello, she treated me as though I had the plague.

Then I was accepted as an NBC management trainee. I had lied my way into the training program by listing members of RCA's board of directors as references. (The personnel department never checked.) I was one of six selected from literally thousands of applicants. Georgia was impressed. That weekend we began dating. Shortly thereafter, the little peach moved in with me.

I was on a roll. And cocky.

"Head of television network sales at thirty," I told Georgia one night while fondling her incredible kazoos, "and head of the *entire* television network by the time I'm forty. No, more like thirty-nine. I want to be president by the time I'm forty-one. The youngest president of the National Broadcasting Company was forty-three. That gives me a year or two leeway."

"You're wonderful," said Georgia, delighted that in the not-too-distant future she herself stood a chance of wallowing in the lap of luxury.

"Didn't I tell you I'd make it to the top?"

"You sure did."

"And it's only the beginning," I promised.

"From your lips to God's ear," she said, and added, "Let's fuck."

Several days later she would tell her friends, "See, either a Young Turk or a kike. But kikes are best. They'll give you everything you want. You just gotta know how to pick 'em."

And then I was fired.

"Fired!" snapped Georgia, looking down at me. I was seated in our only armchair, a secondhand number from the Salvation Army.

"Yes, fired," I moaned. "I can't believe it. I just can't believe it."

"What was the reason?"

"Efficiency cutback." I was still stunned. "I just can't believe what's happened to me."

Georgia said, "Well, I'll tell you something else you won't believe."

"What's that?"

"I'm pregnant!"

I looked up at Georgia. "Pregnant?"

"Pregnant."

"*Pregnant!*" I yelled.

"*Pregnant!*" she yelled back defiantly. She was standing in the center of the room with a wretched scowl on her face and her hands on her hips.

I went directly to St. Patrick's Cathedral.

I entered the cathedral, crossed myself, lit a candle, and crossed myself again. I walked halfway down the main aisle, knelt on one knee, and crossed myself again. I sat down in a pew, looked up, and said, "Hey, God, what the fuck is going on?"

I was exasperated, and I told Him so. "There are times, God, when life is absolutely mystifying. Take the National Broadcasting Company. After spending thousands of dollars to *train* me, they *fire* me! And when I asked them why, you know what they told me? To make things more efficient! Too many employees. Too much overhead. So they kicked my ass out with the last-in secretaries, and the last-in typewriters, and the last-in wastebaskets. Motherfuckers.

"And then take this little two-faced cunt I'm living with, God; this nice little Catholic girl with the big kazoos who's spent her whole life learning about rhythm fucking—this sleazebag is telling me she's pregnant! Now I ask you, God, what am I supposed to do? What the fuck am I supposed to do? Never in the history of my religion has a Jewish boy left a girl when she was pregnant. So what am I supposed to do?"

I waited for over an hour, but I didn't hear any answers. God was apparently just as confused as I was.

Or else He just plain didn't give a fuck.

Then, after five days and nights of unadulterated terror, Georgia informed me that her period had begun. "I guess I was just late," she groused disgustedly, as though Mother Nature's act was not one of cleanliness, but of spite.

Good old Mother Nature. She fucked Georgia Barclay royally. That old bitch made the little cooze play her trump card at the wrong time and in the wrong place. Now Georgia didn't have any trump left. The simple southern twat would have to start all over again and trap another Turk or kike, which wasn't an easy task under the best of circumstances. And she wasn't getting any younger.

Anyway, that night, while Georgia slept, I packed. In the hours before dawn I tiptoed quietly out of the apartment. I carried all the possessions I owned: a duffel bag filled with clothes, a guitar, and a radio. I walked past St. Patrick's Cathedral, dropped my duffel bag, and crossed myself. I said, "Thank you, God." I felt sort of hypocritical saying it, but I said it anyway.

I was a very happy boy.

* * *

"Why did you leave the National Broadcasting Company?" asked the man from the CIA.

"I wanted to broaden my experience," I answered.

"Broaden your experience?" he repeated. I noticed he was writing viciously on his pad of paper. That bothered me.

"Yes, sir," I mumbled, fumbling for additional reasons. "I—ah—wanted to get a wider scope of experience in the communications industry."

"What did you do after you left the National Broadcasting Company?"

"Let's see," I said, stalling. "What did I do?"

I decided not to mention my sales job at the Teleprompter Corporation, where I was fired for never selling any teleprompters, or my sales job at Brentano's bookstore, where I was fired for never selling any books. (I spent my time reading them.) I did mention setting up my own television production company in order to develop TV properties—which was partially true. It wasn't exactly a production company. It was just me, my TV set, and a telephone.

"How many employees did you have?" asked the man.

"Three."

"How did you finance your production company?"

"Through the royalties I received as a songwriter."

"So you're a songwriter too?" asked the man from the CIA. The subject seemed to titillate him.

"Yes, sir."

"Have you written any songs that are well-known?"

"Yes, several," I said. I was lying again. Only one of my songs had ever sold any records to speak of.

"I also dabble in music. Would I know any of them?" There was envy in the man's voice.

"Possibly," I said. It might have been my only honest answer of the day.

"Try me," he said playfully.

"Okay. 'Palisades Park.' "

"Never heard of it. Who performed the song?"

"A singer named Freddie Cannon."

"Never heard of him."

I shrugged my shoulders.

"All right, what happened after you formed your TV production company?" asked the man, the impersonal edge back in his voice. "Is that what you're doing now?"

"No, I've disbanded the company, but I still spend most of my time trying to create a TV game show. There's a lot of money in TV game shows, and I *know* I can think of something a hell of a lot better than the stuff that's on the air now."

"I don't watch much television," said the man, scanning his notes. And then he looked up and asked, "Does that bring us up to date?"

"Yes, sir."

"You haven't left anything out?"

"No, sir."

"Good," he said, placing a fresh tape in the recorder. (Jesus, I thought to myself, *another* tape!) When the man was satisfied that his machine was functioning properly, he asked, "Are you a homosexual?"

The question startled me. "No," I replied, a shade too quickly.

"Do you have friends who are homosexuals?"

"No," I lied again. Of course I did. I'll bet he did, too. The man in the cardigan sweater was beginning to irritate me.

"Do you take drugs?" he asked.

"No, sir."

"Did you take any form of drugs prior to coming here for this interview? A doctor's prescription, perhaps?"

"No, sir."

"At some future date, would you be willing to take a polygraph test—a lie detector test?"

"Of course," I said cheerfully.

"Fine," said the man, turning to a clean notebook page. "Just a few more questions. Are you a communist?"

"Are you kidding?" I huffed. "Do I *look* like a communist?"

"A simple yes or no will suffice."

"No, I'm not."

"Are you, or were you ever, a member of the Communist Party?"

"Never."

"Do you have any friends who are members of the Communist Party?"

"No."

The man scribbled some notes, and, without taking his eyes off his writing, asked, "What do you think a communist looks like?"

What did I think a communist looked like? Someone like my Uncle Albert, I imagined. Wire-rimmed spectacles attached to a big hooked nose. A black, unwashed beard stained with the residue of yesterday's meals. A beret and a torn woolen turtleneck sweater under an old army jacket. Baggy, creaseless corduroy slacks and dirty Hush Puppies. Exactly like my Uncle Albert. Except that Uncle Albert was a militant right-winger. He was one of the only Jews in the John Birch Society —a charter member, as a matter of fact. My Uncle Albert, the fartbiter.

I concluded one really couldn't tell what a communist looked like.

"I guess I really can't describe what a communist looks like," I confessed.

"Neither can I," he replied, switching off the tape recorder.

"Is that it?" I asked.

"That's it."

The man stood up, handed me my overcoat and scarf, and opened the front door. "You'll hear from us," he said, "one way or the other."

I stepped outside. The man shut the door behind me. It had begun to snow. I looked at my wristwatch: eleven-thirty A.M. I had been talking to the man in the cardigan sweater for almost two and a half hours, and it seemed to me like a gigantic waste of time.

I buttoned my overcoat collar, pulled my scarf over my chin, dug my hands into my pockets, and walked to the bus stop.

Three

March 17, 1965.

I was standing under a goddamn tree, alongside a highway in Alabama, in a torrential downpour, eating lunch. My sandwich was falling apart in my hands. Soggy, rain-soaked pieces of white bread slipped away between my dirty fingers, and I couldn't do anything about it. I couldn't do anything about anything. All I could do was stand under that goddamn tree.

We had been walking for two days and nights—Montgomery was still another two nights and a day away—and I was a royal mess. My Brooks Brothers ensemble—button-down oxford shirt, rep tie, dark blue blazer with brass buttons, gray flannel slacks, and black socks— was soaked through, and had been for over twenty-four hours. My penny loafers were beginning to disintegrate. Where the hell did I think I was going? To a Yale class reunion? To an advertising-agency party on Madison Avenue? I was going to Montgomery, Alabama, that's where I was going.

We had stopped for lunch. (I loved that: "lunch." A ham sandwich between two pieces of stale bread, under a tree in a rainstorm.) How, I wondered, had I ever allowed fate to place me under that goddamn tree in the first place? What was I doing in the middle of shit-drenched Alabama anyhow? I was there because nothing made any fucking sense, that's why I was there. Of course, it wasn't that way when I started out. When I started out everything made sense.

* * *

Ten days before, I had departed from Los Angeles for Montgomery, Alabama. There was a car pool at the Montgomery airport. A young black boy drove me to Selma, along with four black clergymen from Illinois. I sat in the car's front seat sandwiched between the driver and one of the clergymen. During the ride, one of the ministers leaned forward from the back seat, tapped me on the shoulder, and asked, "Why are *you* here?"

"Pardon?"

"I said, why are you here? Why you?"

I didn't mind telling him. "Well, Father . . ."

"Reverend," he said, correcting me. "Reverend Jackson's the name."

"Well, Reverend Jackson, maybe it was that beefy, red-necked, motherfucking sheriff I saw on television yesterday afternoon. Maybe it was because I got so mad watching him and his asshole posse bashing in black heads."

* * *

It *was* on television, right there for everyone to see.

I was sitting in front of my old TV set, like I was most every Sunday afternoon, trying to adjust its rabbit ears while searching for the NBA game of the week. Instead, I found a major in the Alabama State Police shouting, "This is an unlawful assembly. Your march is not conducive to the public safety. You are ordered to disperse and go back to your church or to your houses."

The major was addressing six hundred black civil rights marchers who had halted at the crest of a small bridge. Someone in the crowd of marchers shouted back, "May we have a word with the major?"

"There is no word to be had," replied the major.

A tense silence crept across the television screen and into my living room. I backed up and sat down in my armchair, never taking my eyes off the old TV set. The confrontation I was watching was far more electrifying than any basketball game could ever be.

It all took place on U.S. 80. At one side of the small bridge stood fifty state troopers wearing riot helmets. They carried a variety of billy clubs, nightsticks, and double-thick, extra-long blackjacks. Behind the state troopers was Sheriff Jim Clark and his posse: several dozen white vigilantes on horseback. Cocky. Flushed. Laughing nervously. Feeling good about having those state troopers in front of them, I suppose.

On the other side of the bridge—"the nigger side," as the townies would later refer to it—was a group of black onlookers, a handful of people standing near an old school bus. Some seemed to be praying, although I could have been mistaken. There were TV and newspaper people on that side too, lots of them, watching through their camera lenses and binoculars as if it were a rocket launch.

Suddenly, the major turned to his state policemen and yelled, "Troops advance!" As the whites cheered from the sidelines, the blue-uniformed state troopers moved forward and into the marchers. The marchers tried to hurriedly gather up their belongings and avoid the state troopers' nightsticks and billy clubs. And then the sheriff and his posse rode onto the bridge, bashing black skulls and shoulder blades with a gleeful, violent gusto.

Then abruptly, as if on cue, the troopers and posse stopped everything and put on gas masks. Soon, tear-gas canisters exploded, and a mustard-colored cloud spread across the bridge. Everything below the horseback riders' stirrups disappeared. The blacks disappeared. I sat in my living room, mesmerized, watching men wearing rubber masks, atop legless horses, riding in circles in a waist-high sea of dirty, yellow mist. As they rode, the masked men flailed their billy clubs and nightsticks at unseen creatures in the murky haze beneath them.

And then the cloud of tear gas evaporated, and I could see the blacks again. I saw their bloodied faces and clothing, the women and children clutching each other, and everybody running and stumbling, trying desperately to avoid the vicious swipes at their heads.

Trying to get off that goddamn bridge.

And then my telephone rang.

* * *

I twisted my shoulder so that I was facing the Reverend Jackson, and said, "I've never done anything like this before. I've never been big on causes, or demonstrated anywhere, or anything like that. I came down here to Selma because I want to be in the crowd that marches to Montgomery. I want to be in the crowd because I want that crowd to be so big it'll be impossible for the state troopers and that asshole posse to stop it. This time I want that goddamn sheriff to be scared shitless."

"Amen!" said the Reverend Jackson.

We drove the rest of the way in silence, through white Selma, and then into black Selma. We stopped in front of a church in the middle of a nondescript block of worn-out stores and houses. A sign over the church entrance declared the building to be Brown's African Methodist Episcopal Church. Crowds of surly, belligerent blacks and toady whites were milling about in front of the church. The four ministers and I were taken to a room in the church where we were told to register. A few minutes later, the five of us were assigned to a house that we would use as our sleeping quarters. And then we were on our own.

For the rest of the day I loitered near the church, despising every minute of it. I quickly realized that I—like my Brooks Brothers ensemble—was completely out of my element. And everybody bothered me. Everybody.

The antagonistic blacks bothered me, but it was the whites who *really* got on my nerves. I sat there on the church steps observing the whites fawning over the blacks, running their errands, doing everything but wiping their black asses. The whites would have done that, too, if given the chance. And if you would have told any of those brownnosers that the black asses they wished they could tend were going to come back and haunt them someday—SNCCing them, and Black Panthering them, and figuring out how to get a bloody revolution going so they could *really* jam it up those pearly white yin-yangs—they would have come apart at the seams. They would have called you a fascist weirdo racist, or some other equally enlightening sobriquet. Anyway, the righteous riffraff I had met were depressing me something awful. Shit, if I could have gone home right then and there, I would have. But I couldn't. I had made a commitment, and the commitment would stand. So I sat in front of Brown's Church with the rest of the lickspits and watched day turn to night. It was anything but thrilling.

And then I learned that not everyone would be allowed to march to Montgomery. If you had come to Alabama with that goal in mind, then being there was only half the battle. The other half was getting chosen, and I needed to be chosen. I *had* to march to Montgomery.

I asked around and eventually pieced together what was going on. It seemed that one hundred blacks and fifty whites would walk from Brown's Church in Selma to the steps of the state capitol building in Montgomery. The march would be fifty miles long, and Martin Luther King would walk only the last ten. The demonstration was to bring to the world's attention the lack of black civil rights in the United States of America. It would be an historic event, and, naturally, everyone wanted to be part of an historic event. Consequently, selecting the marchers from the thousands who had traveled to Selma would be an arduous task. Countless black churchmen insisted on marching to Montgomery—important priests and ministers with enormous and wealthy congregations. And choosing the fifty whites, who were needed to indicate to the world that white people were as concerned with voter registration rights in the South as blacks, would be even harder. Powerful white politicians with large black constituencies demanded to be allowed to march. So did famous white entertainers. But King wanted the common man to do the walking; not the opportunistic politicians, or the ambitious ministers, or the publicity-obsessed show-biz folks. So King kept postponing the march, trying to figure it all out. He stayed in Atlanta, talking to his aides and agonizing over who should, and shouldn't, walk those fifty miles from Selma to Montgomery. I stayed

in Selma and hung around Brown's Church, wondering what to do with
myself. The days dragged on, tedious and purposeless.

The nights were worse.

During the evenings I would sit in the stuffy, crowded church
listening to endless gospels and interminable sermons. Every night one
march leader after another would walk up to the podium and request
volunteers for this committee or that chore. I would offer my services
regularly for everything (just to *do* something), but I was never chosen.
I wondered why. Was I dressed too fashionably?

And then one night, to my surprise, I was asked to come to the rear
of Brown's Church.

I was led behind the stage to a small office that was inundated with
people, papers, boxes, and telephones. Two large black men brought me
to a crammed desk. Sitting at that desk was a man named Frank
Surrocco.

Surrocco, I found out later, had attended the University of California at Berkeley and then disappeared into the civil rights movement.
He was pale and gaunt—about my age, thirty-five or thirty-six—and
white.

For what seemed an age, Surrocco worked feverishly, paying absolutely no attention to me.

In due time, I grew tired of standing meekly in front of his desk.
But just as I was about to turn and leave, Frank looked up and said,
"Feel like working?"

I said I did.

He asked me why.

"Because I'm bored to death," I replied. "I've been volunteering
for *everything*. I've been waving my hand in the air every single night,
and nobody in this goddamn church seems to care. In fact, I was
thinking of going home tomorrow."

"Is that so?" said Surrocco. "Well, it's a good thing you didn't go.
We've been keeping you for something special. For bigger and better
things than the shit you've been volunteering to do."

"Why?"

"Because the last person you look like is a civil rights worker,"
answered Surrocco.

My Brooks Brothers ensemble.

And then Surrocco told me what he wanted me to do. He wanted
me to drive to as many Hertz and Avis offices as I could, rent as many

flatbed trucks as I could, and bring all the trucks back to Selma. "You'll be given a rented car and a helper," he said. "The two of you should drive as far away from Selma as you can before renting the trucks. I don't want anyone out there to suspect the trucks are for the march— or, at least, I want to hold off their suspicions for as long as possible."

"Your partner will be black," said Surrocco, "so you negotiate the rentals. It'll look natural. You're the owner—the employer—and the black guy works for you. Understand? Let your helper drive the rented truck and follow your car back to Selma. The two of you will have three days to rent at least seven trucks. A dozen would be better. But we *must* have seven. Do you have any questions?"

"Yes. What are the trucks for?"

"To haul shit."

"Haul shit!"

"Honeywagons," said Surrocco. "Crappers. Toilets. Portable out-houses."

"Oh," I said, feeling extremely foolish.

"And don't think that just because you're renting trucks to haul crappers around, you're doing something demeaning," said the tele-pathic Surrocco. "Because you're not. You can't have a fifty-mile march without goddamn crappers. We can't be littering the beautiful Alabama countryside with civil rights shit, can we? And we can't have frigging crappers tagging along behind the marchers unless they're on frigging trucks, right? So when you get right down to it," said Surrocco, lighting a cigarette, "Dr. King can't do his thing unless you get those toilet trucks. And they aren't going to be that easy to get. It might be a tad dangerous. Are you with me so far?"

I nodded, feeling a sudden ambivalence toward the assignment— delighted to be doing something, but not so delighted to be doing something "a tad dangerous."

"Yeah, I'm with you," I said. What the hell.

"Good," said Surrocco. Then he introduced me to my helper. "His name is Father Raymond Chester," announced Surrocco, pointing to a short, squat black man standing behind him.

The man named Father Chester was dressed in a work shirt and blue denim overalls. In his early forties and built like a brick shithouse, the last thing he looked like was Father anything. He had no neck and a very surly expression on his face. The expression struck me as having been there from birth. It made me uneasy.

"Don't let this ugly-looking priest scare you," said Surrocco. "He just looks mean. *All* priests look mean. And a lot of them *are* mean. But not Father Chester. He's really just a big, fat pussycat from the City of Brotherly Love."

"Oh, really?" I said to Father Chester cheerfully. "I'm from Philly, too!"

"Big deal," replied Chester in a very surly tone of voice.

* * *

The next day at dawn, Father Chester and I left Selma to look for rent-a-car offices. We drove north to Tuscaloosa and Birmingham, and west to Montgomery and Columbus, Georgia. We found the rent-a-car offices and quickly developed a routine.

I would tell the rent-a-car clerk I needed a large, open flatbed truck for a construction job I had just contracted. While I signed the papers and charged the expenses to my credit card, Father Chester would loiter off to the side, shuffling around, waiting for me to finish. When everything was in order, I would instruct Father Chester to go outside, get the truck, and follow me back to the alleged construction site. I would usually add some remark like, "And goddammit, boy, don't go lagging so far behind that you get yourself lost like you did yesterday."

Father Chester would mumble, "No, *suh!*" and the rent-a-car clerk and I would roll our eyes and exchange one of those ain't-niggers-dumb looks.

After we cleared the neighborhood, Father Chester and I would hightail it back to Selma as fast as we could and deposit the newly acquired truck in front of Brown's Church.

We drove everywhere, returning to Selma three or four times a day with our rented toilet trucks. After two days and nights on the road, Father Chester and I had commandeered eleven trucks, and we had become quasi-heroes. Father Chester vowed we would rent an even dozen before we quit. "We're goin' straight into the heart of Dixie to do it," boasted the surly priest from Philly. "Chuckie and I are goin' straight down to Mobile to get that motherfuckin' twelfth."

But in Mobile we ran into trouble.

The word was out.

A white guy and a nigger were renting trucks all over Alabama and taking them to Selma for the march on Montgomery. The white guy was saying the trucks were for something else—construction jobs, shit like that—but the trucks were really for the goddamn march.

Father Chester and I were spotted heading for Mobile, and the local Ku Klux Klan was alerted. A dusty old Pontiac, with three men in the front and three in the back, trailed us to a Hertz office on the east side of town. The car's occupants watched as we entered the rent-a-car office.

While I was signing the papers for the twelfth truck, the telephone rang. The clerk answered it. He looked at me and said, "Are you Barris?"

I said I was.

He said, "It's for you."

It was Frank Surrocco.

Surrocco told me that the Klan knew the rented trucks were for the march, and that they were on the lookout for us. He warned us to be careful, and said, "Forget about the twelfth truck. Just get back to Selma as fast as you can."

I told Frank we would try our best and hung up. During my telephone conversation, I had noticed the dusty Pontiac parked across the street. I saw the locals inside the car looking at me through the Hertz office window. "A tad dangerous," I remembered Surrocco saying. A tad, my ass.

I told Father Chester what Surrocco had told me, and nodded toward the idling Pontiac. Father Chester had already spotted the automobile. We unfolded a road map, pretended to study it, and whispered to each other our options for getting out of Mobile alive.

Father Chester wanted that twelfth truck, and so did I. We decided to leave our rented car parked in front of the Hertz office and return to Selma in the rented truck, sneaking away down the back alley. We hoped that by the time the red-necks in the Pontiac realized we weren't going to use the car we'd be long gone.

The two of us walked through the office to the rear parking lot, climbed into the truck, and drove off. I thought our plan had fooled the boys in the Pontiac, but it hadn't. Twenty minutes later, on the two-lane U.S. 80 to Selma, I saw the dusty automobile in my side mirror. I told Father Chester. He mumbled a short prayer, mentioning something about God protecting "two idiots from Philadelphia," and said, "Boy, drive your fuckin' ass off."

It was late by then—about ten at night—and the two-lane highway was practically deserted. As soon as there was a clear stretch of road up ahead, the dusty Pontiac made its move, pulling out into the left lane and starting to catch up to us. In my side mirror I could see the man in the front passenger seat roll down his window. He held a shotgun.

"They've got guns!" I yelled. I was paralyzed with fear, unable to do anything but look at the road ahead and the shotgun in the mirror, the road ahead and the shotgun in the mirror, as if I was watching a tennis match.

"Don't just sit there, you stupid son of a bitch," hollered Father Chester. "Ram him!"

I veered the big truck into the left lane. The Pontiac's driver drifted back behind our tailgate and stayed there; both of us tear-assing to Selma, single file, on the wrong side of the highway.

I held the Pontiac in my side mirror until I saw an automobile coming toward us in the distance, its headlights growing bigger and bigger. I stayed in the wrong lane until I couldn't stay any longer, and then I swerved the truck back to the right side of the highway. The Pontiac veered over to the right, too, avoiding a head-on collision. Our truck and the Pontiac remained in the proper lane until the automobile coming in the other direction—blaring its horn in anger and fear—passed by.

Then everything started all over again.

And so it went—minute after agonizing minute—for over two hours, zigzagging back and forth across U.S. 80.

Just as we finally saw the Selma city-limits sign, Father Chester hollered, "Keep your head down!"

"Why?"

"Just do it!" he shouted.

I started to drive in a crouch. Suddenly, while we were both bent over, the man in the Pontiac aimed his rifle at the rear of the truck and fired a frustrated farewell blast that blew out most of the rear window. Neither of us was hurt, but I shit my pants when the window went. Not a lot, but enough. I was that scared.

"They shoulda thought of that sooner, the dumb fucks," growled Father Chester. "They would have gotten us eventually. And if they hadn't killed us with buckshot, they sure as shit would have frightened us to death."

When we arrived at Brown's Church, I was drenched with sweat. So was the surly father from Philadelphia. But the two of us hugged each other anyway. "That was great drivin', you little motherfucker," said Father Chester, and I beamed from ear to ear.

* * *

Frank Surrocco recommended to Martin Luther King that Father Chester and I be allowed to march to Montgomery as a reward for our honeywagon exploits. King agreed. That's why I was standing under that goddamn tree in a torrential downpour. That's why I was holding a soggy sandwich that was falling apart in my hand. And me unable to do anything but stand under that tree and wonder why I was the lucky guy who got to go to Selma.

* * *

We marched for three days, reached the outskirts of Montgomery on the third evening, and slept in the Church of St. Jude's parking lot. During the night the temperature dropped about twenty degrees. I couldn't sleep at all.

The next day we marched into Montgomery with twenty-five thousand new arrivals who had joined the festivities that morning at St. Jude's. It was a joyous occasion. Everyone linked arms and sang "We Shall Overcome." (God, was I sick of that song by then.) There were speeches in Montgomery, and bands, and balloons, and television cameras and newspaper photographers. There was a tremendous feeling of being a part of something enormous; something bigger than life, something that would eventually mean something—though exactly what, no one was particularly sure.

And then it was over.

And everybody went home.

* * *

I flew to Atlanta and checked into the Peachtree Plaza Hotel. The bellhop let me into my room. When he had gone, I threw my bag on a chair and stared at my face in a mirror. I looked like shit. "You look like shit," I said. Then I bathed for one hour and slept for fifteen.

The following afternoon I boarded Eastern Airlines Flight 204 to Washington, DC. I was assigned seat 1A. Occupying seat 1B was a man named Byrd. He was very tall, had red hair and freckles, and was thirty, though he looked younger.

Jim Byrd was my immediate superior—my control agent—in the Central Intelligence Agency.

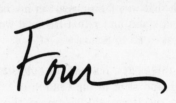

Four

"Here's your mail," said Jim Byrd.

Byrd always went to the trouble of collecting and delivering his agents' mail for them when they returned from a job. It was always the first thing he did—hand you your mail. The march to Montgomery was only my second assignment away from home for any length of time; a stint in Harlem doing some surveillance on a Malcolm X cell had been the other one. I had been away from Los Angeles for more than a week on that mission, and Byrd had handed me my mail then, too.

My mail contained the usual tripe. Nothing to get excited about except for a letter from Penny Pacino.

Penny's letter was full of scattered and silly thoughts, just like Penny. And it was funny, like Penny. And it was also warm and loving, like Penny. I had first met her many years earlier. She was the friend of a girl I was dating, and the girl had brought Penny along one afternoon when we were apartment hunting. After that day, I never bothered calling the girlfriend again. Instead, I called Penny. (Needless to say, my ex-girlfriend was furious, and said I was nuts to chase after someone like Penny Pacino.) But I didn't care. My life after that became full of silly letters from Penny, or unexpected visits, or hugs when I needed them most—or marriage proposals. Penny was forever trying to marry me, and without success. I liked Penny—maybe even a lot—but, as I always told myself, not *that* way. (I sometimes wondered if I'd ever like any girl in *that* way. On my lengthy roster of fears and phobias, marriage held a pretty lofty position.)

This letter was much like all the others. "What is it you do that makes you stay away so long?" she wrote. "I don't like whatever you're doing. Do something that keeps you in the neighborhood. When are we getting married? I *miss* you. Love, Penny."

I missed her too. I always missed Penny when I was depressed, and, God knows, I was depressed. I stuffed Penny's letter in my coat pocket and said to Jim Byrd, "You sure picked the eleventh hour to telephone me. And the way you explained it, for Christ's sake, it sounded like a matter of life or death—like a revolution was about to begin. I raced down to Selma so fast I think I forgot to turn my television set off."

"It was on," said Byrd. "One of the boys turned it off."

"And then," I added, beginning to get angry, "I sat around Selma for what seemed like years, doing nothing."

"We had to move fast," said Byrd. "We didn't know when the march would actually take place. How did it go?"

"It sucked. As far as I'm concerned, it was a total waste of time."

"That's not for you to decide," Byrd answered calmly. "There's nothing in the rules that states you have to agree with the purpose of a mission. All you have to do is perform it correctly. They assign, and you perform."

"Who are *they?*" I asked.

"None of your business."

"Well, fuck *them.*"

"You're tired," said Jim Byrd.

"I am not."

"You'll feel better in a day or so."

"The *fuck* I will."

I sat in my seat, simmering. Maybe Jim was right; maybe I *was* tired. Maybe I would feel better in a couple of days.

Out of the corner of my eye, I watched Byrd mix his bourbon on the rocks with his sturdy right forefinger. I liked Jim Byrd. If "they" could be like Jim Byrd, I would enjoy the Company a lot more. It was the "theys" I couldn't stand.

Jim Byrd sighed deeply, and said, "Can I have your report?"

I found my file folder and gave it to him. The folder was filled with names and information concerning those names; information that would be used for input, leads, and evidence—if necessary—against the many people from Selma in my folder.

Jim Byrd and I parted in Washington. He was going to the CIA headquarters in Langley, Virginia, and I was returning to California. Before we separated, Jim said, "Remember, you've got to be patient. You're paying your dues now. As far as I'm concerned, you have the makings of a really good agent—*if* you find the right niche. I'll keep my eyes and ears open. If anything comes up I think you'd like, I'll come find you."

I smiled a feeble smile and thanked him. We shook hands, and I walked away. Several hours later I boarded my plane for Los Angeles and thought things over.

* * *

The first time I saw the Washington Monument was in April 1963. I was looking through the porthole window of an airliner, and the sight gave me goosebumps. Patriotism flooded my body. My country, right or wrong. And on this trip, I was a goddamn guest of my country, right or wrong. All expenses paid by Uncle Sam: New York to Washington and back, including a night in a hotel. And maybe even a job, too.

As a spy!

And so it began. Actually, there's no need to detail my step-by-step indoctrination into the Central Intelligence Agency. Suffice it to say that I passed all the testing and interviews. And, later, the FBI investigation and clearance. And, still later, my intelligence education in Washington, Langley, and on the "farm," our nickname for the Company's advanced-training center. I did surprisingly well, performing gallantly and taking to "spooking" with a zest and proficiency unmatched by most of my classmates. I was a straight A student in operational methods and the execution of clandestine affairs. When it came time to pick a major, I decided on Counter Intelligence.

"Don't forget," said our instructor, poised to move his pointer across an information-packed blackboard, "the Foreign Intelligence staff is concerned with intelligence-*collection* operations; the Psychological Warfare and the Paramilitary staffs with *action* operations; and the Counter Intelligence staff with the *protection* of the Foreign, Psychological Warfare, and Paramilitary operations. The difference between action and collection operations is that an action operation *always* has a visible effect, whereas *neither* Counter Intelligence nor collection operations should *ever* have a visible effect."

No visible effect. Spooks.

Toward the middle of 1964, I had requested permission to be assigned to the International Organizations Division, which was headquartered in Los Angeles. The I.O.D. supervised CIA surveillance of labor, students, and the news media in the United States and throughout the world, and it was reputed to be a challenging department that involved a great deal of traveling. My request was eventually granted, and I was sent to the West Coast on an interim basis until my permanent assignment came through.

I arrived in Los Angeles on September 3, 1964, and began the job of an agent for the Central Intelligence Agency. And how was the job, once I was actually doing it? It was boring, is what it was. And when it wasn't boring, it was sleazy. I was nothing more than a penny-ante eavesdropper; a high-class tattletale. I wasted most of my days in the pursuit of becoming a professional snitch, and spent most of my evenings writing endless bureaucratic reports justifying those wasted days.

But I had never felt really disgruntled until Selma. I had always believed in the notion that working for the CIA would be fun, interesting, challenging, exciting, adventurous, and patriotic. I enjoyed my romantic concept of the spy—of espionage and counterespionage. I had done some serious fantasizing about mysterious cloak-and-dagger trips, skulking through the streets of foreign capitals, humping East German lady agents—that sort of thing. Instead, I had been assigned to a half-assed Muslim meeting in Harlem and a fifty-mile rain-soaked civil rights march in Selma.

A real hoot.

* * *

Anyway, by the time the plane landed in Los Angeles, I had decided to be patient, and to hope that Jim Byrd would soon come up with something worthwhile. Something with a little excitement to it. Besides, it wasn't too difficult to be patient in Southern California. The weather was great, the girls were tanned and pretty, and TV production was booming—this last being the underlying reason I had applied for the transfer in the first place. I was still obsessed with the notion that I could create a saleable television game show. Consequently, when I wasn't eavesdropping someplace, or writing a goddamn CIA report, I was attempting to create new TV program ideas at my desk at the American Broadcasting Company studios in Hollywood, where I was moonlighting as a night clerk in the programming department. The extra money was nothing to rave about, and the odd jobs were brainless and boring, but at least I had a toe in the door of the area I most enjoyed: television.

And when I wasn't developing new TV game show ideas, I was trying to sell the game shows I had already created—including a low-budget pilot I had filmed for ABC tentatively titled "The Dating Game."

But to no avail.

I mean, how many times can you call TV brass in New York or Los Angeles and say, "Well, whaddaya think?" or, "Any word yet?" or, "Can I show you something else?" In due time, when my name was mentioned, the executives had either just stepped out of the office, were out of town, or were out of the country. It was becoming painfully obvious that there wouldn't be any television in my future.

Just as this terribly distressing fact was sinking in, I received an even more distressing letter. It was a memorandum from the Central Intelligence Agency regarding my newly determined permanent assignment. It was to be at one of the Company's more dismal desks: Caracas, Venezuela. What caused me even greater concern was the number of inoculations I would have to suffer. The list was a mile long. One or two, like the cholera shot, really hurt, and spun off incredible reactions.

But what could I do? Resign from the agency and stay in Los Angeles, the worst city to be in with time on your hands? Stand in unemployment lines for months on end with all the dorks in Hollywood? Go back to New York and pound the pavements through the suffocating, humid months of July and August, when all the creeps come out of the woodwork and sit around the Plaza fountain and stare at their feet? At least I'd have something to do in Caracas. And maybe a revolution would occur, and I could become some kind of hero. Then, there was always Jim Byrd's promise to find me if "something with a little excitement to it" opened up—if Byrd hadn't forgotten I existed.

So, on a sunny day in the middle of November 1965, I packed my bags, stuck my airline ticket to Caracas in an inside suit-coat pocket, and was about to lock the front door of my apartment when the telephone rang. I walked back into my living room and picked up the receiver. It was Leonard Goldberg calling from New York.

Leonard Goldberg was, at that time, vice-president in charge of daytime television programming for the American Broadcasting Company. He said, "We have some problems with our daytime lineup, and we need one or two quick replacements. We've been reviewing some of our pilots, and I think we have a place for 'The Dating Game' on the schedule."

"What do you mean?" I asked, knowing pretty much what he meant, but unable to believe it.

"I mean I want to put 'The Dating Game' on the air."

"*My* show?"

"Your show. The one you created. The one you call 'The Dating Game.' That *is* your show, isn't it?" Goldberg asked somewhat facetiously.

"Yes! Yes! 'The Dating Game' is my show."

Goldberg asked how soon I could have it ready.

"How soon do you need it?" I replied hoarsely.

"How about six weeks?"

"Six weeks. Yes, sir. I'll have the show ready in six weeks. Six weeks from now the show will be ready. Absolutely perfect. Ready for air."

"It's your first show, Chuck. Do you need any help from us?"

"No. No, thank you. I can do it."

"Fine."

"Can I ask you something, Len?"

"Sure."

I was terribly nervous and could hardly speak, but I did manage to say, "You *do* know you're talking to Chuck Barris, and you're *sure* you want to buy my program, 'The Dating Game'? For coast-to-coast television?"

"Yes," said the vice-president with good humor.

"For how long?"

"You'll be on a thirteen-week contract," he replied.

"You mean I'll be on the air for at least thirteen weeks?"

"Yes."

"And if the program succeeds, I can be on for another thirteen weeks?"

"Yes. You can be on for thirteen *years* if the program holds up that long."

"Jesus."

"Keep me in touch with your progress," said Goldberg, "and good luck."

"Thank you," I said.

And then I hung up the telephone.

And then I threw up.

* * *

Not on my phone stand but down the hall in my bathroom sink. Afterward, leaning against the porcelain, I wondered what had prompted such a violent reaction.

Earlier—about two or three months before—I had talked the network programming department into coughing up the paltry sum of seventy-five hundred dollars out of their precious development fund to make a no-frills pilot of an idea of mine: a show to be called "People Poker." I argued that the network could save the huge royalties and fees they paid outside program suppliers by permitting an insider to create and produce new properties, and they grudgingly agreed. It was to be a test! If I succeeded, the network would have more money to spend for new programs, and I would be a hero. If I failed . . .

"People Poker" required two contestants to play poker using human beings as playing cards. There would be three categories to choose from, five people to a category, plus a "wild card." On the pilot show, I used sixteen women: five brain surgeons, five police women, five hookers, and—as a wild card—a bouncer from an East Los Angeles bar. I planned to mix up the lot, hang numbers around their necks, and stand them all on a tiered platform. The two contestants would study the crowd's faces and attempt to figure out what each one did for a living. (I got the idea riding the New York subways, where I would pass the time trying to decide the occupations of the characters sitting and standing around me.)

The winner would be determined after each contestant had made five choices. The contestant with the best poker hand would win a prize: five of a kind over four of a kind, four of a kind over three of a kind and a pair, three of a kind and a pair over two pairs, et cetera.

The contestant would select any woman he wanted, and then guess what she was. If the contestant was right, he was allowed to go again. If he was wrong, he was stuck with whatever he picked, and consequently would be forced to pick another of the same category when it was his turn again. If a player selected the wild card, he or she automatically lost the "card" to the opposing player, who could then use it any way he desired. That's how it worked. Rather, that's how it was supposed to work.

Unfortunately, I had not planned things carefully. I had failed to pay attention to details. Although I had given the set designer the basic facts, I hadn't thought it necessary to check his work. I didn't discuss the subtle points of the show with my director. I had left the briefing of the sixteen women to my contestant coordinator, with only the rudiments of the game's rules to guide him.

As a result, the pilot was a disaster.

The set was a mishmash of flats and scrims. Although the sixteen people were standing on the tiered platform I had ordered, the platform was stationed to the rear of the stage, seemingly miles away from the cameras and the studio audience, and out of sight of anyone who might be the slightest bit interested in studying their faces. The director delighted in focusing his cameras on everything I didn't want to see. My screams unnerved him. He was unable to comprehend the panicked suggestions I was shouting in his left ear. (He suffered what appeared to be a nervous breakdown shortly after the second commercial break.) The policewomen were not pleased with being on the same stage as the hookers, most of whom they had arrested at one time or another. Yelling broke out, followed by pushing and shoving. One of the women fell off the platform and twisted her ankle.

I left the studio, walked across the street to a bar, and downed a double Scotch and soda. Out of sheer frustration and disappointment I threw the glass at a wall, causing a shower of glass that landed mostly in the bartender's hair. He was an extremely large man. I was amazed at how easily he vaulted the bar and landed precisely one inch away from me. He grabbed my sport-coat lapels in one hand and pulled me to my toes. His other hand was balled up in a gigantic fist. He stared at me, wondering, I guess, which part of my body to hit. I begged for mercy. I said that I hadn't the slightest idea why I did what I did. I must have looked pathetic. The bartender lowered me to the floor. He called me a dumb fuckhead. I have used that expression ever since to describe anyone I didn't like.

The v.p.s at the American Broadcasting Company were pissed. "Some producer *you* are," said one. I was in the doghouse for months. I sat by myself in the company commissary. I avoided looking at other people looking at me by writing reams of notes on yellow, lined legal-size pads of paper. I made lists: revised personal budgets, junk food I vowed to give up, goals, chores, countries I dreamed of visiting—things like that. And I would think of ideas for game shows. One idea in particular. The idea consisted of three screaming teenage girls seated on one side of a partition, unable to see the three pimply-faced boys on the other side of the partition. One of the three boys would be a teenage rock-and-roll idol. The girls would ask the boys questions, hoping to find a perfect date by their answers. The girl with the best questions would get to choose. In my wistful fantasies, I would imagine the teenage girl screaming—or, better yet, fainting—if she happened to select the rock-and-roll idol—and doing the same if she didn't. I tentatively titled the program "The Dating Game."

I tried doing practice shows with friends, then with strangers. Nothing worked properly. The teenage girls were obnoxious. So were the boys. It was difficult to determine the girl with the best questions since all the questions were abysmal. Nobody screamed or fainted. Perhaps that was because we were unable to practice with rock-and-roll idols. I was discouraged.

And then one day Leonard Goldberg appeared in the executive dining room. He stopped at my table and chided me about the "People Poker" disaster. He asked, jokingly, what idea I was working on for my next fiasco. He did so while peering over my shoulder at the doodles on my yellow pad. He saw my symbols for stools, partitions, and screaming teenage nitwits. I explained my program idea to Goldberg. He said, "Why limit the show to teenagers?" and walked away. Good question.

In the weeks to come, I revised my idea. One screaming teenage girl, not three, on one side of the partition. And it wouldn't always be a screaming teenage girl. I would use women of all ages interrogating eligible bachelors who were their contemporaries. It worked like a charm.

I traveled to New York and visited Mr. Goldberg. I told him I appreciated his taking the time to see a corporate black sheep such as myself, and then I explained the new "Dating Game" idea to him. He was interested, and, within a month, he phoned me back to say that he wanted to make a pilot of "The Dating Game." I was so excited I couldn't eat for two days.

With my CIA salary and money borrowed from relatives, I set up an office on Ventura Boulevard. I hired five cronies. (Some of them would be with me almost twenty years later.) We installed two telephones. The staff grew to seven. Another telephone was installed. The staff was enlarged to ten. The telephone installer became one of the crowd. We all worked long hours, seven days a week. We had numerous crises. We drank lots of six packs, and I played the guitar to relax.

We did the pilot in one evening a week before Thanksgiving. It went off without a hitch. I thought the show was sensational. The ABC veeps thought so too. They spoke to me afterward. One of the veeps said, "You can be proud of yourself," and suggested I drop by the next morning to discuss what might be in store for the project. (All of us in the Ventura office—including the telephone installer—knew what was in store for the project. A spot in the daytime network lineup, that's what was in store for the project. We all hugged. I hugged the telephone installer.)

The next morning, I drove to the ABC studios. The veeps met me with handshakes and back slaps, and told me they were not going to schedule my show. "That's not to say it's not a good show," said one of them. "It *is* a good show. An excellent show. We just don't have any openings at the present time. We've decided to exercise our hold on the program. We're going to put "The Dating Game" on the shelf for six months or so, and review our options sometime in the future."

I drove home angry and disappointed and sick and tired. My cronies were waiting for me on the pavement in front of the office building. When they saw my car, they all burst out in smiles. I held up my hand, thumb down. Their smiles disappeared. They turned and walked into the building. The installer spent the day pulling out the telephones. I closed the office.

In the month that followed I disappeared into the CIA routine, seeing neither family nor friends. Then came the telephone call from Leonard Goldberg. "You'll be on a thirteen-week contract," he said.

"Thank you," I said. And threw up.

Part Two

One should not be driven along by
a momentum other than one's own;
one should create, and not be
created.
                    —Ernest Raymond

Fire

On the third "Dating Game" show, one of the three bachelor contestants called the girl on the other side of the partition a cunt.

On the fourth program, a girl asked one of the three bachelors, "What would I like most about you?"

He answered, "My cock."

The program was not proceeding in good taste.

"The Dating Game" always had that inherent danger. Spontaneous shows give birth to spontaneous asides, and—depending upon the intelligence of the performer—the asides may not always be within the bounds of acceptability. That's the chance you take with spontaneity. And if ever there was a spontaneous, unrehearsed, explosive television program, it was "The Dating Game." The show consisted of a single young lady sitting on one side of a high partition, unable to see the three eligible bachelors seated on the other side. But she was able to hear them. The pretty girl would interrogate the occasionally handsome bachelors for five minutes or so, trying to determine which of the unseen gentlemen most appealed to her. After the questioning time had elapsed, she would be asked by the program's master of ceremonies to choose one for a blind date. The girl's only basis for choosing a suitable bachelor was her instinct, grounded on how the bachelors had answered her questions. The girl would make her choice, and then squirm with anticipation, waiting to see if she had made the best one. But before the girl was allowed to meet the bachelor she had chosen, she was forced to face the two she had *not* chosen.

One at a time, the runners-up would come around the partition, usually tugging at their pants bottoms or slicking down their hair with sweaty palms as they walked. The girl would appear delighted or dismayed—delighted if the reject seemed to be a nerd; dismayed if he was a movie star or a particularly handsome dude. And then, waiting with bated breath, the girl would brace herself for the moment when she would be introduced to the man she had selected to share her "fun-filled night on the town." The date was usually an evening in Hollywood. (The couple was chaperoned and chauffeured, and returned to their respective apartments—usually before midnight. There *were* exceptions to the rule, but I generally never heard about them.)

Anyway, when girl met boy—in front of millions of coast-to-coast television viewers—she and he would suffer some form of traumatic reaction, either one of extreme disappointment or ecstasy. An indifferent response was catastrophic. If the program generated consistently indifferent responses, it would fail.

"Indifference is antithetical to creativity and romance," I said one afternoon at a network evaluation meeting. "Show business," I pontificated, "should avoid indifference at all costs."

"Even when taste is involved?" asked one of the network television executives, an annoying sort who appeared to be most concerned with nonexistent problems.

"Yes," I recall replying—not too brightly—"even when taste is involved. Taste is a word, and can to a certain degree be semantically stretched."

"I *don't* agree," said the network executive. And then the twit added a classic statement. He said, "You don't fuck with taste."

You don't fuck with taste.

"I guess you're right," I said, attempting to end the conversation.

"Just keep that in mind," said the twit.

"I will," I promised.

The network executive smiled philanthropically.

Meanwhile, my third and fourth "Dating Game" shows had definitely fucked with taste. They were unairable, and I would have to pay for their production costs out of my own pocket. My life as a television producer was starting to teeter on the edge of a precipice, and a short life in show business appeared imminent. Thankfully, the fifth "Dating Game" program was acceptable, ending an exasperating—and expensive—first week of production. At least, I thought, things couldn't get any worse.

But things got worse.

The second week's shows were more horrendous than the first. It seemed contestants were getting a kick out of being flagrant on coast-to-coast television. Angelic little girls and seemingly benign gentlemen were metamorphosing into garbage pails in front of our very noses—and there didn't seem to be anything we could do about it.

The sixth, seventh, and eighth "Dating Game" shows were nightmares.

* * *

EXCERPT FROM THE SIXTH "DATING GAME" SHOW

PRETTY GIRL CHEERLEADER: Bachelor Number One, one of my biggest difficulties is spelling. How do you spell relief?

BACHELOR NUMBER ONE: F-A-R-T.

PRETTY GIRL CHEERLEADER (without batting an eyelash): I see. Bachelor Number Two, what nationality are you?

BACHELOR NUMBER TWO: Well, my father is Welsh, and my mother is Hungarian, which makes me Well-Hung!

PRETTY GIRL CHEERLEADER: Well, aren't you the clever one? Okay, Bachelor Number Three, what's the funniest thing you were ever caught doing when you thought nobody was looking?

BACHELOR NUMBER THREE: I was caught with a necktie around my dick.

EXCERPT FROM THE SEVENTH "DATING GAME" SHOW

GORGEOUS HIGH FASHION MODEL: Bachelor Number Three, make up a poem just for me.

BACHELOR NUMBER THREE: Dollar for dollar, and ounce for ounce, I'll give you pleasure 'cause I'm big where it counts.

EXCERPT FROM THE EIGHTH "DATING GAME" SHOW

WHOLESOME GIRL: Bachelor Number Three, what is your favorite sport?

BACHELOR NUMBER THREE: Fishing. Do you like to fish?

WHOLESOME GIRL: No, but I'm good bait.

BACHELOR NUMBER THREE: Do you nibble, or swallow it whole?

WHOLESOME GIRL (giggling): I swallow it whole.

BACHELOR NUMBER THREE: You must have a *very* big mouth.

WHOLESOME GIRL (beside herself with glee): Okay, that's enough, Bachelor Number Three. Bachelor Number One, I play the trombone. If I blew you, what would you sound like?

BACHELOR NUMBER ONE: Ohhhh . . . ohhhh . . . ohohohoOHOH!

WHOLESOME GIRL: Terr-ific! Okay, Bachelor Number Two. What side order of food do *you* wish I were most like?

BACHELOR NUMBER TWO: Falafels.

WHOLESOME GIRL: Why?

BACHELOR NUMBER TWO: Because I like a girl with big falafels.

* * *

On Thursday of that infamous second week of production, I tried what I thought was an entertaining and novel idea for "The Dating Game." Instead of questioning three hidden bachelors, the young lady would interrogate a famous Hollywood trio of well-dressed chimpanzees. When the girl would ask the bachelors a question, three offstage male voices would answer for the trio of simians, and, consequently, the girl wouldn't suspect that she was talking to chimpanzees. To our audience, who could see both sides of the partition, the girl would appear to be trying her best to determine which chimp would be a fun escort for a night on the town. The chimps were my idea. I presumed the variation would be funny. It was—but for the wrong reason.

It was because of a gumdrop.

It seems the chimps' trainer always fed the animals gumdrops before they performed. The gumdrops calmed the chimps down, or made them happy, or something. In any case, the chimpanzees had been seated in their chairs, the gumdrops had been given to them, the curtains were about to be opened, and the game was about to begin. Then, just as the curtains opened, the middle chimpanzee's gumdrop fell into his crotch—somewhere deep down between his legs. The chimp was determined to find the hidden gumdrop. He began searching for it among his testicles.

Meanwhile, the first chimpanzee had taken to unscrewing one of the two decorative knobs on the sides of his chair. In due time, the monkey unscrewed the knob completely, and he immediately threw it out into the audience. This startled the bachelorette. She was in the process of asking a question when she saw a chair knob fly out from the other side of the partition and hit an elderly lady in the stomach. She wondered what manner of man would do such a thing.

In the meantime, the middle chimpanzee was still obsessed with retrieving the gumdrop. With a half-crazed expression on his face, he yanked feverishly at his scrotum. Our audience was unaware that the chimp was looking for a gumdrop. They simply thought the animal enjoyed playing with himself. A lot. Constantly and aggressively. With both hands. And with his head straining to get down to his crotch so that he could see the action up close. (Although the studio audience was roaring, there were those out there in TV-land, I'm sure, who later questioned the judgment of a television producer who found it humorous to display such a perverted chimpanzee on coast-to-coast TV.) And the situation didn't get any better. The chimp began to unbutton his fly, thinking the gumdrop might have fallen inside his pants.

I became light-headed.

And then the other chair knob flew out into the audience, conking an elderly man in the neck.

I ended the game.

The frazzled young lady who had been asking the questions chose Bachelor Number Three. The third chimp came around the partition and nipped her leg.

Jesus, I said to myself, at least things can't get worse.

But they did.

On our tenth show—the last program of the second week—a very shy and nervous girl sitting on one side of the partition had this bit of dialogue with a very shy and nervous man sitting on the other side of the partition:

> SHE: What does a rabbi do on his day off?
> HE: A rabbit?
> SHE: No. A *rabbi.*
> HE: How the fuck do I know?

* * *

The tapings were over. All the stage lights had been turned off except for the traditional forty-watt bulb in a shadeless standing lamp at center stage. I was sitting in the empty control room, two flights above the stage, looking down at that bulb. Everyone had gone except the night watchman, who was sitting below me in the shadows by the stage door, reading his newspaper. I wondered why he didn't find a more suitable place to read. There was so little light by the stage door. As I pondered this distracting bit of nonsense, I saw a second man emerge from the shadows.

It was Jim Byrd, from the CIA.

We ate dinner at Martoni's Restaurant, on Cahuenga just above Sunset Boulevard. Martoni's was fun in those days, when Mario and Tony ran the joint. The restaurant was always packed with crazy characters from the music business. It was packed the night Jim Byrd and I were there. The two of us sat in a corner booth, hidden from most of the excitement, twirling spaghetti with white clam sauce into our mouths and washing it down with red wine and cold beer.

Byrd said, "You look haggard."

"I feel haggard," I replied.

"Why are you dodging our assignments these days?"

"I want to be a television producer."

"You can do both, you know."

"I'm having plenty of trouble doing one."

"Come off it. You have enough energy for the two of us. At least think about it. Why get rusty and let all your good training go down the drain? I know how you work—you're good. You complain a lot, but you're good. And you hang in there. That's a very good sign. I like an agent that hangs in there." Jim wiped his chin with his napkin and said, "I'm putting a team together, and I want to bring you in with me. I told the D.O. about you, and he said it was all right with him. You wouldn't be hanging around Malcolm X meetings anymore, or trailing a bunch of hippies all over the South. You'd be doing *good* things."

"Like what?"

"Like . . . good things," he answered. Jim sat up straight, his eyes scanning the room. "Do you want to go to Mexico City with me next weekend?"

"Why?"

"To see what I do for a living these days."

"Jesus, I can't, Jim. I've got my hands full trying to get my new television program on its feet. I've taped two weeks worth of shows—

ten, all told—and I think if I'm lucky I'll be able to salvage three of them. The way I'm headed, I'm either going to go broke paying for shows I can't air or get canceled by the network." I took a gulp of beer. "I can't sleep at night," I went on, "and when it's time to go to work, I get nauseous and break out into a cold sweat. By afternoon I'm half dead. I take a nap and always have the same nightmare. I dream the network censor is chasing me around the studio with a hatchet, screaming, 'Come here, you little bastard, I want to cut your nuts off.' Then he grabs my nuts with one hand and pulls them about a yard away from my body, until they look like two super-long rubber bands, and with the other hand he swings his fucking hatchet. That's about the time I wake up, eyes like two pissholes in the snow. Then it's time for me to go to the studio, where a couple of dozen swinging singles can't wait to say 'fuck you' on national TV. And in the midst of this pandemonium, you want me to take off for a cute little weekend of fun and games in Mexico City!"

"You'll enjoy it," said Byrd, smiling. "I know you, and you'll enjoy it." He leaned back into the booth's red leather cushions, looking happier than I had ever seen him before. His red hair and freckles; his funny little smile; the perennial schoolboy glint in his eyes—everything pointed to someone who liked what he was doing. "Remember when I told you I'd keep my eyes and ears open for something you'd like?" he said. "Well, I guarantee you'll like this. And you'll only have to answer to me, unless you get so good at what we're doing that you'll want to work alone. And then you'd probably report to some higher control. But that would be down the road. For now, you would be with me, doing very exciting things." Byrd waved at the waiter and asked for the check. "Do me a favor?" he asked, looking me right in the eyes. "Think about going to Mexico City with me next weekend."

Jim paid the check, and we left the restaurant. Standing in the parking lot, waiting for our cars, I asked, "Exactly what *are* you going to be doing in Mexico City?"

He said, "I'll tell you on the airplane, if you decide to come." He told me he would be leaving for Mexico City the following Saturday morning, and gave me a number to call if I changed my mind and decided to go.

We shook hands and parted.

* * *

That night I slept poorly. Sometime during the hours before dawn I had another nightmare. I dreamt we were taping "The Dating Game" and the crotchety censor from Network Standards and Practices was back again, sitting next to me in the control room, holding his hatchet. He was on the telephone, speaking to the president of the American Broadcasting Company. I heard the censor saying something about wanting to arrest me. The show was in progress, and I was having a hard time following both what was being said on the stage and what the censor was saying to the president. Then I noticed that the single girl asking the questions was not a pretty, young bachelorette but a toothless old hag, and that the three bachelors sitting on the other side of the partition were nude.

"They're sitting there *nude!*" whispered the censor, cupping the telephone so that I couldn't hear what he was saying. But I heard anyway. "That's right," he continued, "nude! I think Barris should be locked up. After all, he *is* the responsible party."

"Who the hell told the goddamn bachelors to take off their goddamn clothes?" I yelled.

"None of us," said a faceless writer. "That must have been their idea."

When I turned to explain to the censor that the nude bachelors were not our idea, he was gone. In his place was a large red-faced man in a polyester business suit, raincoat, and porkpie hat. Attached to the pocket of his suit coat was a gold police badge. He held a billy club in his right hand that he kept slapping into the palm of his left. The man resembled Selma, Alabama's Sheriff Clark. "I'll show those naked niggers," he said, and stomped out of the control room. I didn't recall that the three nude bachelors were black. I walked over to the floor-to-ceiling control-room window and looked down at the stage. The bachelors were black.

I whirled around and said, "Who the hell—?" and realized the control room was completely empty. When I turned to look down at the stage again, I saw the large red-faced man in the polyester suit appear, take his billy club, and beat the three naked bachelors to death.

I woke from my dream elated. I had discovered the answer to my unruly-contestant problem.

* * *

The next afternoon I translated my nightmare into a plan. "Ladies and gentlemen," I said to the "Dating Game" bachelors and bachelorettes assembled in a room backstage, "before we get started with this evening's taping, I would like to take this opportunity to introduce you to Mr. Peter Jenks, of the Federal Communications Commission. I advise all of you to pay close attention to what he has to say. If afterward you decide you'd rather not participate in tonight's taping, please feel free to leave. And now, here's Mr. Jenks."

Peter Jenks stepped out from a corner and walked to the center of the room. Jenks was the consummate bureaucrat. He reeked of law and order. Government was obviously his bent, paperwork his life. His smile was devoid of mirth. His morals were as straight as the part in his hair. He said, "I don't know if any of you are aware of this or not, but it is a federal offense to make lewd or licentious remarks on a radio or television network broadcast. And, as you all *do* know, ignorance is no excuse." Mr. Jenks paused the appropriate amount of time to allow his first two sentences to sink in. "Broadcasting," he continued, "is regulated by the government, and the government takes a dim view of profanity on the airwaves. The penalty for such behavior is a year in prison or a ten-thousand-dollar fine, or both. Anyone making an off-color remark during the production of tonight's program will be arrested immediately. The taping will be halted, and the suspect, or suspects, will be removed from the stage. I will then handcuff the accused and personally escort him or her, or both, to the federal prison for booking under edict number three-sixty-four of the Broadcast Act of nineteen hundred and sixty-three. Are there any questions? No? Fine."

Peter Jenks was an actor. I hired him to portray a character I had created: the red-faced man of my nightmare, the policeman who beat the three nude bachelors to death. Jenks' job was to scare the shit out of "The Dating Game" contestants with threats regarding their use of foul language on the show. And he did. No one ever questioned Mr. Jenks' authority or the validity of what he said. We never had a problem of taste again on "The Dating Game"—at least, not for a good many years. But by then, the tenor of the times had changed, and a little bad taste was in good taste. And, since it's easier to unleash vulgarity than to keep it harnessed, my television programs flourished during those permissive years.

And then the times would change back again.

They always did.

And suddenly morality would be right up there with God and country. Pure thoughts and bodies would become the nation's obsession. Soon everybody would start eating only Dover sole for dinner and drinking skimmed milk. Everybody would be wearing Adidas sweat suits and sneakers when they went shopping on Fifth Avenue. Everybody would be swimming endless numbers of laps, lifting tons of weights, jogging from city to city with the same otiose ease as in fetching the morning paper. Everybody would find it necessary to walk a mile in fifteen minutes or less, lest he or she be considered a sloth. Everybody would be into perspiration, determined to sweat out their sense of humor as if it were last night's alcohol. The consumption of whole milk, ice cream cones, hot dogs, salt, butter, waffles, syrup, two eggs over easy, and Hershey Almond Bars would be comparable to ingesting arsenic or strychnine. It would be a bizarre era in which Americans would be infected with a grinding mania to do everything in their power to live forever. Everyone would become bor-ring in the process, and seem to enjoy becoming that way. And if that doesn't make any sense to you, it didn't make any sense to me either.

But then what did I know?

I'll tell you what I knew. I knew that I was continually suffering from a low-grade sadness about my genetically miserable timing; the realization that I had been too old to enjoy free love during the sixties, but was still young enough to have to endure the fitness bullshit of the eighties. Every morning I prayed the *New York Times* would feature a front-page story proclaiming that exercise would shorten your life by ten years and that junk food was surprisingly beneficial for everyone's cardiovascular system. But they never did.

The bastards.

At least I had solved the problem of our "Dating Game" contestants' excessive use of profanity and lewdness during the program's tapings. But, just when I thought my problems were over, a lady living in Los Angeles sent a letter to the *real* Federal Communications Commission stating that "The Dating Game" was a sham.

"A what?" I asked my lawyer.

"A sham," he repeated. "She says your claim that everybody on 'The Dating Game' is single is a lie. She wrote that she saw her husband on the program and, since he's still her husband, he's obviously not as single as you purport the bachelors to be."

"But," I whined, "all the contestants sign affidavits *swearing* they're single or divorced."

"Then they lie," said my lawyer calmly. "A network vice-president has called for all your files, tapes, legal documents, et cetera. You know how nervous the networks have been since the payola and quiz scandals, and this woman has made a serious accusation."

"But she's nuts! We're scrupulously honest. I *know* how nervous the networks are."

"Then prove that you're scrupulously honest," said my lawyer. "Unfortunately, the burden of proof is on you."

"What if I don't prove it to their satisfaction?"

"You're in trouble."

"What can they do to me?"

"Cancel your show."

"Jesus," I moaned, "I've only been on the air for a few weeks."

My lawyer handed me a copy of the lady's letter to the FCC. It was handwritten, the penmanship that of a five-year-old. The accusations were clearly moronic.

Later that day I spoke to the bachelor involved. He confirmed that he *was* legally divorced. I was furious. Wasn't it obvious to the American Broadcasting Company executives after examining the document that the letter was stupid? Couldn't the goddamn network vice-president have taken a moment of his precious time to check the credibility of the accuser? Would the tranquillity of my life be at the mercy of every letter-happy ex-spouse who owned pen and paper?

I fired off a two-page telegram to the goddamn network vice-president. It was an emotional telegram, and perhaps I should have thought twice before sending it. Somewhere within it was the following: "It's as if some demented lady sent you a letter insisting that all the bachelors on 'The Dating Game' were hunchbacks, that 'normal' people were not allowed on the show, and that the program was unfair to 'normal' people and should be taken off the air. And as a result of her puerile letter, you *immediately* had our files and tapes confiscated before even a cursory investigation was conducted to see if, in fact, the dim-wit's allegations were true. The hypothetical imputation that we program hunchback bachelors exclusively makes about as much sense as the lady's absurd declaration that we recruit married men. A married man on 'The Dating Game' is about as beneficial as a hunchback on 'The Dating Game'!"

To this day, I cannot for the life of me understand why I used hunchbacks as an example. It was the worst possible choice I could have made. Mr. Sylvan Siegel, the vice-president in question at the American Broadcasting Company's television network, was a hunchback.

* * *

At about the same time Siegel was exploding with fury in New York, a pretty young starlet was walking into my Hollywood office with a complaint. She said that a man had stopped her in a restaurant in Los Angeles and presented her with his card, which stated that he was a talent scout for "The Dating Game" television program. The so-called talent scout claimed he was considering recommending her for the show, and suggested she come by his office for an interview. She did, and he raped her. "I am," she said, "on my way to the police."

I didn't believe her.

I believed her story about the imposter, but not that she was going to the police. The "starlet" spoke gangster English and had a distinctly sleazy appearance. Her makeup was an inch thick and her tits were crammed together and half-exposed, bulging out of a World-War-II-style peasant blouse. Whether she was the sort who would have totally disliked the assault was questionable. She appeared to be angry, but I instinctively felt her injured feelings were a trifle manufactured and could be mollified by some form of recompense. In other words, she had come to my office in search of hush money. Blackmail. And so, with a damp and trembling hand, I shoved a hundred dollars into her purse and promised she would definitely be on the show. I begged her not to do anything rash, and assured her that we would catch the culprit and take care of him "in our own way." I hinted at Mafia-type revenge, which seemed to please her. I also alluded to the possibility that she might receive the same sort of treatment if she mentioned the incident to the press or the law. She left my office in decent spirits.

When she had gone I slumped into my desk chair, at wit's end. Had I done the right thing? Had I nipped the problem in the bud?

No, I hadn't.

Before the day had passed, three other young ladies had called my office with similar complaints. Same man. Same card. No rapes, but heavy molestation.

"What are you going to do?" asked my secretary.

"Go away," I answered. "I have to go away and think."

"Where will you go?"

"I'm not sure," I replied, but I was sure. I was going to Mexico City.

* * *

"Great country, Mexico," said Jim Byrd as Western Airlines Flight 272 —nonstop to Mexico City—leveled out at thirty thousand feet. "Great patriots. The history of the country is full of them. Allende, Hidago, Aldama, Jimerez. Fought like hell, even though they never had anything to fight with. Always behind the times." Byrd stretched forward and peered out the window across the aisle. "Must be the Sierra Madre mountains down there," he said, and flopped back into his seat. "They watched us take California and Texas and couldn't do a thing about it. Except give us Montezuma's revenge. Can't say as I blame them for being pleased when a gringo comes down with the revenge. It's small retribution for losing California and Texas."

"How do you know so much about Mexico?" I asked.

"I always study a place before I visit it. Never know what you might learn. And it just might save your ass someday."

Jim and I sat in the first two seats of the middle section, in front of all the other passengers. Good old Jim, I thought to myself. Never one to mingle in crowds. Always a loner. Look for the most secluded seat in a restaurant, train, plane, movie theater, or terminal, and you'll discover Jim Byrd. Usually scribbling notes, talking into a tape recorder, or just thinking.

"First-class seats are the best places to talk," he said, as though he were reading my mind. "Nobody can hear what you're saying. There's enough room between the rows of seats and enough engine noise to make eavesdropping impossible."

"How long will we be in Mexico?" I asked, vaguely concerned about my problems with "The Dating Game."

"Today, tomorrow, and Monday," he answered, "if everything goes according to plan."

"And if it doesn't?"

"Tuesday and Wednesday."

I ate a chunk of pineapple and thought again about those aggravating "Dating Game" problems. I felt guilty for leaving the fort in such disarray.

We adjusted our wristwatches to Mexico City time. "And what are we going to do in Mexico City?" I asked Jim halfheartedly, my mind elsewhere.

"Kill Salvador Panagra Renda," he replied.

Seven

January 27, 1966.

Salvador Panagra Renda was in his late thirties. He wore brown tortoiseshell spectacles and sported a thin mustache on a slender brown face. He was a frail man; bald, studious, and soft-spoken. But when he spoke, others listened. He wasn't as charismatic as his friend, Ernesto "Ché" Guevara, but Renda always seemed to get the message across. Renda made sense. Renda aroused. He galvanized and electrified the intelligent, the learned, the liberals, the conservatives, the students, the teachers, the vulnerable, the impressionable. Salvador's friend Ché was the headline hunter. Not Salvador. He preferred the shadows, the darker corners of the room away from publicity. His was a low profile, a satisfaction in results, a dream of a communistic South America led by Fidel Castro. Ché had that dream too. So did Castro, and while the latter consolidated his power base in Cuba, Ché and Salvador spread the word. They were good at spreading the word—too good. Instructions had come down from the shadowy heights of the Central Intelligence Agency. Salvador Panagra Renda, the unknown one, and Ernesto "Ché" Guevara, the celebrity, were to be eliminated. James R. Byrd was assigned Renda.

"How are we going to do it?" I asked.

"I don't know yet," answered Byrd. His answer startled me.

We landed in Mexico City. The smell of airplane fumes was everywhere. As we approached the customs booths, I broke out in a thin sweat. I had never passed a phony document, and I was convinced that if the forged papers Byrd had given me on the airplane didn't get me arrested, my sweaty, guilty face would. I handed my "Bernard Field" passport and visa papers to the customs official. He stamped its pages without looking up. The official kept the white immigration form and returned the pink copy to me lethargically. The Mexican customs clerk appeared too tired to care, as worn and rumpled as his uniform.

Byrd and I disappeared into the terminal.

I said, "You must have been pretty certain I'd come to Mexico City to go to all the trouble of making up a set of false documents for me."

"I was certain," said Byrd. "You're a sucker for excitement."

"And I hate uncomfortable situations."

"What's so uncomfortable about the CIA?"

"Nothing—at the moment," I replied. "It's being a television producer that's uncomfortable right now."

We found the sign that read *Cambio de Moneda:* currency exchange. Standing by the sign, apparently as planned, was one of our team, a stringer named Roberto Soledad. Ex–free-lance terrorist, ex–CIA operative, and now a part-time agent for the Chilean secret service, Soledad was "moonlighting" for the Company as a payback for past favors. Like the time some of the Company's agents saved Soledad's life in the Dominican Republic. Roberto Soledad owed Jim Byrd one, and the time had come to collect.

Soledad guided us to the limousine he had rented. It was parked in a no-parking zone.

"You're lucky you didn't get a ticket," Byrd said.

"I was in a hurry," sniffed Soledad.

"Don't be," barked Byrd. Jim Byrd's demeanor had changed rapidly since he stepped on Mexican soil. He had become brusque and snappish, the schoolboy glint in his eye replaced by humorless concentration.

Roberto Soledad's rented limousine may have been the oldest limousine in Mexico City. Its ashtray lids were gone. So were its cigarette lighters. One rear window worked. The radio aerial hung limply from its socket, draped over the front fender as if shot. The shock absorbers were history—a sudden dip in the road meant instant back problems.

"What a piece of shit," complained Byrd ill-temperedly.

"It's all they had," whined Soledad.

In front of our hotel, the Camino Real, was a decorative fountain and pool. The pool was in terrible turmoil. Its submerged jets had gone berserk, causing great quantities of water to thrash about violently. A maintenance man's mistake had produced treacherous geysers and evil whirlpools in the normally placid pool. I stared at the deranged body of water, fascinated.

"Así es la vida," said the doorman. I smiled and nodded, uncomprehending.

We registered as W. Colsen and B. Field, using fictitious Los

Angeles addresses. The clerk gave Jim our room keys and a lot of literature about the hotel's restaurants and shops. We dropped our shoulder bags in the room, met Soledad in the lobby, and drove to the Restaurant Bellinghausen in the fashionable central shopping district called the Pink Zone. We arrived there a little after four o'clock. The restaurant was still jammed with the afternoon lunch crowd. The head-waiter led us to a table for five on the patio at the rear of the restaurant, and the three of us sat down. At four-thirty, Jimmy Brazioni and Manuel Benitez joined us. The Renda hit team was complete.

* * *

Manuel Benitez was a mole. Ostensibly, he was a messenger boy for the CIA working out of Mexico City, transporting information from the Company's headquarters there to Mexican contacts and vice versa. Yet it was common knowledge in the Company that Benitez was working both sides of the street. Now and then, Manny would let the opposition peek at what he was carrying *before* he made the delivery. The CIA knew what Benitez was doing and continued to let him carry docu-ments—unimportant ones. The Company also knew that Benitez met Renda now and then. And, of course, the Agency was aware that Benitez could be bought; that his services usually went to the highest bidder. The Company had been holding Benitez in abeyance—waiting, as they liked to say, for the Big Play. With the announcement of the Renda job, the Big Play had arrived.

No one knew how or why Salvador Renda had established contact with Manuel Benitez, only that he had. And that Renda usually called Benitez when he arrived in Mexico City. That's how the Company knew Renda was there: Benitez had passed the word to his CIA con-tacts. "Renda phoned," Benitez had said, "and told me he was coming. He said he was going to stay for about a month. While he's here, he wants to use me for small courier jobs around the city."

Benitez had in this case obviously made a practical business deci-sion: he had decided the United States would pay him more money than Cuba. It was a sound judgment on Benitez's part.

Obviously, Renda didn't know how utterly corruptible Benitez really was, or to how many different alliances Manny had already pledged his unswerving loyalty. The knowledge that Renda was un-aware of Manny's faithlessness was both surprising and critical to the success of our operation. It was also dangerous. A great part of the Renda assassination plot was riding on the highly questionable premise that Manuel Benitez could be trusted if the price was right. Still, it was foolhardy to believe you ever had Manny pegged. The Cubans could always come in with a higher offer. (I found out later—much later—that the CIA had planned to pay Benitez handsomely if he performed his job successfully. And then they planned to kill him.)

During lunch at the Restaurant Bellinghausen, we discussed how we could go about assassinating Salvador Renda. The tentative plan called for Benitez to lure Renda to the target site by promising to let him see important CIA papers regarding Cuba. Shortly after Benitez and Renda reached the site, Roberto Soledad and Jimmy Brazioni would kill Renda. If anything went wrong—if Soledad and Brazioni were eliminated—Jim Byrd would kill Renda. If Byrd was eliminated, *I* would kill Renda. If it ever got to me, and I failed, the mission would be considered a disaster. The knowledge that I was in line as a hit man excited the hell out of me. I was finally doing something adventurous. And patriotic. And *meaningful*. At the time, the fact that I might have to kill a human being was irrelevant to me. Or so it seemed.

During the long discussion, I studied Brazioni, Benitez, and Soledad. Jimmy Brazioni had nothing in common with Manuel Benitez. In fact, the two were exact opposites. Brazioni was tall, well-proportioned, fair, and handsome. Benitez was short, squat, dark, and ugly. Whereas Benitez was totally untrustworthy, Brazioni could be trusted. Brazioni appeared to despise Benitez, and I was fairly certain the feeling was mutual. Conversely, Brazioni seemed to like Roberto Soledad.

Jimmy and Roberto were alike in many ways. Both men loved to kill people, and both did it well. Brazioni and Soledad were equally adept demolition experts, with a penchant for explosives as a means of getting the job done. They both loved action. They had both been banned from the United States for life. No one knew exactly why. No one asked. Though Brazioni and Soledad were not allowed to set foot on American soil, they were allowed to kill for America—and they were paid handsomely for their services. At the time we were in Mexico City, Jimmy Brazioni was affiliated with the Patria y Libertad, a neofascist terrorist group working in and out of Chile. Years later, in 1973, Brazioni would be instrumental in Chile's military coup. Some would say that it was Brazioni's burst of machine-gun fire that killed Chilean President Salvador Allende. Eight years after our lunch in Mexico City, Brazioni would look me in the eye and tell me he was nowhere near Allende at the time of the assassination. But for some reason I wouldn't believe him.

Sitting in the Restaurant Bellinghausen, Jimmy Brazioni said,

"Neither the Patria nor anyone else has an exclusivity on me. If the job pays well, Jimmy Brazioni is available."

"The job pays well," said Jim Byrd.

"Then I'm in," said Brazioni, lifting his wine glass.

"So am I," said Brazioni's friend, Roberto Soledad.

"Me too," muttered Manny Benitez.

"Good," said Jim Byrd. "Here's to a successful job and long lives." We all clinked our wine glasses. (In 1980, every member of the Renda hit team except me would be dead. I would never find out how anyone died, only that they had.)

We finished our drinks, and the waiter passed out the menus. They were in Spanish. Byrd, Brazioni, Soledad, and Benitez spoke the language fluently. I didn't, but wouldn't admit it. I ordered what I thought was broiled chicken. When my platter arrived, Brazioni said, "Why the hell would anyone eat *that?*"

"Because I like it," I said, staring at the atrocious-looking objects on my plate.

"You like the ankles of a pig?" asked Manny Benitez, flashing a gold-toothed smile.

"Yeah, I do," I said. I never touched the goddamn things. I drank a couple of beers instead.

It was hard to believe that on this pleasant, sunny afternoon in Mexico City, I was discussing the murder of another person, orchestrating the death of a meek, mild-mannered man from Cuba.

By the time we finished lunch, the basic plan was complete. Manuel Benitez would contact Salvador Renda the next morning and suggest they meet the following day at noon. Benitez would say he had some important papers he wanted Renda to see before he delivered them to his CIA contact, and he would ask Renda to meet him in front of the Museo Nacional. When they met, Benitez would lead Renda to a bench away from the museum's main entrance. After they were seated, Soledad and Brazioni would walk over to them and kill Salvador Renda.

"It sounds too simple," said Roberto Soledad. "What if he doesn't come? Or what if he becomes suspicious and brings others? What happens then?"

"Beats the shit out of me," said Jim Byrd.

Brazioni burst out laughing. So did Jim Byrd. Soledad looked at Brazioni, then at Byrd, and then began laughing himself. Benitez didn't crack a smile.

* * *

Sometime during the following evening in Mexico City, Roberto Soledad returned to the airport. In the terminal, near the currency exchange booth, he met a contact. Soledad gave the contact three pink I-94 immigration exit visas, shook hands with the man, and returned to his hotel room. The contact placed the exit visas into a stack of similar pink forms collected by customs officials from a planeload of travelers boarding a Pan Am flight bound for New York and Paris. As far as the Mexican authorities were concerned, W. Colsen, B. Field, and J. Bigatel (J. Byrd, C. Barris, and J. Brazioni) had departed Mexico City that night; Sunday, January 28, 1966.

Meanwhile, in our headquarters—the garage of a pasty yellow house on a narrow street named the Calle A. Poe—Jim Byrd gave me my second forged passport and a new forged exit visa. I was now James Cooper. We raised fresh beer bottles to our new names, to the success of the next morning's assassination, and to a good night's sleep.

Later on, I drank four more bottles of beer in our hotel room to make me sleepy. But for hours I remained wide awake, staring at the ceiling and listening to Jim's snoring. Christ, I thought to myself, goyim sleep the night before *anything*. Olympic gold-medal competitions, open-heart surgery, executions, night-bombing raids over Dresden, trips to the moon, assassinations . . .

* * *

That night, the first thing Manuel Benitez did after leaving the pasty yellow house on Calle A. Poe was meet a friend on a nearby street corner at exactly nine o'clock. They walked to the front of the Museo Nacional. Benitez's friend was stocky and dark, and, though it was a warm night, he wore a black knit sailor's watch cap and a black sailor's pea-coat. For a hundred and forty dollars, Manuel Benitez told the man in the pea-coat that Salvador Renda would be shot the next morning. "On that bench," said Benitez, pointing to the target site. The man nodded and disappeared into the night.

The next morning at the museum, Byrd, Brazioni, Soledad, and I walked to the stone bench in the plaza in front of the museum. Benitez was sitting there with the bearded man in the watch cap and pea-coat.

"That's not Salvador Renda," I whispered to Byrd, looking at the man sitting next to Benitez.

"How do *you* know?" scoffed Jimmy Brazioni.

"I *know!* That's someone else!"

"Relax," hissed Jim Byrd.

I told Byrd to stop telling me to relax. I insisted that the man in the black knitted watch cap was not Renda. *"You* should know that," I whispered. "You studied the pictures the same as I did."

"I said, relax!" shouted Byrd angrily. "You're scared shitless."

"I am not."

"You are so. You're a scared little piss-ant."

The others heard Jim Byrd chastise me. The bearded man and Benitez began laughing. So did Brazioni and Soledad. A black dog, sleeping in the middle of the plaza, lifted his head to see what was going on. After a second or two, he lowered his head and went back to sleep.

"Whosa goink tawinna de Rosea Bowla?" asked the bearded man in the pea-coat. He spoke with a strange accent. "Ees eeta goink tabeea U-See-Ella-Aye ora Meeshageena?"

The question struck Benitez and Brazioni as funny. "Who's gonna win the Rose Bowl, UCLA or Michigan?" repeated Brazioni. He laughed loudly and said, "Your friend is a funny guy, Manny."

Manuel Benitez smiled. His gold teeth glared in the sunlight. He said, "I am glad, Jimmy, we became friends before it was too late."

I was perplexed. I wondered what was so hilarious about a question concerning the Rose Bowl. Besides, the game had already been played. UCLA had won 14–12. And before what was too late? And why were Benitez and Brazioni suddenly such good friends?

And then, still seated on a marble bench, the bearded man and Manuel Benitez drew big .44-caliber pistols out of their jacket pockets and shot bullets into me, Byrd, Brazioni, and Soledad.

"I told you!" I screamed, confused and dying. "I told you!"

The dog lifted his head.

* * *

The morning heat smacked me awake.

I had been dreaming again.

I was panting, and sopping wet. I turned my head to the left and saw Byrd in the other bed, still sleeping like a goddamned baby. I reached for my wristwatch. It was ten minutes before six. I tiptoed to the balcony, quietly slid the door open, and stepped outside. The air smelled of diesel fumes and dog shit.

I was scared.

The dream was an omen. I was convinced that Benitez had told our plans to someone during the night, and that we would all be shot dead in less than three hours. But none of the team would ever believe me. If I explained my nightmare, and told them I was sure it was a portent of things to come, they'd laugh. Especially Brazioni. And Byrd would say, "Relax," just like he'd said in my dream.

An hour later the four of us met for breakfast. Benitez was elsewhere, allegedly meeting Renda. Self-consciously, I told Jim Byrd about my dream, out of the corner of my mouth so the others wouldn't hear me.

Jim said, "Relax."

"Jesus, Jim, every time I tell you something, all you ever do is tell me to relax."

"Then do as I tell you, and relax. If you're superstitious you shouldn't be in this business. Besides," Byrd continued, dunking a piece of toast in a puddle of egg yolk, "we all had that dream last night."

A few minutes before nine that morning, Jim Byrd, Brazioni, Soledad, and I walked onto the Museo Nacional Plaza. On a bench on the other side of the plaza sat Manny Benitez and Salvador Renda.

Even from a distance we could tell it was Renda. We had all studied his pictures. He had thinning gray hair on a high, receding forehead. Small, almost frail-looking, Renda hardly appeared dangerous—something I would discover about most extremely dangerous men.

Renda and Benitez were chatting enthusiastically, waving their arms, pointing forefingers. Neither one saw us.

Or so it seemed.

We walked two abreast, Brazioni and Soledad in front of Byrd and myself. The four of us pretended to be chatting. We walked along the opposite side of the huge plaza, away from Renda and Benitez, turning right at the far end, and then right again at the far corner. We were now on the same side of the plaza as Renda and Benitez. They were dead ahead, a good distance away. We started forward in a straight line that would lead us directly to Renda's bench. I knew that when we approached that bench, Brazioni and Soledad would step quickly ahead of us, turn, and execute Salvador Renda. I knew that Renda had less than a minute to live.

It was an agonizingly long minute. Before the four of us traveled the final fifty feet, we stopped to check the plaza one last time. The square was somewhat crowded, more so than when we had looked it over the day before. Our hit team, with its cameras, maps, and checkered slacks, appeared to be just another group of tourists. Several

couples were approaching the museum's entrance. A few individuals
strolled about, stopping now and then to snap pictures of each other
or the museum. A half dozen visitors sat on the marble benches that
bordered the plaza. But no one was sitting near Renda or Benitez. It
was perfect.

And then a strange thing happened.

Groups of schoolchildren began to file into the plaza. They were
wearing outfits in their school colors, and they kept coming up the
curved marble steps in never-ending ranks. Squealing and giggling,
yelling and laughing, their teachers herding or trying to herd them all
together.

"Where the fuck did *they* come from?" groaned Brazioni.

"It's Monday," I said. "Shouldn't they be in school?"

"Maybe it's some sort of holiday," said Soledad nervously.

"Keep walking," snapped Byrd.

We kept walking. As we approached the bench, Byrd slowed
down, and so did I. Then we stopped. Brazioni and Soledad continued
on. I looked around the square. Where were Renda's bodyguards? Did
he actually come alone?

By the time I looked back at the bench, Brazioni and Soledad had
reached it. They were standing in front of Renda, facing him. Brazioni's
shoulders were hunched together. He was shooting from the hip. Soledad's right arm was fully extended, unloading his gun at point-blank
range, the end of the barrel inches away from Renda's face. All I heard
were little popping sounds. Renda slumped to the back of the bench,
his head flopping to the side. Someone screamed. Then people were
running in several directions. Benitez was gone. So were Brazioni and
Soledad. I watched Jim Byrd walk to the bench, lean over, look at
Renda dispassionately, then walk away.

It was all over.

I stood in the plaza alone, with a hundred schoolchildren, dozens
of tourists, and a dead man. Suddenly, I had to see Renda: I had to peer
at his dead face, to verify his death for myself. I walked toward the
bench. As I walked, I heard schoolchildren crying out. I saw some of
them pointing at Renda, running toward him. Many reached Renda
before I did. I continued walking toward the dead man, fascinated.
Saying to myself: my God, he's dead.

I pushed my way through the children and their teachers and
looked down at Renda. He sat as if he were dozing. His eyes were
slightly opened, his mouth an oval. There were visible bullet holes in

his forehead, right cheek, and neck. A dark brown stain widened across the front of his sport shirt. A pool of blood grew larger and larger on the bench by his right hand and thigh.

"He's been shot!" someone said in English, uselessly. "He's been shot, and he's dead!"

I backed away and left the plaza.

*   *   *

I walked as fast as I could without appearing to be walking as fast as I could. My mind was a jumble of vivid impressions. The holes in Renda's face. The puddle of blood on the marble bench. And one particularly silly thought: none of the team had said good-bye—they had simply disappeared. No one had looked over his shoulder to see if the others had gotten away safely. Everyone had just evaporated.

I walked for almost half an hour. I passed a small park and saw pairs of men practicing bullfighting. I sat on a bench and watched the grown men romping about in pockets of shade under the tall trees of the park. Not far away on the boulevard, irritable taxi drivers blew their horns at each other, and dejected people walked to work. I had a violent urge to stand on that park bench and shout, "We did it! We killed Renda!" I wanted to tell the bullfighters what we had just accomplished, and the angry taxi drivers, and the worn-out clerks and salesgirls plodding along the sidewalks to their miserable jobs. I wanted to describe to everyone how exciting, and how scary, the assassination was. I was suffocating; I needed to scream the story so that I could breathe. I wanted to shout into someone's face the minute details of our accomplishment. A stranger would suffice—anyone at all who would allow me to boast of how I had just helped murder an enemy of the United States of America. But I couldn't tell a living soul, and it was agony.

"You'll get over it," my grandmother would have said. And I did. Each and every time. But it wasn't easy. That part never was.

*   *   *

The plane ride back to Los Angeles was uneventful. I had a chance to think about things—to unravel my thoughts. Although it had been a long weekend, it seemed that I had been in Mexico City only a few hours. I had been petrified most of the time, but I would have gladly done it again. It was fun. It was more than fun; it was *living*. In Mexico City life had risen to the surface of my skin. Every sensation had been magnified a hundredfold. I may have been sickened by the death, but I never doubted why I was there. I might have been frightened, but I was never bored. I might not have been a hero, but I had shown a certain amount of courage. I liked that.

I sat in my seat, eating peanuts. Already, memories were collecting like flies on flypaper. The ancient limousine. The plaza. The dog. The pigs' knuckles at the Restaurant Bellinghausen. The dream. The pasty yellow house on Calle A. Poe. Walking the perimeter of the plaza. The schoolchildren. The popping sounds.

* * *

Gene Banks, a "Dating Game" staffer, met me at the airport.

"How was your vacation?" he asked.

"Great."

"It was short. Did you get a chance to relax?"

I said that I had.

Back at the office, things were relatively sane. The hunchbacked vice-president had apparently calmed down. And the dirty remarks made during the tapings of "The Dating Game" were no longer a problem; my actor friend, Peter Jenks, was impersonating the bogus FCC inspector to perfection, and licentious remarks had become a thing of the past. The show's tapings were now lily white. Even the wizened censor had all but disappeared.

The only dilemma that now remained was what to do about the fraudulent "Dating Game" talent scout. He continued to lure women to so-called preliminary auditions and then molest them with wild abandon. I hated him with a passion, and dreamed nightly of getting my hands on the slimy bastard. Or, better yet, of having some of my cronies get *their* hands on him. Then, a week after I returned from Mexico City, a girl called my secretary to verify an appointment with someone from our "Dating Game" staff named Stan Gillis.

I asked my secretary who Stan Gillis was. To my knowledge there wasn't anybody in our company named Stan Gillis.

"He's obviously our friend the fake talent scout," my secretary replied.

My heart skipped a beat. I told my secretary to tell the girl to keep her appointment. "Just ask her when and where she's planning to meet this Gillis guy."

The girl informed us that the meeting was to take place at ten o'clock that evening at the Ocean Diner in Santa Monica and that she would be wearing a red dress. She described herself as somewhat thin, sort of well-built, and with blond hair.

At nine forty-five that night, an emaciated girl in a fire-engine-red dress was sitting in a booth in the back of the Ocean Diner on Pico Boulevard. There was not a semblance of a breast on her chest, and her flagrantly-dyed blond hair was teased into a gigantic beehive. She rubbed the palms of her hands together nervously.

I sat at the counter with three friends of mine, drinking coffee. My friends were all very large. And very black. And all ex-convicts. My pals and I had done some jobs together when I was working for the Company in New York, the details of which I'll keep to myself. (Suffice it to say that if an arm needed breaking, they broke it. It was a function of their parole agreements.) Our motley quartet was dressed as if we were coming from a softball game: we wore baseball hats, matching T-shirts with "Shulman's Bakery" on the back, and we carried baseball gloves, softballs, and two Louisville Slugger baseball bats.

At exactly ten o'clock, a mousy-looking man entered the diner. He scanned the place, smiled when he recognized the skinny girl in the back booth, and quickly joined her. Ten minutes later the pair left the diner. We tagged along behind them. The mousy man led the skinny girl to a 1960 Cadillac parked in a dark and lonely corner of a vacant lot. A very dark and lonely corner. "How come we never got this lucky when we were snappin' bones in Harlem?" whispered one of the ex-cons.

The mousy man was opening the car's door for the skinny girl when we arrived. One of my friends whacked the door closed with a baseball bat, pushed the girl aside, and grabbed the Mouse by his throat. "What's goin' on?" the Mouse gurgled.

My enormous black friend said, "I'll motherfuckin' talent-scout you, you motherfuckin' asshole," and slammed the Mouse up against his Cadillac. The Mouse groaned.

I thanked the skinny girl and suggested she go home. She did. Moments after she left, my enormous black friend brought his enormous knee up into the Mouse's nuts. The Mouse fell to the ground in the fetal position, hands cupping his crotch. While the Mouse writhed in the parking-lot dirt, the three ex-cons took turns bashing in the Mouse's Cadillac. The boys destroyed the headlights, the windshield, the side windows, and the taillights. Then they slashed the car's tires. That's when I finally spoke to the Mouse. I said, "Don't bother us anymore, you little pervert, or next time *you'll* be the fucking Cadillac."

The Mouse never bothered us again.

But Rollie Ripple did.

* * *

Rollie Ripple was a well-known radio correspondent and reviewer based in Hollywood. His opinions on the entertainment scene were beamed coast-to-coast two times a week. Ripple was a pipe-smoking egoist, a ham, and a flirt. He was pompous and crude. And he was nicknamed the "Hatchet Man."

When Rollie Ripple talked about you, you knew you were being talked about. Ripple was never complimentary. He was vicious. He sought out vulnerability—the gray areas, the soft underbelly—and then he struck. He had a great future in intimidation and innuendo. And now the Hatchet Man had zeroed in on "The Dating Game" and Chuck Barris Productions. My cocky fledgling company, full of braggadocio and dreams, was just right for a Ripple exposé. Besides, Ripple had thought of an ingenious plan that would be fun to implement. He would pose as a prospective "Dating Game" bachelor. He would use a clever nom de plume and hopefully go undetected through our contestant selection maze. As he proceeded through the program's various auditions, he would take notes. Eventually, he would surface and tell all, in typically venomous fashion. His machinations, he was sure, would result in not only good radio copy, but quite possibly a *Newsweek* feature, or maybe a *Time* cover story. (Ripple always dreamed of breaking into print.)

The day Rollie Ripple appeared at our offices, my contestant coordinator buzzed me on the intercom and said, "Rollie Ripple is here posing as a prospective contestant. He's calling himself Bill Jones."

"Who's Rollie Ripple?" I asked.

"A real prick. He's a radio commentator who cuts up everyone he talks about."

"So?"

"I just wanted to know what you wanted to do about it."

"Nothing," I said. "Let him go through. Let's see what happens."

The next day I watched Rollie Ripple play a practice game with other "Dating Game" contestant prospects. Ripple was fat and forty, and his demeanor was that of a church deacon. He sat on his stool with a haughty scowl on his round, red face. His curved pipe hung over his fat lower lip, and his stomach hung over his belt. His pants were yanked up above his socks. One of the collar buttons on his button-down shirt was missing. His tie had a stain at the bottom. I looked at Ripple's holier-than-thou face and wondered what he would think if he knew what we knew. Our researchers had found out that Ripple read *Screw* magazine and loved to date teenyboppers.

I listened to Ripple answer the questions of an auditioning bachelorette. He was terrible, but I put him on the show anyway. He was terrible there, too. And then he surfaced. Three days after he appeared on "The Dating Game," he strolled into my office. My secretary told me that a Mr. Rollie Ripple would like a word with me. "He says you might know him as Bill Jones. He says he was on 'The Dating Game' a few nights ago."

I said, "Send him in."

Ripple appeared with a tape recorder.

Through a cloud of pipe smoke, Ripple confessed that he had tricked us. He had used an alias on the show. He told me he had gone the route undetected, from application to performance. "Frankly, I was surprised I wasn't found out. I never expected to get so far as to actually be on the program," he said with a pretentious grin. "I didn't think I was that good." (You weren't, you fartbiter.)

There were pipe ashes in Ripple's crotch. He caught me looking down there, looked himself, and then flicked the ashes away with thick, stubby fingers. His tone of voice changed as he flicked. It became very grim. "I have most of the information I need for the feature I plan to do," said Ripple, looking up from his crotch. "I want to ask you a few questions to fill in some of the spaces. I hope you don't mind." Ripple turned on his tape recorder without waiting to find out if I minded or not.

Though it was superfluous, I told Ripple I didn't mind. "But," I said, baiting my trap, "you haven't really experienced the entire 'Dating Game' phenomenon. True, you were one of three bachelors answering questions. But to know it all, you should see what it's like to be on the *other* side of the partition. You should experience how it feels to *ask* questions. You should quiz three pretty young girls. We don't usually do that, but in your case I would make an exception. You would know 'The Dating Game' from every conceivable angle. Also," I added with a leer, "you'd have a night on the town with one of those cute little girls."

"Could I do that?" he asked.

At the next production meeting, I told my staff I wanted to tape a program where a man would question three girls. "The man," I said, "will be Bill Jones, a.k.a. Rollie Ripple."

"We'll get three terrific ladies for him," said someone.

"Wrong," I said. "What I want for Ripple are three of the cheapest, sleaziest-looking nubiles you can get your hands on."

"You're not serious," said my contestant coordinator. "You can't play tricks like that on important people. Especially not with the likes of Rollie Ripple."

"Oh yes I can," I replied.

And I did.

So there he was, the infamous Rollie Ripple, sitting in the chair normally used by the bachelorette, augustly smoking his curved white meerschaum pipe, asking exquisitely erudite but terribly wearisome questions of three of the seediest, dumbest trollops ever to adorn a coast-to-coast television program. The event was well worth the inevitable penalty I would have to pay.

At last the game ended, and the moment came when Ripple would meet the flea-bitten harridans he had been talking to but hadn't seen. At last I would have my revenge.

Ripple chose Bachelorette Number Three. She just happened to be the trio's sleaziest. His eyes widened when he met Bachelorette Number One. They grew even wider when he met Bachelorette Number Two.

And then Bachelorette Number Three came around the partition.

And guess what?

It was love at first sight.

I attended the wedding. It took place on the lawn of Ripple's house in Beverly Hills, under a flower-bedecked arbor. Someone played a violin. I was best man. Rollie Ripple gave me a big hug, and so did the bride. (The bride had obviously tried to transform herself from a cheap, nubile sleaze into a sophisticated, debonair woman fit for the likes of Ripple.) While she was squeezing me, she whispered something in my ear. She said, "If you ever blow my cover, you little cocksucker, I'll jam your pecker into a meat grinder." I promised the blushing bride I would never blow anything of hers.

Ripple's tender story was heard across the country, detailing how he found true love on "The Dating Game."

Sometimes I think about Rollie and Flossie, and wonder how they are. I understand they lived happily ever after.

As my grandmother would have said, "Go know."

* * *

Producing "The Dating Game" was wearing, but never dull. There was a new crisis every day; some funny, some pathetic, some scary. Happily, none of the girls were raped; and, to my knowledge, none became pregnant. A great number, however, were laid. The news, when it came, was a shock to me. I had thought we were running a moral ship. (The revelation that not everyone participating in the show was as puritanical and sexually repressed as I was came to my attention much later during a "Dating Game" reunion party in Hollywood. We had invited as many ex-Dating Gamers as we could find to a hotel for champagne and dancing. Throughout the evening, former "Dating Game" bachelors would approach me, smiling slyly, winking conspiratorially, slapping my back, and saying things like, "Thanks for the great piece of ass. What a guy!" For a while, I had no idea what they were talking about. Eventually I figured it out.)

*   *   *

The months that followed Rollie Ripple's wedding were full of high emotion and intense excitement. I spent much of my time wondering if we were doing everything we could to make "The Dating Game" a success. If a particular show didn't work, why didn't it work? What had we done wrong? I spent long nights at my desk, staring at contestant forms. I studied the pictures of smiling bachelors and bachelorettes. I talked to those pictures as if the contestants they represented were sitting in my office with me. "Why were you so good in the audition," I would ask the picture, "and so lousy on the show? How come I couldn't figure you out? How can I make sure someone like you doesn't fool me next time? And you, you little cocksucker, you sat on your stool like a rock. Why couldn't I see what a moron you were *before* I booked you?"

The Polaroids never said a word.

Eventually, paranoia set in. I was convinced we weren't doing enough; that "The Dating Game" would be canceled after its first thirteen weeks. I began to rationalize defeat. At least after thirteen weeks I would have enough money to pay off the small debts I had accrued and still have some left over for a rainy day. But would I sell another television game show before that rainy day came and went? I was sure I had the three ingredients that my hero, Tom Stoppard, felt were necessary for creative existence: an unsinkable quality, eccentric persistence, and an irrepressible vitality. But I wasn't sure I could think of another television game-show idea.

And then one day I received a telephone call from the *executive* vice-president of ABC. The exec had a problem. He told me he was about to cancel "The Tammy Grimes Show" after only three outings. Tammy's national rating was a disappointment. The exec needed a replacement, and he needed it in a hurry. The replacement would move into the seven-thirty-to-eight time period on Saturday night—a plum of a spot. But what show would he place there?

"Perhaps 'The Dating Game,' " he said, with incredible seriousness. "But the nighttime 'Dating Game' cannot be the same as the daytime 'Dating Game.' If you can think of something you can do on a nighttime version that would be exciting, unusual, and *different,* I'd consider putting your program in prime time. It would be the first game show ever on prime-time television. A big risk, but I'm prepared to gamble. I mean, what the hell is life all about?"

(What, I wondered, *is* life all about? Thomas McGuane called life a "shit sandwich" and said we all took bites.)

"Price is no object," continued the exec, "within limits, of course."

"Of course."

"I need an answer in exactly seventy-two hours."

"Three days!"

"Right," said the executive v.p. "If I don't hear from you by then, I'll move elsewhere. So put on your thinking cap, Chuck, and get back to me A-S-A-P."

It wasn't fair: it seemed the network biggies were always forcing creative decisions out of me, and giving me no time to come up with them. I spent the next forty-eight consecutive hours in my office, hoping that sitting at my desk would help me think of the idea that would mean prime time for "The Dating Game." I wanted to endear myself to God by showing Him my nose was firmly to the grindstone, hoping that He in turn would reward me with a clue. I fervently hoped God would look kindly upon me for not wasting time eating, or drinking, or making merry. Or even going home. I seemed to recall that God liked guys who wore hair shirts, and I was suffering the best I could. God would give me the answer. The fucker wouldn't let me down.

But God was apparently out to lunch. At least He wasn't hanging around 1313 Vine Street in Hollywood. The fucking heavens never did open up. It was obvious I would have to figure it out myself.

> And so it is written: As long
> as man hopes, he will go on
> turning out hopeful finales.
> —Gunter Grass

From your mouth to God's ear, Gunter, if you can find the dork. In any case, forty-eight hours of hoping had passed, and I still couldn't think of a thing to do.

What *could* we do?

We were using the prettiest, most personable girls in California, and the handsomest, most extroverted bachelors. The questions were about as keen as we could suggest. What else could we do? Add a forty-piece symphony orchestra?

Time moved on, as it is wont to do. In desperation, I went to our empty television studio and sat there, hoping it might help. I picked a tenth-row seat, twelve seats in. Ten plus twelve equals twenty-two. My lucky number. Maybe sitting in a charmed studio seat would help to flash some eleventh-hour stroke of genius into my head. I was on my fifty-third hour and needed all the help I could get. I stared at the barren stage and the four canvas-covered television cameras and thought and thought and thought.

And then someone grabbed my throat in an arm lock and began to strangle me. I clutched at the strong arm that was smashing my windpipe into the back of my neck, trying desperately to pry it loose. I couldn't. I struggled silently in my good-luck seat.

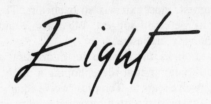

Eight

The horrible arm dropped away from my neck and tweaked my crotch. I staggered to my feet, coughing violently, and whirled around.

It was Jim Byrd. I threw a punch at his mouth, which he easily blocked. "*Jesus motherfucking Christ,*" I screamed, "*you prick! What the fuck do you think you're doing?*"

"Be alert. You must *always* be alert."

"You're a stupid fucking turd, you know that?" I yelled, massaging my neck.

"Let's get something to eat," he said calmly.

For the first time in over two days, I left the premises, and we went to Martoni's. It was early, and the dinner crowd hadn't arrived yet. Jim and I sat at the bar. He asked for a bourbon and soda with a beer chaser. I ordered a double J.B. on the rocks with a beer chaser, embarking on the exceedingly masochistic pursuit of getting ripped. I was tired, empty, disappointed, and visibly pissed. It would be the self-flagellating binge of the defeated.

"Anger is acknowledgment of failure," said Byrd. "I read that somewhere. In a Paul Theroux book, I think. I like Theroux. Ever read anything of his?"

"No," I replied, and told Jim my "Dating Game" problem. He didn't ask, but I told him anyway. I explained how nice it would have been to find the solution; and, if I had found one, what a profound opportunity it would have been for me, my staff, and the show in general. We all would have prospered.

Byrd burped and ordered another beer.

I groused about the last two agonizing days and nights on the creative rack; days and nights of unadulterated pain and deprivation without a fucking thing to show for it. And now, I said to Byrd, it appeared as though time had run out on me. There were only ten of my seventy-two hours left to think of something—an academic point, since I had obviously already given up. I also told Jim it was good to see him. Then I paused to let Byrd get in a few words.

"I want you to do jobs for the Central Intelligence Agency on a more regular basis," he said.

"Jesus Christ, Jim. Why?"

"I need you. I'm in charge of a fairly large wet operation now, and I could use your potential skills."

"Great."

"And you have the perfect cover," Jim continued, mixing his bourbon and soda with his right index finger. "You're a respectable packager of television shows with what appears to be a successful television program on the air."

"I'm not so sure about that."

"You can take legitimate business trips," Jim went on, "and no one would suspect any hanky-panky."

"Oh, *that* again." Jim was beginning to annoy the hell out of me. His fucking CIA shit. His fucking boyish good looks. His goddamn red hair and freckles. The fact that he never made a mess mixing his bourbon. I just wasn't in the mood.

"Didn't you have fun in Mexico City?" he asked.

I looked up from my drink and saw Jim Byrd's smiling face.

"So what if I did?" I whined, being as contrary as possible. "Anyway, I haven't any reason to make business trips."

"Yes, you do."

"No, I don't."

"Yes, you do. Look," said Jim, gulping some bourbon, "I don't mean to be butting into your business, but I've been watching 'The Dating Game' all week. I've noticed that you send the winning couples to asshole places like nightclubs in downtown Hollywood, or maybe half-ass restaurants in Beverly Hills. Isn't that so?" He took another gulp of bourbon and was surprised to see there was none left. "You see, my point is this," said Byrd, waving to the bartender. "Why don't you stop messing around with rinky-dink California cities, and send the winning couples to the big leagues instead? Send them to exciting places, *romantic* places—places like Paris, Rome, Vienna, Capri, Bali, Hong Kong, Hawaii . . ."

"For Christ's sake, Jim," I moaned, "nobody's going to allow us to send a girl and a guy off alone to some foreign country. The girl's parents'll raise holy hell. So will the network's goddamn Standards and Practices Department."

"Send a chaperone," said Jim. "Hire nice little old ladies who have nothing better to do with themselves. They'll jump at the chance to travel to Paris, all expenses paid. Or send your own employees. As a bonus. Anyway, the trips would only be three or four days long. Nobody'll be gone forever. And every now and then, *you* be the chaperone. Every now and then, schedule a date to a city where the Company has a little business to transact—and *you* go as the dates' chaperone. That's a legitimate business trip, isn't it? And it's the perfect cover."

"And who's going to pay for all of this?" I asked. And then—as if struck by a gigantic bolt of lightning—I saw the answer to my question. I saw the answer to Jim's question. I saw the answer to the executive vice-president's question. I saw the answer to my prayers! I jumped off the bar stool and roared, *"That's it! Yahoo!"* I danced around my bar stool, shouting, *"That's the fucking answer! That's the fucking answer! That's the fucking answer!"*

We were asked to leave the restaurant.

Outside, in the restaurant's parking lot, I gave Jim Byrd a big hug. "You're a genius, Jim. A goddamn genius!"

"I know."

"Of course!" I yelped. "Paris, Rome, Capri. Exciting, romantic, fun-filled dream dates! Something we *don't* do on our daytime show. On our prime-time "Dating Game" program the winning couples will go on *dream dates!* To Tahiti, Florence, Venice, Amsterdam . . ."

"Moscow," said Jim.

* * *

Six weeks later, "The Dating Game" became the first television game show ever to appear on prime time. And I became the first CIA agent ever to become a chaperone. And, later, the first chaperone ever to become a killer.

For the rest of that year, I trained for the time I would go out alone to assassinate on my own. I started by doing secondary jobs for the Company: I was backup on a hit team in Naples, I watched a job in Guadalajara, and I traveled to Brussels for a kidnapping. I visited all of those cities—and more—either as a "Dating Game" chaperone or as a producer evaluating locations for one of the program's "dream dates." When I was a chaperone, most of my CIA work was done after the couple returned to the States.

In the early part of the following year I planned to chaperone a lucky "Dating Game" couple to London. While there, I would transact some business for the Uncle. The trip to London would be my baptism into the double life I would lead for the next thirteen years. It would also be my first assignment in which the responsibility for the success of the mission rested solely on my shoulders. I would work alone. I was to make a "collection," and then "eliminate the delivery boy." In other words, pick up some top-secret shit, then kill the courier.

* * *

May 1967, 6:00 A.M.

From my bathtub, I listened to the sounds of London. I heard the growl of a motorbike carrying someone to work. The diesel engine of a lonely taxicab. The milkman's electric truck. The clinking of bottles placed in doorways. I slid deeper into the warm water, my cigar hovering inches above the waterline. I delighted in the bathtubs of Europe. Why were they so much better than American tubs? European bathtubs were always the perfect length, and deeper than the tubs at home. And the water always surged from the faucets with great authority, making the temperature easier to control. As I puffed and soaked, I ran the "Dating Game" couple through my mind: a stick of a girl and her lummox of an escort, a Pacific Eight halfback. The girl was an emaciated telephone operator from Malibu, California (Weren't the show's bachelorettes supposed to be pretty?); the boy, a gargantuan clod from the University of Oregon. (Didn't the school have entrance requirements?) They were both nineteen, and, at that precise moment, sleeping (I hoped) in their *respective* hotel rooms. Though why anyone would want to sleep with that stick was beyond me. Clearly someone had.

"I was raped," she had told me, seconds after we were introduced.

"Raped?" I replied, stunned.

"A week ago," she said, and nothing more.

The Lummox came to London without a sport coat or tie, toting instead a heavy multicolored mackinaw. A restaurant on Whitehall would not allow him through the door. I loaned the Lummox a tie and my blue cashmere blazer. He thanked me and slipped into the blazer, ripping the back seam open. I wrote the coat off as a business expense. But that was the night before. They were sleeping now.

I dressed and left my room. The night clerk, still on duty, blinked good morning, and a bellboy, sitting by the hotel's entrance, nodded sleepily. Outside, the morning air was pleasantly refreshing. I walked along South Audley Road to Curzon Street, taking care when crossing the street to look the proper way for oncoming automobiles.

I had little trouble finding the small, antiquated restaurant in Shepherds Marketplace. Though it was early, I could see it was packed with the morning breakfast crowd. I spotted the man in the pink polo shirt right away, sitting at one of the round café tables in the front of the restaurant. ("He'll be wearing a pink polo shirt.") The man was younger than I had expected—in his late twenties, perhaps. He was taller than I, clean-shaven, with straight brown hair that covered his ears. I approached him and asked if the Red Sox had won.

"Yes. One to nothing."

I sat down to the right of the man. We were in extremely tight quarters. He asked in a clipped English accent how long I intended to stay in London.

"Until tomorrow," I answered. "I hope to leave tomorrow evening."

"If you're free for dinner," he said, flicking a piece of lint off his trousers, "I suggest you try Mr. Chow's."

"Is there a time when it's not crowded?"

"Late," answered the man. "About ten forty-five."

"I'll be there at exactly ten forty-five. Are there any other places? Just in case?"

The man mentioned the Red Lion Pub at a few minutes before eleven, and the Connaught Hotel at exactly eleven-fifteen. "Do you know where they are?"

"Yes," I replied, jotting down the locations on a small pad of paper.

The man left, and I ate a hasty breakfast. Halfway back to the hotel I encountered the "Dating Game" couple.

"We're on our way to breakfast," said the Lummox.

"We're on our way to breakfast," repeated the Stick.

"We were looking for you," said the Lummox.

"I'm glad we found you," said the Stick.

The Stick appeared thinner that morning than she had the night before. Suddenly, I was worried about her, and I inquired whether she had slept well.

The Lummox said, "Sure she did," and grinned the inherited oafish grin of lummoxes from time immemorial.

"Did you sleep with each other?" I asked.

After a moment's pause, the Lummox laughed.

What the fuck did *that* mean? That they had? That they hadn't? And if they had, and the Stick was impregnated, would she complain to the press? Would the resultant publicity doom "The Dating Game" once and for all? Could we blame the pregnancy on her alleged rapist from the week before? Would the public accept that explanation? And if the Stick was already with child, what could be done about it? An abortion? That would be going from bad to worse. The business of chaperoning was a pain in the ass.

"When does your plane leave?" I asked the glazed couple standing before me on Curzon Street.

"At noon," replied the Lummox.

"Well, I hope the last three days were fun," I said, trying to be chipper. "I hope I wasn't in the way. Nobody likes an old busybody hanging around."

"You're not old," said the Stick.

"Aren't you going back with us?" asked the Lummox.

"No, I'm afraid not. I have some business in London that will keep me here for a few days."

"Really?" said the Stick. She looked disappointed.

"Well," I said, trying even harder to be cheerful, "it's been fun."

"It's been more than fun," said the Lummox. "It's been a slice of life."

A slice of life.

"It has," said the Stick. And then she said, "Ciao."

"Ciao," I repeated. I hugged the Stick's bony frame and had my hand crushed by the Lummox. "And, whatever you do, don't miss your plane."

"We won't," they said in unison.

I turned and walked away.

The couple had seemed genuinely sad that I was leaving them. I didn't care. Fuck 'em.

I dawdled the day away and had dinner in the hotel dining room, continually distracted by an odds-on congenital liar seated at the next table. The suave asshole was trying to convince his girlfriend of his fidelity. "I was giving her bloody *dictation!*" the Liar said, his mouth inches away from the girl's face. "That's what secretaries do, don't they? Take bloody dictation."

"Sure," said the girl sarcastically.

"Well, that's what we were doing," huffed the Liar, sitting back in his chair. "I was working her bloody ass off."

"You were *screwing* her bloody ass off!"

"Shhhhhhhhhh," he said, pushing his palms out.

"Well, you were!"

"Oh, come off it," the degenerate-looking roué said.

"Swear on your daughter's life. Go ahead. Swear on your daughter's life that you weren't screwing your secretary's bloody ass off this past weekend."

My soup spoon stopped somewhere between my mouth and the bowl. He wouldn't do that. He wouldn't swear on his daughter's life.

"I swear on my daughter's life," said the Liar. He held his right hand over his heart, his left hand straight up in the air.

I finished my meal, paid the check, and left the restaurant. On my way out, I stopped at the table of the quarreling lovers, nodded to the girl, and said to the man, "Sorry to hear about the death of your daughter," and continued on my way.

                              *   *   *

I walked aimlessly. At ten-thirty, I took a cab to Mr. Chow's Restaurant, entering the establishment at exactly ten forty-five. The man in the pink polo shirt wasn't there. I quickly stepped outside and took another cab to the Red Lion Pub. The pub was jammed with tweedy clerks and red-faced workmen. But no man in a pink polo shirt. Apparently, he was being trailed, or thought he was.

I walked briskly to the Connaught Hotel. At eleven-fifteen I pushed through the revolving doors and entered the hotel's lobby, only to be immediately bumped by the man in the pink polo shirt heading in the opposite direction. "The church," he said. "Across the street. The courtyard. In five minutes." He shot me a desperate look and darted through the revolving doors.

My heart began pounding like a bass drum.

Five minutes later, I was standing in the church's dark courtyard. The man in the pink polo shirt called to me from the building's shadows.

"I've been followed all night," he said when I reached him. Though it was a chilly evening, his face was covered with beads of sweat.

"Who's been following you?"

"I'm not sure."

"Do you have it?" I asked.

"Where's the money?"

"Sorry."

I reached inside my raincoat, brought out an envelope, and gave it to the man in the pink polo shirt. He opened the envelope and counted the money.

"It's all there," I said.

He finished counting and put the money in his pocket. "Here." He handed me a box of Polaroid color film. The kind you can buy in any drugstore. "It's in there," he said, reading my suspicious face.

I said, "Thank you," and jammed my automatic into his mouth. The front of the silencer broke teeth as it went in. The man's eyes became immense. Too surprised to be worried. I pulled the trigger three times. The man's eyes remained surprised while the back of his head splattered against the wall of the church. As he slid down the wall to a sitting position on the pavement, I reached into his sport coat, retrieved the envelope I had just given him, and started out of the church courtyard. I stopped when I saw a car parked at the curb near the courtyard gate. The automobile hadn't been there when I had entered the courtyard five minutes before. Two men were sitting in the car's front seat. My stomach tightened. I turned and walked in the opposite direction. I located another gate leading out of the courtyard. When I reached it, I saw a second automobile. Four men were sitting in that one.

* * *

I stepped behind a tree and leaned against it, tingling with fear.

Mother of Christ. What the fuck was I going to do now?

I did nothing. I just waited in the church courtyard, too frightened to think clearly. After what seemed like an age, I heard the two automobiles start up and drive off.

Where had they gone? Was it all a trap? Were several of the occupants of the two automobiles lurking in the shadows somewhere, waiting to kill me as soon as I left the tiny mews? Jesus, I thought in panic, I can't stay here forever. I can't have anyone discover the dead man while I'm just a few feet away!

Holding the pistol in my raincoat pocket in a death grip, I walked out of the courtyard. I was relieved to see that other people were on the street, and that none looked as though they wanted to kill me. I walked-ran to my hotel. Once inside my room, I chained the door and flopped onto the bed. I didn't bother taking off my raincoat or hat— I just lay there, staring at the ceiling. Who were those men? What did they want? Why were they blocking off the churchyard exits? Why did they leave? Had they followed me to my hotel? I jumped up, turned off the room lights, and went to the window. I flattened most of my body against the wall, pulled a section of the drapes aside, and peeked through the curtains. I reminded myself of someone in an old movie thriller: James Cagney; George Raft. I saw nothing of consequence.

Then I remembered the box of Polaroid film the man in the pink polo shirt had given me. I found it, opened the box lid, and ripped off the silver foil that protected the film. A small white plastic vial dropped to the floor. Inside the vial was a rolled-up section of microfilm.

I went to the bathroom, opened my toilet bag, and found a tube of Vaseline. I greased the bullet-shaped vial with the lubricant, dropped my pants, and slid the vial up my ass.

* * *

I left London the next morning, unharmed and apparently unnoticed. Six hours later, I was in New York, sitting in the back of a very long black limousine. Inside the limousine were Jim Byrd and an immaculately attired man in his late fifties. His name was Simon Oliver. Oliver, I would later learn, was Division Control; my superior, as well as Byrd's. Simon Oliver manipulated over a hundred CIA agents at home and abroad.

Byrd asked if everything had gone according to plan.

I said that it had. I felt very tired and irritable, and silently pleaded with my superiors to handle me with care.

"May I have the microfilm?" asked Simon Oliver, extending his open palm.

I said he most certainly could, but that he would have to wait until I could use a washroom.

"Why?"

"Because the microfilm's up my ass."

Simon Oliver sighed, then asked what I thought was a stupid question. "Are you sure?"

"If *you* had a fucking vial of microfilm up *your* ass, you'd be sure!" I answered.

In retrospect, that may have been the most damaging reply I ever uttered in my entire CIA career. It caused Simon Oliver to hate me, and, once Simon Oliver hated you, he hated you for the rest of his life.

I was aware even then of Oliver's reputation. He was reputed to be a grudge-bearer who never forgave an insult. He was also a renowned bigot and führerlike martinet. Simon Oliver expected his agents to report to him in the manner of a Prussian lieutenant. Maybe because I *did* know about Oliver's despotic idiosyncrasies—or maybe because the assassination and the trip back from London had made me tired and testy—I purposely taunted my pompous superior. From that moment on, Simon Oliver would always despise me. "He's a wiseass kike," he would say whenever my name was brought up. "A fairly competent professional, but pushy. You know what I mean? Those kind are more trouble than they're worth. One of these days he'll stumble, and I'll buy drinks for everybody."

Twelve years later Simon Oliver would attempt, in a backhanded way, to get me killed. But that was twelve years later. During this limousine ride in 1967, Simon Oliver simply detested me, and I considered him, in reciprocation, an insufferable fartbiter.

"Well, congratulations on a successful mission," said Jim Byrd, sensing the tension. "Why don't you tell us the details."

I described what had happened, up to and including the two automobiles that had trapped me in the church courtyard.

"They were ours," said Simon Oliver, stuffing a Dunhill pipe with Dunhill tobacco.

"*Ours!*" I cried.

Oliver jammed the tobacco down into his pipe bowl with a gold Dunhill penknife-tamper. "Yes, ours."

"Well, they scared the living shit out of me, for Christ's sake. If one of them had come into the courtyard, I would have blown his brains out."

"That's why they didn't come into the courtyard," said Oliver, smiling. He had a mean smile.

"Well, what were they doing there?"

"They were (puff puff) there (puff puff puff) for your (puff puff) protection," said Simon Oliver, lighting his pipe with a gold Dunhill pipe lighter. "After all (puff puff) you *were* a virgin. It *was* your first (puff puff puff) solo assignment."

"A goddamn lot of protection they gave me," I said. "If that guy shot me in the churchyard, those bozos sitting in their cars would have been a lot of help."

"They would (puff puff) have killed *him,*" said Oliver. "And (puff puff) saved the (puff puff puff) film."

Swell. "They followed the contact all evening, did they?" I asked.

"Right," said Oliver, looking at me from the corners of his eyes.

"Well, your boys did a great job on him. The bastard was so rattled from the tail, he almost didn't show."

"But he *did* show," Oliver said, sporting his thin, humorless smile.

* * *

I flew home to Los Angeles in a dreadful mood. The last thing I needed was Simon Oliver's aggravation. But then, I would be reporting to Jim Byrd most of the time, and I loved Jim. True, the bureaucracy of the agency would always drive me up a wall, but being a hit man was a fascinating avocation—an unbelievably exciting pastime. The entire proposition of being an accomplished killer seemed to instill in me—perhaps inappropriately—omnipotent powers, outrageous confidence, and a superhuman ego. I was larger than life, bigger than the biggest man. If I didn't like you, I could actually kill you, with anonymity and impunity. If not now, then later. At least, that's what I led myself to believe. Consequently, I had the fool's courage to stare down the toughest truck driver; to ignore the snidest remarks. These psychic rewards, plus the thrill of accomplishment and the rush of patriotism—no matter how warped the inception—provided me with indescribable satisfaction. These were the advantages I enjoyed in the Central Intelligence Agency. At least then.

After landing in Los Angeles, however, I quickly forgot about Oliver, Byrd, and the pros and cons of the CIA when I received some extraordinary news. While I was away, the American Broadcasting Company had purchased a second game show I had created. They were going to schedule the program in both their daytime and nighttime lineups.

The program's name was "The Newlywed Game."

"NEWLYWED GAME" QUESTION AND ANSWER

HOST: Who will your husband say is *your* favorite classical composer?

WIFE: Neil Sedaka.

* * *

"The Newlywed Game" would become, like "The Dating Game," both a daytime and nighttime success. I was overwhelmed with our good fortune. Although less than two years old, my production company was already producing eleven half-hours a week of network television. My net worth had skyrocketed from just about zero to over five million dollars. I wondered how long this dream-come-true would last.

"How long will this dream-come-true last?" I asked a psychic.

The psychic fiddled with her ouija board and said, "Ten years."

I was ecstatic. I never considered the possibility that the psychic might be wrong, although she was. The programs ran sixteen years on American television, and were still going long after the psychic died.

"The Newlywed Game" was based on a simple idea, and an easy one to produce. All we needed for each show were (a) four couples married less than a year and (b) nine questions. The show's premise—how well newly married husbands and wives know, or don't know, each other—was basic and highly identifiable. The wives would first be asked a set of questions, and then their husbands would be brought onstage and asked the same set of questions. They were supposed to supply the same answers they thought their spouses had given. Then the process was reversed: the husbands would be asked the questions, and the wives brought on stage later to see if they could match their spouses' answers. A couple was awarded points when their answers matched. The couple with the most points at the end of the show would win a toaster. Or a small refrigerator. We couldn't make the prizes too luxurious; when we did, the program turned violent.

We knew that from experience. We upgraded our prizes once for a few weeks—with disastrous results. A missed answer would cause couples to become dangerously pernicious. They would immediately lose their sense of humor and begin bashing each other on the head with their thick cardboard answer cards. Besides, there wasn't a need for big prizes. The possibility of being on coast-to-coast television was tempting enough to lure the newlyweds to our studios. Which isn't to say that playing for a toaster, and losing it, didn't create ample cause for broken homes. Sure, the show caused some divorces. Forty percent of our "Newlywed Game" couples, in fact, never celebrated their tenth anniversaries. But then, neither did forty percent of the rest of the country's married couples. In any case, if a newlywed couple loved and respected each other, they probably would never have thought about doing the show in the first place. And even if they had, we would most likely not have selected them for the program. They would have made lousy contestants. Loving couples would never think of embarrassing each other, or batting their mates on the heads with thick answer cards.

* * *

"NEWLYWED GAME" QUESTION AND ANSWER

HOST: What household chore will your wife say you do exactly the same way as you "make whoopee"?
HUSBAND: Wash the dishes.
HOST: Your wife said take out the garbage.
HUSBAND: Take out the garbage?
WIFE: Yeah. You just do it. There's nothing fancy about it. You just put it in and put it out.

* * *

In 1968, while "Newlywed Game" wives were discussing how they made whoopee, the world was falling apart at the seams. The U.S. Navy intelligence ship, *Pueblo,* was captured by North Korea. Students were rioting in Paris. Martin Luther King was assassinated while standing on a Memphis motel balcony. Riots and police brutality bloodied the Democratic convention in Chicago. In March of that year, I chaperoned a winning "Dating Game" couple to West Berlin. It was a questionable destination for a "Dating Game" date, I admit. West Berlin was hardly the most romantic city in Europe. But after the couple returned home, I led a hit team that was supposed to kill the German terrorist, Rudi Dutschke. The mission failed. Our information was incorrect, and we couldn't find him. In May, I chaperoned a "Dating

Game" couple in Venice, returning afterward to West Berlin. But I missed Dutschke again.

Three weeks later, the boys at the Company telephoned me in Los Angeles. They wanted me to go back to Germany and try again. I begged off, saying I had recently taken too many "business trips," and that any more in the next few weeks might provoke suspicions.

Besides, I had a problem. My production company was hot, and I didn't want to lose our momentum. Produce a hit television show and the Network Biggies will listen very carefully to what you have to say. Produce *two* hit television shows, one after the other, and the NBs will take almost anything you have to offer, sight unseen. But what to offer?

That was the problem.

I concluded that "The Dating Game" and "The Newlywed Game" were hits because the television audience could identify with the contestants. Almost everybody had, at one time or another, dated, and many were married. And if they weren't already married, they had parents who were, and who knew what marriage was all about. Everyone could relate to what the contestants on "The Dating Game" and "The Newlywed Game" were going through: the discomfort, the embarrassment, the relief, the anger, the humor, and, sometimes, the thrilling conclusions that dating and young married couples both suffer and enjoy.

I had often explained to my staff that great numbers of people usually eat while watching television. "If," I would say, "you can make something happen on the program that will stop their forks halfway between their plates and their mouths at least once each half hour, you'll have a hit television show."

* * *

"NEWLYWED GAME" QUESTION AND ANSWER

HOST: How long is your husband's inseam?
WIFE: Seven inches?

* * *

Both "The Dating Game" and "The Newlywed Game" had the fork-stopping ingredients television viewers loved: spontaneity, drama, titillating sexual innuendo, identifiability. What other shows, I wondered, would contain those same ingredients? My musings brought me three new ideas: "The Family Game," "How's Your Mother-in-law?," and "Dream Girl of 1968."

"The Family Game" was easy: we would produce the show just

like "The Newlywed Game." Instead of married couples trying to match answers, we would have parents and kids competing against other parents and kids. Parents and kids. All of us were one or the other. All of us would surely be able to identify. It was a simple idea, easy to produce.

"How's Your Mother-in-law?" was a different story. The idea was far more complicated, which worried me. (Usually, the more intricate the format, the less chance of success.) But in this case I felt the concept was potentially hilarious and shouldn't be discarded because of its complexities. "How's Your Mother-in-law?" would attempt to place the legendarily frightening and meddlesome battle-ax on the hot seat. I felt that everyone would sympathize with the young sons-in-law and daughters-in-law. I was also confident that television audiences would delight in seeing mothers-in-law squirm. In order to make mothers-in-law squirm, we needed squirmable situations. We went searching for those situations in much the same way as private detectives. By careful and painstaking interviews with sons-in-law and daughters-in-law, we would uncover highly questionable and sometimes terrifying behavior on the part of mothers-in-law. (For example, we found one mother-in-law who forced her son-in-law to strip to the waist every time he entered her house. Once he had stripped, the mother-in-law would spray deodorant under his armpits. Only after completion of this unusual ritual would the son-in-law be allowed to walk into the mother-in-law's living room.) Armed with loads of bizarre information, we would confront the three mothers-in-law on coast-to-coast television and ask them to explain their extraordinary actions. In the final segment of each show, three well-known comedians would represent the mothers-in-law and pretend to be their lawyers. The comics would defend the deviant behavior of the mothers-in-law in front of a "jury." The jury would be composed of five unemployed actors and actresses costumed in white wigs and black gowns. If the jury found a mother-in-law guilty of being a general pain in the ass, her son-in-law or daughter-in-law would receive a prize. If she was not guilty—if the son-in-law or daughter-in-law deserved what they had coming to them—then the mother-in-law would win a prize.

The third idea, "Dream Girl of 1968," was a beauty contest. The program would commence January 1 and run for fifty-two weeks. An elimination process would reduce the contest pool from hundreds of pretty girls to a mere handful. This handful would then compete for the title of "Dream Girl of 1968." The winner would be chosen during the last week in December. I was hoping to capitalize on America's uncommon mania for beauty contests by having one every week of the year. Of all the shows I created, "Dream Girl of 1968" had the two most outstanding benefits. One was the structure of the show. It would be mandatory that the program run a full year. (Most television network daytime game shows were guaranteed a mere thirteen weeks on the air, with a network option to continue.) The other benefit was the enormous potential the program offered with regard to getting laid. Eight girls a day, five days a week, fifty-two weeks a year. Beautiful, single women; starlets, opportunists, girls that were just plain horny. Even considering my awkward and clumsy approach to females, the odds were definitely on my side.

I took my three show ideas to New York, making sure I went on the week that the monthly television rating books were published. I already knew, from inside sources, the books would show "The Dating Game" and "The Newlywed Game" at new all-time rating highs.

* * *

"NEWLYWED GAME" QUESTION AND ANSWER

HOST: Where will your husband say the very worst romantic session took place?

WIFE: Probably in the bathtub. 'Cause the water kind of shrivels it up.

* * *

"How many new shows do you have for me?" asked the vice-president in charge of daytime television network programs for ABC.

"Three," I answered. "Do you want to hear what they are?"

"No."

"How many do you want?" I asked.

"All three."

* * *

By 1969, we were producing more network television shows than any other production company in the world: twenty-five half-hours a week of national TV. Life had become wilder than my wildest fantasies. I made more money that year than my entire family had in all their collective lives. As a result, my life-style changed drastically.

I moved from my modest apartment in West Los Angeles to a penthouse in a posh section of town called Los Feliz. I traded in a very used '63 Buick Skylark convertible for a brand-new powder blue '69 Mustang convertible. I had my teeth fixed. I bought a rather dapper wardrobe. I fell into the habit of taking a "relaxing" drink at the office at the close of the day. I began picking up expensive dinner checks. I was less shy about asking girls out, and found less and less resistance on their part. Needless to say, my convertible, my penthouse, my office in Hollywood, my show-business affiliation, and my newfound riches didn't exactly hurt my sex appeal. I don't think I would have done one-twelfth as well as a struggling dentist in Erie, Pennsylvania.

* * *

"NEWLYWED GAME" QUESTION AND ANSWER

HOST: What one fact made your last "whoopee session" uniquely different from all the others you've had?

WIFE: It was unique because it was in the hallway on a newspaper.

HUSBAND: Oh God, think of our son.

WIFE: What son?

* * *

By the end of 1969 I had another new game show on television ("The Game Game"), my first prime-time special ("The Mama Cass Show"), and my second automobile (a maroon Jaguar XKE convertible). I also had my tenth pregnant girl-friend. Or so they'd all said. This girl was a blond nineteen-year-old dancer named Monica Fleming. Monica Fleming had the softest pubic hair west of the Mississippi. She was also very pretty, with huge brown eyes and a peaches-and-cream complexion. She was shy and quiet almost to the point of being boring, and she wore pinafores, knee socks, and white cotton panties. (I happen to love pinafores, knee socks, and white cotton panties.) Needless to say, there had to be something wrong. There was. Monica Fleming was religious. She was more than religious; she was an Episcopalian. She was even more than an Episcopalian; she was vestal. I was very surprised that virginal Monica consented to date someone as uncouth and atheistic as I. I was even more surprised when the scrubbed and gleaming maiden permitted me to test the silken quality of her snatch. And you can imagine my astonishment when she allowed herself to become pregnant!

"We shouldn't have, I guess," said Monica Fleming, moments after I ejaculated.

"Why not?" I asked dreamily.

"This is my fertile week."

"Who cares?"

"I guess I do. I don't use any kind of birth control."

"*What!*"

Monica Fleming repeated what she had just said.

"Jesus," I moaned, "why do you tell me this *now? After* we've made love? Why didn't you tell me *before?*"

I suppose it didn't matter how dear Monica, with the fleecy clam, answered my question. It was going to cost me, and that was that. It always ended up costing me. I calculated that over the years (Monica's expenses included) I had spent close to $20,000 on abortion and abortion-related expenses, including air travel to and from illegal doctors, hotel rooms for traumatic confrontations before and after the event, aspirin, liquor, gifts, etc. And God knows how many of those little embryos were really mine.

"What a waste," said Penny Pacino.

"Tell me!" I moaned.

"How was Puerto Rico this time?" she asked.

"Slimy." It always was. Looking for the address down some garbage-filled alley. The seamy little office up a flight of smelly stairs. The greasy woman who opens the door, and the obsequious doctor. The money up front while the lady with the duck in the oven sits mortified in a corner. The scary ride with the doctor into the country to his hideaway "hospital." The hypodermic injections. The waiting.

"How's your latest fertile turtle?" asked Penny.

"Scraped and cleansed, and packing for New York."

"Leaving town, is she?"

"Yep."

"Why?"

"She's disillusioned with Hollyweird."

"I can imagine," huffed Penny.

I said nothing, hoping the subject would disappear.

"I don't mean to be pickle-nitting," said Penny, "but—"

"Nit-picking."

We were at UCLA, walking through the sculpture gardens. Penny Pacino and I always accompanied each other through the university's sculpture gardens when either of us was feeling down and out. This time I had called Penny. I was the one who was dejected.

"You look cute," I said to Penny.

"I *always* look cute. What the hell was I going to say?"

"You were going to say, 'Why don't we get married?' "

"Exactly," said Penny. "Why don't you want to marry me? You say I'm cute, and since you're the master of romantic understatement, that means you must think I'm gorgeous. You always run to me when you're in trouble. You've known me since I was a puppy, so you know

I'm not going to change. The day after I marry you I'm not going to grow warts on my nose, or anything like that. Besides, you're almost *forty!* And after all . . ."

"After all, what?"

"Well, I'm beginning to wonder . . ."

"Wonder what?" I asked.

"I'm beginning to wonder why you haven't married *somebody* by now."

Good question.

We sat down under a tree. Penny leaned her back against the tree trunk and I stretched out with my head on her stomach. Why hadn't I married? Well, shit, I mused, my parents didn't seem to be too thrilled about *their* marriage. In fact my entire family, save my grandmother, was a mess, so why would I want to start *another* family of messes? And Christ, I would hate having in-laws. I wasn't terribly thrilled with my own mother and father. I certainly didn't need another pair. Besides, I still didn't know what I wanted to do with my life. Did I want to stay in television? Or be a writer? Or a professional killer? Or build a gigantic corporation? Or something else? I guess I should have decided by now, but I hadn't. Anyway, even if I wanted to get married and raise a family, it wouldn't have been the smartest thing to do. It would be just like me to marry and get my wife pregnant, and then get whapped by some fucking terrorist I was supposed to whap. Best I keep humping brainless starlets and spend occasional hairy weekends in Puerto Rico. Or get a vasectomy. Jesus, what a goddamn life. "*Shit! Piss! Fuck!*" I wailed.

"What?" said Penny, scared to death by my sudden outburst.

"Don't ever ask me about marriage again!" I shouted.

"I won't," she whispered.

That night, when Penny and I made love, she was crying. It was dark, but I could feel her tears.

"I'm sorry I yelled at you, Pen."

"I'm not crying because you yelled at me."

I almost asked Penny to marry me right then and there.

But I didn't.

*   *   *

The next night I went to the run through where the lady farted.

It was unfortunate that the lady farted at that particular run through, since it was a rather important one—one in which the last thing I wanted was a farting lady. The reason the run through was so important was that the vice-president in charge of daytime television programs was going to attend. His name was Edwin T. Vane, and he had flown to Los Angeles so that he could personally see how "How's Your Mother-in-law?" was progressing. After all, "How's Your Mother-in-law?" was one of his first projects, and, since he was a new vice-president, it was of substantial import that he kick off his regime with hits.

Edwin T. Vane, a graduate of Fordham University, was in his thirties, had a delightful wife named Claire, and endless amounts of sons. Mr. Vane was a religious man who neither smoked nor cursed, drank now and then, had a fair sense of humor, loved television game shows, was loyal to his family and friends, was honorable, had been an officer, and was always a gentleman. He generally wore three-piece suits, was the essence of decorum, and had a low tolerance for the lewd and licentious. Naturally, I took great care to see that everything was functioning properly and in good taste. Lewd and licentious posters were stripped from prominent offices, lewd and licentious employees were told to keep it clean, and everyone was ordered to wear shoes until Mr. Vane had gone.

The run through had been progressing at a decent pace, with hardly any problems and quite a few belly laughs. We were auditioning mothers-in-law. They sat on bridge chairs—several rows of them—usually flanked by the daughter or son on one side, and sometimes the daughter-in-law or son-in-law on the other. The mothers-in-law were asked various questions. We would judge how extroverted they might be by their answers—the more extroverted and hyper, the better. And then the lady farted.

She was sitting in the middle of the first row. She was in her early fifties, dressed primly with a little hat on top of her head. Her arms were folded in her lap. Both of her elbows encroached on the persons sitting on either side of her. She smiled all the time. Even when she farted.

The first one was a low, short burst. A pzzzzft! And then another. And another! Unable to imagine that someone in the room was actually farting, I was perplexed as to what was causing those periodic bursts of noise. A creaky shoe perhaps? A rusty chair? Whatever was producing those annoying pzzzzfts was certainly coming from the vicinity of the pudgy mother-in-law sitting in the center of the first row. As the noises began to bring everyone's attention to her, the lady turned white as a sheet. About the time I figured out who was doing what, a production assistant leaned over and said, "It's that lady straight ahead, sitting

in the middle there with the hat on her head. She's cuttin' 'em, one after
another!"

"I know," I replied, watching and listening to her greasers become
longer and louder. Pzzzzft. Pzzzzzzzzzzft. PZZZZZZZZZZZZZ-
ZZZFT! And then the lady slid off her chair—as if a little outboard
motor attached to her ass was propelling her forward—and landed in
a sitting position on the floor, legs akimbo, stocking tops and fat upper
thighs in view. The lady's anal rumblings continued, low and more
resonant now that they were being forced into the rug.

The room fell into total disorder. I sat paralyzed, more in awe of
the lady's unending supply of gas than anything else. Then she fainted.
Not knowing what to do, I left the room and repaired to my office. It
was in my office, dark as it was and me hiding in a far corner, that I
saw the "How's Your Mother-in-law?" producer, Mike Metzger, and
someone else lugging the inert lady down the hall in the direction of
the ladies room. She resembled a rolled-up rug, carried at each end and
sagging in the middle.

I'm not sure what happened after that. I vaguely remember seeing,
from the darkened corner of my office, the daughter and son-in-law
trailing behind the lady, and Edwin T. Vane, the vice-president, peering
into my office looking for me. It was dark and deathly quiet, and he
walked away.

I stayed hidden in my office for a very long time.

                                    *   *   *

In the beginning of 1970, I had a surprise visit from another ABC-TV
vice-president. This vice-president had come to cancel four of my TV
game shows: "The Family Game," "How's Your Mother-in-Law?,"
"Dream Girl," and "The Game Game."

"Your four shows," said the v.p., "have obviously not worn well.
Let's start with 'The Family Game.' "

"Okay," I said, sliding into a state of shock.

"The viewing audience," said the vice-president, "has apparently
grown tired of watching other people's kids make a pain in the ass of
themselves on TV. I suppose they have plenty of their own pain-in-the-
asses at home. Also, it appears that the viewing audience doesn't want
to see other people making fun of someone's mother-in-law. Someone's
mother-in-law is someone's *mother.* "

"True," I said, forcing a smile.

"And one *doesn't* make fun of someone's mother on network TV."

"Seems fair."

"As far as 'Dream Girl' is concerned," said the vice-president, "it appears that it isn't enough to create a show that entertains for half an hour, or even for a year. In order to have a television show that lasts, that has *legs,* it seems one must avoid great climaxes. For one solid year 'Dream Girl' strove for the ultimate climax. The climax took place with the crowning of the queen on the last day of the year. On the first day of this year the process started all over again. The letdown was apparently overwhelming. During this past year, 'Dream Girl' ratings have dipped drastically. No one seems to care to go through the exercise again."

"So it seems."

"And 'The Game Game,' " said the vice-president, "apparently didn't work at all."

"Apparently."

"Consequently, I am in the unfortunate position of having to tell you that the network is canceling all four shows."

"Can't win 'em all," I said bravely.

"I really feel terrible," said the vice-president. "I've never done anything like this before. Never *four* shows at one time."

"It's okay."

It really wasn't okay. I was sick. I just didn't know what to say. It had seemed an endless winning streak, and now it was over. The show cancellations pushed me into a deep depression. I didn't leave my penthouse apartment for nine straight days and nights. I stayed in bed most of the time, getting up now and then for something to eat and drink, usually peanut-butter-and-jelly sandwiches and straight Scotch out of the bottle. On the tenth night, I left my apartment and flew to Paris. I drifted around the Left Bank, drinking and looking for trouble. On the eleventh night, I wanted to kill someone, anyone. For my country. "If I can't entertain my countrymen," I moped aloud, maudlin fool that I was, "at least I can assassinate their enemies." I wired Simon Oliver in Langley, Virginia. (I didn't know where Jim Byrd was at the time.) I was drunk when I sent the wire. I asked if there were any European assignments. I added something pathetic like, "My show-manship may have failed, but not my courage."

The next morning I received a reply. The telegram read: "Do not understand your message."

That afternoon a faceless man with a nondescript name called on me at my hotel. He was from the U.S. embassy. He said he was sent to tell me that "they" were very upset. I was never to make contact like that again. "When they want you," said the man in the gray flannel suit, "*they* will contact *you.*" He said the emphasis was theirs, not his.

Goddamn "them."

Later that night I made fun of a French sailor's red pom-pom. He broke my nose. I told the police, "I'm suffering from acute melancholia."

At dawn I was at Orly Airport, trying to get home. I flew to London, then over the Pole to Los Angeles, traveling economy class from London. I hated flying economy, and normally wouldn't tolerate setting foot in that part of the plane. But I was sick, my nose ached, I was disgusted with myself, I wanted to get back to Los Angeles, and it was the only seat available.

I sat next to an American soldier and spent most of the trip ignoring his overtures to chat. The soldier kept asking what I did for a living. Finally, I told him I produced television shows.

"Do you know Bob Hope?"

"No, I've never met the man," I replied, reluctantly giving up my cherished privacy.

The soldier said that Bob Hope was his hero, his idol, and that his lifelong dream was to see Bob Hope in person. "But as long as I'm stationed in the States, that won't happen," he said sadly. "You have to be stationed overseas to get to see him. He's always doing shows in Korea, or Germany, or Japan. He never entertains the troops in Kansas or Oklahoma. I was stationed at Fort Sill, and now I'm at Fort Benning, Georgia. I guarantee you Bob Hope'll never come to Georgia. Or those sexy girls he brings with him when he entertains. But then, I can't say as I blame him. Who the hell would want to come to Georgia?"

* * *

"Why do you want to go to Georgia?" asked the vice-president in charge of nighttime television programs. His office was all windows, and leather, and framed pictures of the ugliest three children I'd ever seen in my life.

"I want to entertain the troops there, like Bob Hope does," I said from somewhere deep in a massive black leather armchair. "I want to do a one-hour weekly variety show from army and navy bases. I want lots of stars, and sexy models, and a big Les Brown-type band. I want to have thousands of servicemen sitting in front of the stage, whistling and hooting and hollering. I want to produce a 'Bob Hope Christmas Show' for our troops every week on ABC-TV."

"And how do you propose to get Hope?" asked the vice-president, cleaning his fingernails with a sterling-silver letter opener.

"I don't. I *know* there's no way I can get Hope. But I don't need him."

"Oh?" said the vice-president, his letter opener frozen in midair.

"Each week, instead of Bob Hope, I'll have a big star hosting the show. Flip Wilson, James Garner, Don Rickles, those kinds of stars. Not only will the program be a gigantic hit for the network," I promised, struggling to move up to the edge of my seat, "but it's a hell of a patriotic gesture."

The vice-president placed the letter opener on his desk and looked at me over his spectacles. He sighed and said, "Oh, come off it, Chuck."

"Well, it is," I insisted lamely.

"What would you call the show?"

" 'Operation Entertainment,' " I said, standing and saluting the v.p.

* * *

"Operation Entertainment" was my first variety show, and my first weekly hour on prime-time television. The show was a hit, and started my production company on a second wave of success. In 1970, I sold two new daytime game shows: "Cop Out" and "The Parent Game." "The Dating Game" and "The Newlywed Game" were still flying high. By the end of the year, Chuck Barris Productions had purchased an office building in Hollywood. We were on another roll. Major magazines wrote articles about us. *Newsweek* called my employees "a bunch of hippies laughing all the way to the bank." And Joan Barthel did a feature story on our production company for *Life* magazine. *Life* was a weekly then, and the most popular magazine in America.

> When Chuck Barris—television producer, corporation president, chairman of the board, age 40—stepped into the elevator of the office building on Vine Street in Hollywood, he was bleary-eyed and unshaven. He was not wearing his helmet, the one painted with daisies and "Make Love Not War," but otherwise he was dressed for the day as usual: sagging T-shirt, dungarees, scuffed loafers. . . . The elevator stopped on the second floor and he stepped into a hall swarming with people, mostly leggy young girls in miniskirts. He grabbed one of the leggiest and kissed her on the back of the neck, grinned at the others, and shuffled down the hall to a door plastered with signs includ-

ing "PRIVATE," "AMERICAN LEGION" and "CLERGY."
Inside the office where the Barris television empire is based, he
put on a Herb Alpert record, tapped on a bongo drum, then
flopped into a swivel chair and pressed the intercom. "Ice! Ice!
Ice!" he called, and an office boy carrying a brimming ice bucket
appeared. Barris filled a glass with ice and club soda. . . .

[Barris] looked happily around his small office, crammed
with three TV sets, a piano, tape recorders and various musical
instruments; festooned with Indian bells, arrows and daggers,
a dried alligator, a horseshoe hideously studded with china
flowers, a necklace of horses' teeth, a wicker dove, a mega-
phone, a Halloween pumpkin, an old chest X-ray in a baroque
gold frame and lots of flags and signs related to his television
shows. . . .

Chuck Barris is not the oldest game show producer in
television, or the most experienced. . . . But he has been one of
the most successful in the least amount of time. (In the summer
of 1965 he was worth only $72, now over $8 million.)

. . . He's one of the busiest; he is responsible—critics use
that word strongly—for 17 half-hours of television programming each week. He is easily the most offbeat. Among the gray
flannel types at network conferences in New York, he is emi-
nent in his torn sneakers and deerstalker's cap. In the lush
world of expense account lunches, Barris munches carrots at
his desk, or bums half his secretary's provolone-and-salami
sandwich. In a glad-handing business where professional smiles
are often pasted on each morning after shaving, Barris lets his
moods hang out. In an industry increasingly controlled by the
computer and the management consultant, he runs an operation that is loose to the point of disintegration. Most of all, he
proves that even in status-conscious television only one thing
really counts: if a guy has that mass, commercial touch, he can
talk like a rebel and dress like a beachcomber and still make it
big. . . .

Volunteers are insufficient to meet the shows' needs, so a
handful of Barris people, called Bandits—harking back to the
Chinese Bandits, the aggressive defensive unit of the 1958
L.S.U. football team—spend long days on the phone, recruiting
. . . The Bandits are on their low rung of the corporate ladder
only temporarily. If they can't meet a quota of 100 contestants
a week, they are quickly moved out. . . . If they bandit well, they

are quickly moved up—to production assistant (average $250 a week) or even writer ($500) and occasionally all the way up to producer ($1000). Meantime, even as Bandits, they are invited, along with the switchboard operators and everybody else in the company, to the weekly staff meetings. . . .

"Yeah, yeah, yeah!" chorused the crowd in [Barris'] office. People were sprawled all over the floor; some sat on other's laps. "Shadow of Your Smile" blared in the background; some staff members had clarinets and saxophones—Barris jangled a tambourine—and either played or faked along. The Friday morning staff meeting was under way. His musical group, the Stompers, went through "Mame" and "Secondhand Rose" and "Day Tripper," followed by applause and yells. . . .

[Barris addressed the crowd:] "I want to tell you that ABC called up to say they're going to put a commercial for vaginal cream on *The Dating Game.*" Hoots, yells. "They say it's a very nice commercial, though, with flowers and violins. It struck me kind of funny, since they won't let us say 'God' or 'bellybutton' on the air, but"—he shrugged—"so be it."

* * *

And it was fun. Or so it seemed.

Our little TV production company was Camelot; a beautiful, phantasmagoric subculture. It was a meteor flash, a falling star, a precious moment of chest X-rays and vaginal cream, of drunken choruses of "Secondhand Rose," "Day Tripper," and "Put Your Money in a Savings Account," of new cars, new clothes, new teeth, new apartments and houses, champagne toasts, and endless celebrations. Yeah, yeah, yeah. Have fun, folks, because it ain't gonna last forever. And it didn't. It's very hard to be successful and remain sweet if you're a company.

By the end of 1971, Chuck Barris Productions had become a cold, impersonal corporation. The small, exciting "love company" had evolved into a multifaceted business enterprise called Barris Industries. Everything became what it was never supposed to become. Love and camaraderie, loyalty and sacrifice, slowly atrophied and disappeared. Purchase orders, requisitions, and intracompany memos sprouted and flourished like weeds. The honor system was replaced with intimidating threats and edicts. And the year disappeared like water down a rain spout.

And then Penny Pacino tried to commit suicide.

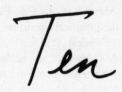

Ten

"Why?" Penny asked me, staring at her cup of black coffee. We were sitting in a booth at Nibbler's Restaurant on Wilshire Boulevard, in Beverly Hills. It was a little after two in the morning on the last day of February 1972.

"Why what?"

"Why were you with that girl?"

"Why not?" I answered, somewhat unsympathetically. Thanks to Penny, the previous evening had been a complete fiasco. Besides, it was late, and I was worn out. Penny had scared the shit out of me, and, now that I knew she was all right, I was really pissed.

"But sitting right *there!*" moaned Penny. "Right in our living room."

"Where was she supposed to sit? And it's not *our* living room. It's *my* living room."

"Ohhhhhhh," groaned Penny Pacino, when the two eggs over light and hash browns arrived.

"Eat it," I said.

"Up yours," she replied.

"How come eleven?" I asked.

"Eleven what?"

"Eleven splits of champagne. What possessed you to try killing yourself by drinking eleven splits of champagne?"

"They didn't have any magnums in the liquor store," she groaned. "But you must admit," she said, with a wan smile, "it would have been a hell of a way to go."

"God protect me," I said to no God in particular, expecting no protection whatsoever. I stared at Penny staring at her coffee. What had I ever done to deserve this woman? This rope around my neck? What had I ever seen in her? She was pretty, but not beautiful. She was smart, but far from brilliant. She was funny, but not hilarious. She was affec-

tionate. She was lovable. But she was also a big pain in the ass. I
wondered why I had allowed myself to become saddled with such a pest
—and for so long. It seemed as though I had known Penny forever. It
had been so many years I'd forgotten how we'd met.

"How did we meet?" I asked.

"I forget," she sighed, staring at her coffee.

Penny Pacino always said we were meant for each other. She had
told me (more times than I'd like to remember) that she had come out
of her mother's womb with my name tattooed on her ass. She was
eighteen when she first told me about that goddamn prenatal tattoo.
And I was thirty-four. That was 1964, eight years earlier.

"What are you writing?" asked Penny through a mouthful of eggs
and potatoes.

I said I was trying to figure out when we met, and to chew with
her mouth closed.

"A bad day at Black Rock," groaned Penny Pacino.

"What?"

"When we met." She looked up from her coffee. "Why was that
cheap tropplop there?"

"She's not cheap," I said, "and it's trollop, not whatever you said."

"She's a tropplop, and why was she there?"

"Penny, we're not married."

"We should be."

"But we're not, and I can date anybody I want. And bring them
to my apartment anytime I want to."

"But you broke a date with me. You said you had to work."

So I wasn't working. So I was entertaining a guest. So the guest
was an attractive woman writer named Gloria Nardo. Gloria had just
said, "I thought you were going with someone."

And I had just replied, "Absolutely not." And then Penny Pacino
had burst into the living room. When Penny saw the erudite Miss
Nardo sitting on the couch, legs crossed, with a half-empty wineglass
in her hand, she went bananas.

"*What*," Penny yelled, "is *she* doing here, man?"

"She's . . ." I began.

"This," shouted Penny to my thunderstruck lady guest, "is *our*
apartment." Penny flipped her finger back and forth between me and
herself as she spoke. "*Our* apartment. I'd like to know what the fuck
you're doing in *our* apartment."

"This isn't *our* apartment," I replied, trying to be calm. "This is *my* apartment." I glanced at Ms. Nardo, hoping that she could see I had the situation under control.

Apparently, that's not how she saw it.

Ms. Nardo was rigid with fear, her face lined with the anxiety of those who suddenly realize their life is in danger. She seemed to be wondering if the maniac had a gun in her purse, and, if she did, whether or not she intended to use it.

"It's *ours,* man!" I heard Penny shout at me. "I *found* it for you. I *decorated* it for you. I spent six months sitting on *that* couch, where *she's* sitting, waiting for *plumbers* to come, waiting . . ." She stopped talking in midsentence and threw the door key I had given her at me. It hit my forehead. (What a great throw, I thought.) "God, you're an asshole," she bellowed, turned, and started out of the apartment.

Throughout Penny's ear-piercing denunciation, I couldn't help noticing how cute she looked. She was furious, but strangely beautiful. It was an unfamiliar beauty, one that I wasn't privy to very often. Penny never raised her voice, never argued (well, hardly ever), and loathed scenes. The only time she became irate was when I "cheated" on her, or hurt her feelings in other ways. Then she would get all flushed and blustery, and her eyes would sparkle, and she would say "fuck" and "man" a lot.

I looked at Gloria Nardo. She was still sitting on the couch in a catatonic state, her glass of wine frozen in midair. I mumbled, "Excuse me," and ran into the hall looking for Penny. She had already taken the elevator down to the street. By the time I reached her, she was sitting on the curb in front of my apartment house, along Los Feliz Boulevard. Four lanes of heavy evening traffic were whizzing back and forth. I could barely hear Penny's sobbing over the roar of the automobiles. I sat down beside her and put my arm around her heaving shoulders.

"Aw, come on, honey," I whispered, "please stop crying."

"*What?*" She was unable to hear me because of all the traffic roaring by our shoes.

I shouted, "*You shouldn't be acting like this.*"

"*Oh, Chuck,*" she hollered, between racking gulps of air, "*I love you so much.*"

"I love you, too."

"*What?*" she yelled.

"*I said you've got to take care of yourself.*"

"*Why?*" she yelled. "*I don't have a goddamn thing to live for. My job stinks. The man I love stinks.*"

"*I don't stink!*" I shouted.

"*The hell you don't,*" Penny shouted back. "*You lie. You cheat. You're constantly pussy-footing around with the sleaziest chicks in town.*"

"Gloria Nardo is *not* sleazy," I said.

"I think I'll kill myself," mumbled Penny.

"*What?*"

"*Nothing,*" shouted Penny.

I drove Penny back to her apartment in her car and took a taxi back to mine. When I returned, Gloria Nardo had gone. There was a note attached to a lamp shade. It read: "She's right. You *are* an asshole." I sat in my living room staring at Nardo's note. Was I really an asshole? I thought about the proposition for over an hour without arriving at a decision. Eventually, I drove back to Penny's apartment. I decided to wake her up and say something nice. When I arrived, I found a printed note in large block capitals under her front door knocker.

GOOD-BYE, CRUEL WORLD.
THE DOOR'S OPEN.

I walked in and found Penny face down on her bed. The litter of empty champagne bottles lay scattered on the bedroom floor. I felt light-headed and rubbery-legged. I thought I was looking at a dead Penny Pacino. And then she said, "Wanna see a stupid girl vomit?"

I helped her into the bathroom and held her head while she threw up. And then I walked her to Nibbler's.

"Ohhhhhhhh," Penny wailed, pushing aside her eggs. "Let's get out of here."

I held Penny around her waist and helped her back to her one-bedroom efficiency. I opened the front door for her. As she stepped inside she said, "I'm feeling better."

I was feeling worse. The Penster was such a sensitive soul. Her anger was like a blowfish, all puffed cheeks and nothing else; something to do on the outside when she was hurting like hell on the inside. I knew Penny was miserable. Not from the champagne, but from a terminal broken heart—from unrequited love evolving from an unsolvable problem. She loved me, nothing ever seemed to come of it, and she couldn't get herself to love anyone else.

But *why* did she love me?

What was there to love?

"For every duck there's a duckess," my grandmother used to say. I guess I was Penny's duck.

I helped Penny get undressed and into her jammies. While I was buttoning her top half, Penny said, "I'm always there when you need me, aren't I?" and started crying again.

"Oh, fuck," I moaned.

"Whenever you're in trouble," she continued, "you call me. And I come." Penny reached for a Kleenex. "Do me a favor," she said. "Call somebody else." She blew her nose. It sounded like a foghorn. "I do everything I can to make you happy," she sobbed. "That's all I ever think about. How to make *you* happy. I buy you all the newest pens and pencils when they come out. I know how happy new pens and pencils make you. And didn't I get you that little suction-cup basketball net and sponge basketball to play with in the bathtub, on those *rare* occasions when you take a bath? Didn't that make you happy? You sure as shit *looked* like you were happy." Penny blew her nose again. "And then when you're really happy, you stand me up, or do something horrible to hurt my feelings. God, what an imbecile you are." She blew her goddamn nose again.

"It's like you can't stand being happy," she continued. "It's like when you're really cooled out and feeling good about yourself, something snaps, and you take off. You just can't seem to handle a lot of happiness for extenuating periods of time."

"Extensive. *Extensive* periods of time."

"I'll fucking say what I want to say, man." The Penster was becoming more angry than weepy. "It's like you think you don't deserve to be happy, right? Or maybe you're *afraid* to be happy. Maybe you're afraid of me because I *make* you happy. Maybe you're afraid that if I make you happy, you'll want to marry me. And that means a commitment, and any kind of commitment scares the hell out of you. You know something, man, you're sick. You oughta see a shrink." Penny blew her nose. "But I do know this. If we don't connect soon, we're not going to connect at all. And that *really* makes me sad. That's why I cry a lot. Because I don't think we *are* going to connect. I think you're going to blow it, and if you do, you'll be the dumbest white man that ever walked the face of the earth. And the sorriest. You really will." She blew her nose. Was there no end to her snot?

I left Penny's apartment about four that morning. It was raining. Beautiful Beverly Hills had become dreary, damp, and cold. Standing

I always put a little Alpo on my crotch prior to a dog act.

With my friend Gene Patton,
aka "Gene Gene the Dancing Machine." (*Vince Longo*)

Paul Picard on the way
to La Bourget airport.

The Unknown comic
(Murray Langston) and I.
(*Vince Longo*)

The Love Company, circa 1966. (*Bert Mittleman*)

With Ray Charles on the set of
Operation Entertainment. (Vince Longo)

On an
assignment
in Paris.

Robert Lawrence Puxton III

Wrapping up another *Gong Show.* (*Vince Longo*)

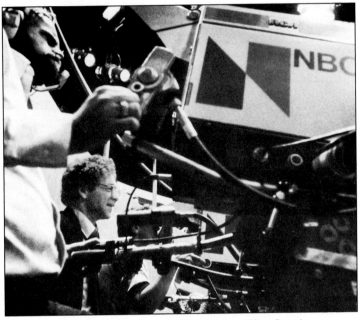

Checking shots at a television taping. (*Vince Longo*)

Patricia Watson in Los Angeles.

I join Jaye P. Morgan on *The Rah Rah Show*. (*Vince Longo*)

(Vince Longo)

and learning how to paint pretty pictures. At least you'd leave behind something nice."

All the way to West Berlin, I thought of what the Duck had said. Whom the gods destroy, they first make mad. Euripides. At least you'd leave behind something nice. The Duck had leaked some buried intelligence. What manner of beast was this creature, the Duck? He reminded me of George Pontifex from Butler's *The Way of All Flesh*. "George Pontifex did not consider himself fortunate, and he who does not consider himself fortunate is unfortunate."

* * *

I took a taxi to the Kempinski Berlin Hotel on the Kurfurstendamm. The hotel lobby was full of people. I wondered if any of them was the man I was supposed to meet, or the man I was supposed to kill.

The manager of the Kempinski Berlin Hotel was named Rudi Bernhardt. I was told that Bernhardt might be useful, but not to worry too much about finding him. He undoubtedly would break his neck trying to find me.

Herr Bernhardt had been told by letter and cable that I was an American television producer whose programs were seen all over the United States, and that I was in West Berlin to plan a "dream date" to the city as a grand prize on a program called "The Dating Game." Herr Bernhardt had been made aware that the locations I selected— the museums, the nightclubs, the restaurants, and the hotel—would be given enormous publicity on the show. He also knew that I was seriously considering using the Hotel Kempinski Berlin. Hence, the prodigious basket of fruit wrapped in cellophane, the bottles of wine, and the sterling silverware on the coffee table in my hotel living room. A note lay on a small silver tray offering a warm welcome and regards from Herr Bernhardt and his staff.

How nice, I thought to myself, wondering if the fucking kraut was old enough to have been a Nazi. Old enough or not, I had never met a German who admitted knowing a real live Nazi in his or her entire life, let alone being one. Not one.

What? A Nazi? Oh, I'm sorry, no, I was never a Nazi. Oh, no. In fact, I never even knew one. I never knew *anyone* affiliated with the Nazi Party.

Amazing. Simply amazing.

And then a man charged into my room.

"Welcome! Welcome!" the man said, shaking my hand vigorously. "Allow me to introduce myself. I am Rudi Bernhardt, manager of the

Kempinski." He had come to my room, he said, to point out the wonders of the hotel, and of the city of West Berlin. He did both succinctly, and concluded his monologue by saying, "I am at your service. Can I do anything, *anything,* for you?"

I said that he could, and asked if he would please make a dinner reservation for two at a restaurant of his choice.

"Of course," he replied, and left, backing and bowing out of the room as he went.

When Bernhardt closed the door, I telephoned Patricia Watson.

Eleven

Rudi Bernhardt had made a reservation for us at a small, intimate restaurant on Budapester Strasse. The rooms were crowded and smoky, the noisy clientele well dressed. I was taken to a corner table in the restaurant. I was pleased to be sitting where I could watch all the others.

It was early. I ordered a dark beer, pointing to another's mug as an example for the waiter, and began to glance through a copy of the *International Herald Tribune.* I noticed on the sports page that I had lost a wager to Jim Byrd. I had bet on Joe Frazier. George Foreman had knocked him out. And I read that in something called "the battle of the sexes," Billie Jean King had defeated Bobby Riggs in three straight sets. Good for Billie Jean, I thought to myself. "Hello," said Patricia Watson.

I looked up, and there she was. She looked pretty, as always. Before I could stand and help, Patricia pulled out her chair and sat down. She said my beer looked delicious, and I ordered a mug for her. We smiled at each other; slow, warm, tired smiles, as if to say, "Well, here we go again."

"So?" I said.

"So, it's simple," replied Patricia Watson. "His name is Hans Colbert. He's an anti-American, pro-Communist trade unionist. He makes a lot of speeches. Little Hans is badmouthing the United States and the rich West German bosses. He wants to unionize the steel mills —things like that. They'll unionize sooner or later—the later, obviously, the better—but Hans wants to do it now. He's calling for major industrial strikes, and the Uncle isn't thrilled about crippling strikes just when West German industry is finally getting back on its feet. And little Hans is involved in other things. There's a good possibility he's being used as a go-between to funnel weapons to some of the better up-and-coming terror groups. Little Hans is causing the Uncle a great deal of trouble, and you know how the Company feels about trouble-some, anti-American German trade unionists.

"Usually the big boys in the CDU and the SDP are able to sit on rabble-rousers like this one, but Colbert is different. He has . . . what would you say . . ."

"The ability to get out from under."

"Noooooo," said Watson, wincing with displeasure. My suggestion had annoyed her. "Oh, what's the word?"

Silence. Damned if I was going to suggest anything else.

"Charisma!" she boomed. "That's it. The little bastard has charisma."

I asked Patricia Watson if she was hungry.

"I guess I should eat *some*thing," she answered.

We ordered. "How's your love life?" I asked.

"Great. How's yours?"

"Awful."

"So's mine," said Patricia. She smiled, straightened up in her chair, and quickly directed the conversation back to business. Watson wasn't one for small talk. She said, "I want you to spend a day or two pretending you're a television producer scouting West Berlin for locations."

"I *am* a television producer," I said petulantly.

"We *are* sensitive tonight."

I was silent.

"You'll meet a man named Keeler," Patricia Watson said finally. "He's an agent with West German intelligence. He drinks too much and smokes too much. His teeth are yellow, and his reliability sucks, so keep an eye on him. But he's still good at what he does."

"What does he do?" I asked.

"He does the groundwork. He's been trailing Colbert. He knows where Colbert lives. He knows his habits. He knows the best place to make the grab, and the best escape route. He also knows how to get the right cars and license plates. And he's strong as an ox. When it comes time to snatch Colbert, let Keeler do it. But," she added, looking me in the eyes, "*you* kill him."

Patricia Watson had beautiful eyes.

* * *

The following afternoon I made the connection with Keeler, and we drove to Colbert's neighborhood. Parking down the street from his house, we began our surveillance. We were waiting for the right time to kidnap and kill Colbert—the moment when, hopefully, Colbert would be alone and his street empty. We waited. And waited. We watched Colbert enter and leave his house. He was generally with someone, and once, when he was alone, the street was crowded with passersby. So we continued waiting, for three days and nights, at #4 Brahmsstrabbe Street.

Keeler had provided the two of us with four stolen cars. We changed cars every day, and parking places every three hours. Periodically, we would drive out of the neighborhood to see if we were being followed. We never were. Of course, the longer we waited, the more dangerous it became. To be lurking in the same neighborhood day after day with the crafty and alert Hans Colbert was not the best of situations. But we had no alternative.

Time crawled by.

Just as staking out Colbert wasn't exactly a thrill a minute, working with Keeler wasn't a bag of laughs either. The bulky German was a taciturn, introspective bore. He tended to sit quietly on the driver's side of the automobile in a cloud of cigarette smoke, seldom taking his eyes off the front door of Colbert's house, even when making notes. Keeler scribbled constantly on a small white pad balanced on a thick knee. His notes concerned the comings and goings of everyone on the block. He observed everything on Brahmsstrabbe, and, to my knowledge, forgot nothing. Why, I'll never know. Maybe it was his way of wasting time.

As the hours and days wore on, I realized I wasn't having any fun at all. What we were doing wasn't exciting or rewarding in the slightest. It was just boring. And, at times, slightly frightening.

So, as we began our forty-third hour in a smoky, refuse-filled automobile parked down the street from #4 Brahmsstrabbe, I made up my mind to resign from the CIA as soon as I could.

* * *

During the third evening—the night of October 15, 1973—Hans Colbert returned home alone. The street was dark and empty. Colbert was enjoying an unseasonably warm night. Keeler drove our car toward Colbert up the right side of the street. As we approached Colbert, Keeler swerved to the left, jammed on the brakes, and jumped out of the car. I slid over to the driver's seat, reached behind me, and opened the rear door. Keeler wrestled Colbert into the automobile's backseat and climbed in on top of him, and I pulled the door shut. Keeler held Colbert down on the floor of the car while I drove quickly to a construction site in the middle of a nearby block. I swung open the fence gates and drove onto the lot, parking in a far, dark corner. I turned off the headlights, reached into my shoulder bag, and found my automatic and silencer. I placed the end of the silencer inside Colbert's left ear and pulled the trigger. Colbert's body jerked with enough force to lift himself and Keeler several inches off the car's floor. I pulled the trigger two more times. The automobile filled with smoke and the smell of cordite. Keeler stepped out of the car and opened the automobile's trunk. I joined him there. We removed two suitcases containing cans of gasoline, and a bag of explosives. I doused the car's interior with the gasoline while Keeler placed the explosives inside the automobile. When we were finished, I threw the empty petrol can into the backseat. It landed on the corpse's shoulders. Keeler closed the car doors. I splashed the outside of the automobile with the second can of gasoline, kicking the can under the car's trunk. Keeler lighted some gasoline-soaked rags, tossed them on the roof of the car, and jumped away. I didn't. The *whoosh* of ignited gasoline singed my eyelashes. If I was stopped by the police, my burnt lashes would tie me to the assassination. Sigfried Keeler turned and looked at me, then he ran off. I went the other way. Halfway down the block I heard the explosion. The entire operation had taken seventeen minutes.

Later, when I thought about it, something odd occurred to me. Hans Colbert had never said a word.

* * *

Between 1973 and 1975, four shows of mine debuted on daytime and nighttime television. One was an evening variety show on CBS called "The Hit Parade." Three were daytime game shows entitled "Spoof," "Treasure Hunt," and "The Music Game." I was working fourteen hours a day, seven days a week. And I was worrying more than I ever had before.

My concerns ran from the mundane to the sublime. I was worried about the American League's new designated hitter rule; about the nation surviving under Nixon; about the American Indians holding out at Wounded Knee. I was wondering why they didn't award a 1974 Pulitzer Prize for either literature or drama, and why I didn't understand a word of Thomas Pynchon's novel, *Gravity's Rainbow*. I worried about my television programs being canceled (an old worry), and whether I would be killed on my next mission for the Company (a brand-new one). I worried and worried and worried. Eventually, I over-amped. I blew a fuse. It was the fuse that controlled my ability to be rational, stable, and moderate. As a result, all of my worries and fears were consolidated and redirected into a life of irrationality, instability, and excess.

I began to overdo everything.

I overate, overtipped, drank too much, stayed out too late, got up too early, and spent too much money. Perhaps it was a feeling that my luck was running out that prompted me to behave that way. Obviously, my television programs and their fat profits wouldn't last forever. I never forgot the TV network vice-president who materialized out of thin air and canceled *four* of my shows at one time.

Once again I moved, this time to a large house in the posh hills of Bel Air. The focus of my attention turned to high brick walls, electric fences, external, internal, and internal-internal alarm systems, security patrols, the training and feeding of large dogs, housekeepers, Japanese houseboys, cooks, pool cleaners, gardeners, and limousine services.

"You're by far the most successful CIA agent ever to graduate Langley," commented Jim Byrd after visiting my new and less-than-humble abode.

I said nothing.

"How many cars do you have?" he asked.

"Three," I muttered, embarrassed.

"You have *three* cars!" he said, shaking his head in awe. "Who needs three cars? How many fucking cars can you drive at one time?"

"Three," I replied scornfully, in the manner of a child. But I thought about Byrd's question.

It started when I sold my Mustang and Jaguar and bought my first Rolls-Royce. The Rolls, I rationalized, would last me the rest of my life. But it wasn't long before I desired a second car—a less expensive one —to drive to places where the poor people hung out. I had discovered that I felt very uncomfortable visiting my less affluent friends in my Rolls-Royce Silver Shadow convertible. So I bought a Volkswagen. I sold it a month later and bought a Mercedes 260 convertible. The poor people were just going to have to accept me in my Mercedes. At least the Mercedes convertible wasn't a Rolls-Royce convertible. (As any fool could plainly see, the tenor of my thoughts wasn't the healthiest in town.)

Owning two cars made it much easier to own three. The third was "just for laughs." For a short time I owned a Chevy truck, then a Toyota Land Rover, a Fiat Spider, a Jeep, a Ford Bronco, an orange Pontiac Firebird, a green classic Porsche "speedster," and so on. Some

I kept a few weeks, others as long as six months. I would celebrate if I put three thousand miles on a vehicle. On those rare occasions when that magic number rolled up on the speedometer, I would stop at the first bar I came to and buy everybody there a drink.

Obviously, I was sick. And getting sicker. Still, I must admit, being rich and quasi-famous was fun. I unabashedly enjoyed having my automobile parked by the front door of restaurants I visited, and I delighted in being seated in the VIP sections of those establishments. I basked in the homage of headwaiters, ushers, stewardesses, tailors, room clerks, limousine chauffeurs, and impressionable girls. I enjoyed receiving mail reeking with envy from high school and college classmates whose faces I couldn't recall, from old teachers and professors who had thoroughly ignored me when I was under their charge, from steelworkers who used to heckle me in Homestead, Pennsylvania, and from two or three former girl friends. One of those inamoratas was the little cockteaser I fell in love with in Pittsburgh—the one who dumped me for a football hero.

Julie Candaleri.

Julie wrote a short letter, a page of carefully spaced words that had neat little curlicues on the ends of the *g*s and *y*s, and big balloons dotting the *i*s. She said she had seen my name on television and watched some of the shows I had created. She wrote that the shows were not very intelligent, but that she was happy for my success. She said that she had two children, and that she and the kids lived in Valley Forge, Pennsylvania. She claimed that she was pretty happy. She signed her letter: "As ever, Julie (Candaleri) Marinaro."

"Fucking cockteaser," I muttered aloud.

"Who's a cockteaser?" asked the girl in my bed, indignantly. I had picked up the floozy earlier that night in Martoni's Restaurant.

"The girl who wrote this letter," I answered.

"Why don't you put the letter down and relax?" suggested the floozy. She was lying naked on her right side, picking pieces of lint out of her navel with her left index finger. I've forgotten the floozy's name. I'm not even sure I knew it then. She was just another dumb piece of ass in awe of being in bed with a real live television producer. "You *never* relax," she grumbled.

"How do *you* know? I met you two hours ago."

"I read about you, and I hear what people say about you."

Perhaps, I considered silently, they are in awe of me, and I don't have to perform, or compete, or be witty or charming. The floozies will do all that. "And what *do* people say about me?" I asked, delighted to talk about myself.

The girl giggled and flopped back into a pile of pillows, her hands joined behind her head. "They say you're a faggot."

"A faggot!"

"Yeah, and they also say you fuck a different girl almost every night . . ."

"Can't seem to get their stories straight, can they?"

". . . and then you rate each girl on a one-to-ten scale, depending on how good a fuck she was. And you keep the ratings in a little black book."

"Little black book?" I was tuning her out. Was a hump worth this torture? Maybe it wasn't the hump I needed—just the company. Any kind of company. Anything but being left alone, staring at my grinning teeth. I was thinking about something Iris Murdoch wrote. "He took his teeth and laid them on the table and felt his face subside gratefully into the face of an old man. He drank the whiskey. His teeth grinned at him."

". . . and I hear you're really weird, too. I hear you have hang-ups comin' out your ying-yang. Boy, I'd sure hate to be your old lady."

"My old lady," I said. I had learned that if, now and then, I repeated the last three or four words of their most recent sentence, the floozies would think I was paying attention. Meanwhile, I could think of other things.

"I guess," pouted the floozy, "being a famous TV producer you get to meet a lot of girls."

"A lot of girls."

"I bet you can't remember half their names."

"Half their names."

"Do you remember my name?"

"No."

"What a fucker," she said.

"Nice to meet you, Whatta," I murmured.

She laughed. Her laugh was a phlegmy wheeze. She was a chain smoker.

And so it went.

I think it was Proust who said you could seduce any woman if you were willing to sit and listen to her talk until four in the morning. Since I had already seduced the gem, I went to sleep.

At six in the morning, the telephone rang. The floozy groaned as

I reached over her to grab the receiver. A hoarse voice said, "Hello, Chuck?"

"Yes?"

"This is Sigfried Keeler."

I came instantly awake. Keeler? The West German intelligence agent!

What the hell was he doing in . . .

Had I done something wrong? Did I know too much? We were all killers, were we not? Was Sigfried Keeler in Los Angeles to eliminate *me?* Unlikely, but not unlikely. If Keeler wasn't here to kill me, then what *was* he here for? I rarely heard from anyone connected with CIA clandestine affairs. Employees of the Company were not accustomed to personal telephone calls from other employees. Contact meant work. So the act of chatting with Sigfried Keeler, at that hour of the morning in Los Angeles, seemed strange at best. One did not expect to find the rumpled, nicotine-stained West German intelligence agent prowling around Hollywood. And how the hell did he get my unlisted telephone number?

"Keeler? Is that really you?"

He said it was. Besides, I recognized his voice. He asked if it was possible to have dinner with me; that he desired nothing more than my company, a few drinks, and a good meal. He told me he was very tired. I said I would meet him that night. I wondered if I had said the right thing. To offset my niggling doubts, I decided to carry a gun.

We met in Beverly Hills at the La Scala Restaurant. We hugged when we met and held each other at arm's length for a few moments. It was surprisingly good to see old Sigfried again. I felt a pang of guilt about the gun that was strapped to my ankle.

La Scala was quite lavish, and crowded with tuxedoed waiters and lively people. We slid into a comfortable booth thickly upholstered with soft red leather and surrounded by expensive bottles of wine.

"A very fancy place," Keeler said.

"Only the best for my friend."

"The friendships one develops in wartime," said Keeler, "are remarkably strong."

"True," I said, strangely touched, and curious about the word "wartime."

We briefly discussed what had happened to us since West Berlin, ordered drinks, and then dinner. We chatted about my television company and America in general. It was all boring, pointless conversation.

The taciturn Keeler was his usual self. He listened without interest, his mind elsewhere, unconcerned with the answers to the questions he asked. He looked exhausted and seemed more distracted than I remembered him to be. He had grown fatter, his eyes were bloodshot, and he was perspiring. And then, from out of nowhere, he asked, "Do you know why you do what you do?"

"What do you mean?" I asked, confused.

"Kill people for the Central Intelligence Agency."

I scanned the restaurant nervously.

"Do not worry," said Keeler, "the table is not bugged. Only in Russia are the restaurant tables bugged. So tell me, why do you do it?"

"Why do I do it?" I repeated. "I've been told, Sig, that every agent attached to every intelligence service in the world asks himself that question sooner or later." I was about to go on, but the waiter brought our dinner.

"We all have our reasons," said Keeler, forgetting that I had more to say. "During the Second World War, I had the pleasure of killing human beings. I say pleasure because it was. The experience was thrilling." Keeler ignored the expensive food and concentrated on his beer and vodka. "In the years that followed the war, I was haunted by those experiences; those killings. I missed that exhilaration. I realized that nothing I had done since the war had been as exciting. Never had my zest for living been so great. Never." Keeler paused. He stared at his food, and said, "That is why I became involved in the murky world of espionage. I wanted to bring a sense of wartime back into my life. I wanted to be exhilarated again." Keeler slouched back in his seat, and drank his beer in a brooding, scowling silence.

Keeler hadn't eaten a thing. I wondered why Keeler was being driven to tell me this collection of personal thoughts, and decided that something must have happened to him. He had probably just experienced a disastrous mission, and it was best to leave him to his own catharsis. Then Keeler started speaking again. " 'Whatsoever thy hand findeth to do, do it with thy whole might. Work while it is called, for the night cometh wherein no man can work.' "

"That's Carlyle!" I said.

"Yes."

"You read Carlyle? Carlyle's one of my heroes."

Keeler said nothing.

"Why did you quote that specific passage?"

Keeler avoided my question, and said instead, "I read in a book, not too long ago, that killing your first man was very much like making love to your first woman. According to this book, both are momentous occasions in which you remember every detail. The book went on to say that one was able to recall both memories with extraordinary clarity, with a special allure—as if the acts had occurred outside civilization. And when the allure is gone, you are condemned." Keeler heaved a despairing sigh. "I am condemned."

"Condemned?" I asked.

"Condemned to live the rest of my life outside civilization." Keeler raised his eyes from his beer glass, turned to me, and said, "You, my friend, will be too."

Three weeks later I learned that Sigfried Keeler had committed suicide.

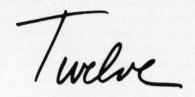

In the murky world of espionage, the tag "suicide" was always highly suspect. Whether Keeler actually did commit suicide, or whether he was "eliminated," was a moot point. The fact was, Sigfried Keeler was dead.

"For the night cometh wherein no man can work."

* * *

It was shortly after I heard about Sigfried Keeler's death that I met *her*. I remember, because I was feeling low about Keeler . . . unexpectedly low for some unaccountable reason. It was during that low period that she came into my life. It was fitting that she should.

She was the lowest of the low.

Her name was Glopp. Lucy Sue Glopp.

I met her waiting for an elevator.

I had been working late at the production company, and it was a little after ten in the evening when I turned off my office lights, stepped into the hallway, and closed the door. That's when I saw her for the first time. She was standing by the elevators.

"Hi," she said.

"Hello."

"My name is Lucy. Lucy Sue Glopp. I hate my last name. I've always hated it. That's why I have to get married as quickly as I can. So I can get rid of Glopp. I'm new here. I quit my job as a cocktail waitress last week. I was just hired this morning. I book contestants. Aren't you even going to welcome me with a handshake, or a hug, or something?"

"Welcome," I said, extending my hand. "I'm Chuck Barris."

"I know who you are, for Christ's sake."

We shook hands. She wasn't the slightest bit nervous, which surprised me. After all, I *was* the boss, and she was meeting me for the first time. New employees were usually nervous when they met me for the first time.

"You're working late," I said.

"More or less. Where are you off to?" she asked.

"I'm going home. And you?"

"To the studio," she replied. "That's why I stayed late. I was waiting for them to finish taping tonight's shows. 'Happiness Game' shows. I guess I shouldn't admit that. I should have said I was working late. Oh, well. Anyway, I'm going to the studio to meet Ronnie."

Ronnie Lake. (Not his real name.) The host of "The Happiness Game." Ronnie was a nice guy, with a slight pompadour and tons of big white teeth. He was handsome but not too bright; a step above Lenny from *Of Mice and Men,* perhaps, but not a big step. Ronnie Lake was a married man. His cute little wife and kids were stashed in a cute little house near the ocean, miles and miles away from the studio. Consequently, Ronnie was free to make passes at all the show models —the ones that pointed to the toasters and refrigerators. Ronnie was always horny, and therefore continually making passes. "Boy," he'd say, with all the acumen of a rock, "I'd fuck a snake with a harelip, as long as it didn't make any demands." Ronnie Lake was your typical television game-show host.

"I'm going to get Ronnie," said the girl standing with me by the elevators.

"You're going to get him?"

"Yep. I'm going to get him. I'm going to make Ronnie leave his wife and marry me."

"You're not serious." And if she was, why would she tell me? If I thought she was a potential troublemaker, I'd fire her. And if she wasn't serious, what the hell were we talking about?

"I certainly *am* serious," said Lucy Sue Glopp. "I've had a crush on Ronnie Lake as long as I can remember. And I'm going to get him, you can bet on it. I'm going to make the bastard leave his wife and kids and marry me. I'm going to get him to marry me if it's the last thing I do."

"You seem quite determined," I said, unsure whether to frown or smile.

She smiled.

She was pretty. And I fell head over heels in love with her. That night, right there by the elevators. But I didn't know it. Not then.

* * *

Actually, Lucy Sue Glopp wasn't pretty—she was striking. On a good day she could look sensational. And, during the year I knew her, she would become more attractive. But I think she was an early bloomer. She may have peaked just before she flew to Hong Kong.

Years later, a famous film director and I were having a drink at my apartment in Beverly Hills. The director would come across her picture in a batch of my photographs. He was in the process of casting a new motion picture, and he wanted an unknown twenty-year-old with an arresting, fresh face for his female lead.

"That one! That's the one I want!" he would boom when he saw Lucy's picture. "She looks exactly like a young Katharine Hepburn. Can you get her for me?"

"That picture's several years old."

"I don't care. Can you get in touch with her? Is she available?"

"No," I would reply.

"Why not?"

"She's dead."

* * *

Lucy Sue Glopp's determination to bust up my game-show host's marriage intrigued me. Instead of being angry, I was amused and somewhat fascinated. I wanted to speak to her the next day, but found neither the time nor the opportunity. So I called her that evening at her apartment. It was a sticky call. She and I knew the real reason I had telephoned her was not for an update on her evening with Ronnie Lake.

"So how did it go?" I asked.

"How did *what* go?"

"Your date with Ronnie Lake. Did you seduce Ronnie away from his wife as planned?"

"That's none of your business."

She was right. It wasn't. But she said it as though it was. I invited Lucy Glopp to my house that evening, for a drink.

"Then what?" she asked. She sounded as if she was talking to an old fool.

I told her that I would take her to the restaurant of her choice. "My chauffeur will come by and pick you up."

She laughed. "Why, Mr. Barris, are you actually asking me out?"

"Yes," I replied, "I am actually asking you out." The entire conversation embarrassed me; yet I was aware of a certain edginess on my part as I waited for her reply. Would she or wouldn't she have dinner with me? I couldn't remember the last time I had felt so nervous about a yes or no.

"And if I don't accept, will you fire me?" she asked. I could hear the smirk in her voice.

I said I wasn't sure.

My chagrin grew. It was the first time I had ever attempted to date an employee. My Uncle Bernie used to tell me never to do that. He would wrap his arm around my shoulders, take the thick, wet cigar out of his mouth, blow a puff of smelly smoke toward the ceiling, and say, "When it comes to twat, here's a cardinal rule you should always remember. Never shit where you eat." I was breaking a cardinal rule.

Fuck rules.

* * *

We never made it to a restaurant that evening. About an hour after she arrived, I entered Lucy Sue Glopp, the girl who hated her last name and wanted desperately to marry so that she could be Lucy Sue Something-else. Lucy Sue Glopp, the girl with the shrill laugh, and the skier's tight, well-built body: small breasts, great ass, long legs. Twenty-one years old, cunning, and mean. Not well liked, but a great hump, and she knew it.

I wasn't a great hump. I was always nervous the first time. (And often the second and the third time.) (And the fourth, and fifth, and sixth times.) I guess I wanted to be extra good the first time, so I was always lousy. But Lucy Sue Glopp got things going.

She was good at getting things going.

* * *

About a week later, Lucy Sue Glopp told me that Ronnie Lake wasn't going to leave his wife.

It was late at night when she told me. I was working in my office. I looked up, and there she was, leaning against the door frame, her arms crossed at her chest, her legs crossed at the ankles. "Ronnie Lake has about as much backbone as a fucking hunk of squash," said a disappointed Lucy Sue. "And you should see Ronnie's wife. She's the ugliest piece of white meat *you'll* ever lay your eyes on."

We went to a neighborhood café. Lucy Sue, antsy and depressed, drank two quick vodka and tonics, trying to drown the disappointment of losing another marriage prospect. "Lucy Sue *Glopp*," she said with a sneer. "God, I hate that name."

"It's not so bad," I said cheerfully.

"The *fuck* it isn't," she growled. She took a big gulp of her third vodka and tonic, and said, "I told him last night, either leave your wife now—I mean right now—or don't bother coming around anymore.

And if you don't leave her, don't bother calling me when you're looking for some poon, because I'll just hang up on you." She whirled the ice cubes around in her vodka glass. "He called this morning and said, 'I jes' can't *dooo* it.' " Lucy gulped the remnants of her drink. "I hung up on the prick."

During her fourth vodka, Lucy Sue took on a mean and corrupt expression, the look my grandmother said goyim got when they were "shicker." Yet there was still something very feline and very sensual about her. She had that *Postman Always Rings Twice* quality; that malevolent, two-timing sex appeal of the girl who works behind the luncheonette counter. The waitress in the tight pink uniform with the great ass you keep checking out over the top of your morning newspaper. The bimbo you fantasize fucking while you eat your eggs and home fries. Lucy Sue Glopp had all those steamy attractions, and something else. She had Eliza Doolittle qualities too—the raw material and the desire to become a lady. At least outwardly. But scratch her surface and you'd always find the slut. She'd never lose that.

"What do you think of my figure?" she asked later that night. We had left the café and returned to her tacky apartment, and she was standing on her bed, drunk and naked.

I said she looked beautiful.

"And my breasts?" she asked, cupping them in the palms of her hands and striking a coy pose.

"Small," I replied.

"But adequate," she added. "If they're big enough to fill a champagne glass, they're adequate. And mine fill a champagne glass easily. If I had a champagne glass, I'd show you."

"I believe you."

Lucy turned so that her back was to me. She looked at me over her left shoulder and said, "Whaddaya think of my ass?"

"It's okay."

"Are you *crazy?*" she slurred. "I have a *great* ass!"

She did.

It was close to three in the morning when I left Lucy Sue Glopp's apartment. The curbs along her street were filled with cars parked for the evening, and my automobile was jammed between two late arrivals. I had barely enough room to maneuver. After a great deal of twisting, turning, cursing, and sweating, I managed to get the front of the car in the clear. I was about to drive away when a taxi pulled up parallel to my left side and stopped. The driver apparently

couldn't have cared less that I was seconds away from departing—
and now, because of him, I was trapped. I shouted, "You're blocking
my fucking car, asshole."

I heard him holler back, "Go fuck yourself."

Within the next five seconds, I was out of my automobile and
coming around the back of the taxicab, my right hand deep in my coat
pocket, wrapped around a container of Mace. "Move this fucking cab,"
I yelled, "or—"

"Or what?" said the Duck.

"Jesus, Mary, and Joseph," I groaned.

"Or what?" he repeated. "Or you'll spray me with that rat piss you
have tucked in your coat pocket?" The Duck had come out of his cab
and was slouched against the taxi's left front fender, cleaning his fingernails with an extra-long nail file.

"Okay, what do you have for me?" I sighed, feeling the adrenaline
settle.

"A message. You're leavin' town, man. Like tomorrow, which is
already today."

"Where to?"

"Call this number and find out." The Duck handed me a piece of
paper. "Use your code name when you call."

"Anything else?"

"Yeah. Somethin' about a dirty house that needs dusting, so bring
a dust rag."

Christ, what does that mean? I wondered. Fucking grown men at
Langley playing spies. Code names. Code messages. "Bring a dust rag."
Now what the fuck is that all about?

"That message make any sense to you?" asked the Duck.

"No."

"It don't make any sense to me either," said the Duck, "but then,
I'm not supposed to be as bright as you."

"Up yours, Duck."

The Duck straightened and shot a look of pure hatred at me. He
twirled his long nail file. I could see that it had been sharpened along
one side to a razor's edge. I tightened my grip on the container of Mace
in my coat pocket, and stared him down. The Duck was a real shithead,
and I would have enjoyed any excuse at all to mace his eyes out.

The Duck relaxed. "And a good night to you too," he said, smiling. But he really wasn't smiling. I watched him get into the taxi. Before

he drove off, the Duck leaned out of his window and yelled, "Someday I'm gonna get you, asshole."

"Hey, piss-ant," I hollered, "don't put any money on it." But he didn't hear me. He drove away while I was shouting.

*　*　*

When I got home, I telephoned the number on the crumpled piece of paper. A sleepy voice grunted on the other end.

I said, "Hi! Sunny Sixkiller checking in!"

"Christ," said the voice. There was a pause, and then, "This is a hell of a time to call. Couldn't you have called earlier?"

"I called as soon as I got the message."

"I don't believe you," growled the other end.

"Hi, Treesh," I said happily.

"What time is it?"

"Three-twenty."

"Oh, God."

"What the fuck are you moaning about?" I growled, my mood changing rapidly. "Making contact with agents at all hours of the day and night comes with the job. If you don't like being awakened at three-thirty in the morning, quit."

"As producer of 'The Dating Game' television program," Patricia Watson said curtly, "I understand you're going to London tomorrow to talk to some hotel people about arrangements for future . . . what do you call them . . . dream dates."

"I *am?*"

"TWA has a flight to New York," she said, "leaving this morning at ten-thirty. You will transfer at Kennedy to another TWA flight an hour later. That flight will get you into London the day after tomorrow at eight forty-five A.M., London time. I'll meet you somewhere at two that afternoon. You'll be staying at the Grosvenor House, and I'll call you there to give you a meeting place. You have six hours to sleep, pack, and get to the airport. I suggest you hang up as soon as possible and start doing something."

"Where are you?" I asked.

She hung up.

*　*　*

Late the next night, high over the Atlantic, TWA Flight 457 to London flew through a thunderstorm, and was struck by lightning. The plane jolted violently for an instant, then resumed its flight plan. I had been sleeping, and awoke with a start. Was the jolt a portent of things to come? Was He trying to tell me something about the mission? Or was He just reminding me (in His own little way) that it would have been nice having Him as a friend instead of being the atheist that I was. Right then and there, on that flight to London, I became an agnostic. At least it was a step in the right direction, or at least I hoped He thought it was. (Although I doubt that He did.) Anyway, I prayed and said, "The older we get, the more help we need, ain't that right, Lord?"

If there is a Lord, He probably replied: "What's this *we* shit?"

*   *   *

I gazed, half awake, out of my taxi window.

It was a rainy Sunday in London. The city was gray and wet. But then it's always raining in London, and the city's always gray and wet. Britishers, with Bibles under their arms, walked to church. An art show hung from a section of Hyde Park gate. The paintings looked depressing. Bored painters examined the bored tourists.

The Grosvenor House Hotel seemed to have aged appreciably since I had last been there. Everything and everybody had grown a good deal older: couches, wallpaper, bellmen, maids, and the plumbing. The telephone was ringing as I entered my room. It was Patricia Watson. "If you come out of your hotel from the entrance that's not facing the park," she said crisply, "and take a right, you'll come across a church mews about two blocks down the street. It'll be on your left."

I told Patricia I knew the church mews well. After all, hadn't I killed a man, and had ten years scared off my life, hiding behind a tree in that mews?

"Meet me there in five minutes," she said. "And bring an umbrella. It's raining."

"I don't have an umbrella."

"Tough."

Seven minutes later I passed through the gate of the mews and walked along a red brick pathway, hunched inside my raincoat. I glanced at the wall where I had killed the man in the pink polo shirt. I remembered the idling cars, the ones parked across from the mews, and the panic they had caused. I saw the tree I had hidden behind. I recalled the feeling of helplessness and fright I had suffered standing behind that tree, and how the memory of those terrifying minutes had lingered for months.

The church mews was empty except for a young lady sitting on one of the green benches under an umbrella. I walked up to the lady and said, "Hi, Treesh."

"Hello. Are you tired?"

"Yes."

She said, "So am I."

"You look terrific."

"Sit down." Watson patted space on the bench beside her. "When you go back to your hotel," she said, "have the concierge hire you a car and driver for tomorrow. Tell the concierge to call the Apple Limousine Service and ask for Andy. Tell the concierge to make sure that Andy knows how to get to the Ye Olde Bell Hotel. It's near Henley-on-the Thames. Actually, it's more near Maidenhead than Henley. Most drivers know where it is. Ye Olde Bell Hotel is a famous landmark. When you get there, go to the bar and order a drink. Wait there until you're contacted. A man named Leonard Chump-Chop will be your contact."

"You're not serious. Leonard Chump-Chop?"

"Is your code name any better? Is Sunny Sixkiller any more learned than Leonard Chump-Chop?"

"Code names," I said disagreeably, "may be the last opportunity for humor in this entire shitty line of work."

"I'm going to sleep," said Patricia Watson.

"Pardon?"

"I said I'm going to sleep. I'm going back to my room to take a nap."

"Where are you staying?" I asked.

"I'm not telling."

"Why not?"

"You'll follow me back and try to talk me into making love, and that's the last thing I want to do."

There was a moment of silence. We both stared at our shoes.

"So that's it?" I asked.

"Yep," said Patricia Watson. She stood and walked away.

I sat for a while on the soaking bench, tired and perplexed. Where had we gone wrong, Patricia and I? What was I doing here in London, planning a murder, when I could have been safe at home in California? I was too preoccupied with these increasingly familiar questions to notice the two men sitting in an idling British Ford outside the park's far entrance.

Unlike the last time I had been in the mews, these strangers weren't on my side.

The strangers were KGB agents, who had been instructed to put a "casual" tail on me. There were two other KGB agents parked in a car at the Mount Street entrance. I had no idea any of this was going on. I would not learn about it all until later—much later.

There were a lot of things I didn't know about.

The Soviets had been keeping track of my whereabouts for over a year, and a dossier regarding my activities had been filling up an entire filing cabinet somewhere inside Moscow Center. KGB in Los Angeles had been listening to my personal telephone calls for months from a truck that loitered on a hill a good distance away from my home. They had heard the conversation with Patricia Watson that had sent me to London.

I had become a CIA agent worthy of Soviet surveillance: a celebrity status among international hit men. My ruse of being an American television producer was over. When and where I had blown my cover would never be known to me, but blown it I had. If I continued my record of successful assassinations, the KGB would soon be forced to decide whether to proposition me or eliminate me.

A proposition would most likely come in the form of an offer to continue working in U.S. intelligence but as a KGB "mole." I would receive money and protection in return for information such as America's overseas political targets, the names of all key U.S. intelligence agents, our general mode of operation, and so forth. But the chance of receiving a Soviet offer to transfer my loyalties—even if I wanted to— was highly remote.

Most likely, I would be blown away.

The next morning Andy picked me up, drove me out into the English countryside along the M14 to Henley-on-the Thames, and left me at the Ye Olde Bell Hotel with Leonard Chump-Chop, who told me the story of Harry Kirby.

In 1973 the Soviets had set up surveillance teams to record the actions of a suspected CIA agent, Harry Kirby, who was working out of the Company's West Berlin office. Kirby was fifty-two years old, a graduate of Yale University, and a seven-year veteran of the U.S. State Department. With the exception of a slight potbelly, Kirby carried his age well. He was a natty dresser who always wore a red corsage in his buttonhole, and was considered by those who knew him to be a charming and witty friend.

The KGB discovered that Kirby was not only a natty dresser, but that he was also a crafty, unscrupulous agent with a broad knowledge of Western European security information. The Soviets further learned that Kirby had access to urban target locations; military personnel strengths and weaknesses; intelligence recruitment strategy; electronic surveillance equipment requirements, and other top-secret data.

Beyond this, the KGB noted that Kirby was a womanizer, that he was a compulsive and high-stakes gambler, and that he was deeply in debt. Kirby owed more money than he liked to admit, for a longer time than was generally considered healthy, and to a stratum of people whose reputations Kirby would rather have forgotten. The Soviets knew Harry Kirby would be easy pickings.

In the spring of 1974, the KGB made Harry Kirby a "Godfather deal"—an offer he couldn't refuse. They promised to cover all his gambling debts (in what was probably the nick of time), and to put him on the KGB payroll at double his CIA salary. They offered to pay old Harry a bonus for switching sides equal to more than Kirby's total CIA earnings over the past three years. "Either accept the deal," they told him, "or you're a dead man." Harry Kirby became a KGB mole.

Eventually, Kirby was planting bugs on CIA walls, "borrowing" top-secret U.S. intelligence containers, and passing all his ill-gotten information on to a Colonel Yuri Slasky, 13th Department, Line F, Section Victor, KGB, Moscow Center. Colonel Yuri Slasky was a prick. I had heard all about him. Slasky was said to be a rabid anti-American, anti-Semitic cocksucker who—from as far back as the days of the OSS—had killed more CIA agents than any other living Soviet. Now seventy-five, Colonel Slasky controlled Kirby's every move, and the two formed a treacherous and highly successful team.

It was my job to kill both.

* * *

I had never been assigned a doubleheader before, and I wasn't sure I was pleased. The rewards were greater—but so were the risks. Twice as many details had to be covered, and twice as many things could go wrong.

At seven-thirty the next morning, I stood across the street from a Parisian apartment house at #53 avenue Montaigne. I had been told that Harry Kirby was staying in one of the old apartments that bordered the building's inner courtyard, and that he would lead me to Colonel Slasky. I had a week to complete the operation; in eight days, Kirby and Slasky would be gone.

Within a few minutes, Kirby arrived. As usual, I had studied his pictures so carefully that I felt I knew the man personally. I watched

Kirby enter his parked automobile and warm the engine. I slipped into my rented Renault to do the same. When he drove off, I made a U-turn on avenue Montaigne and followed his automobile. In less than seven minutes, I had lost him.

The next morning I lost him again. I spent the rest of the day depressed and angry, promising that I would resign from the CIA as soon as I could after this mission.

The third day, Harry Kirby didn't appear at all. There was nothing I could do but come back the next morning and wait for him again. The fourth morning passed without Kirby. Then, just as I was about to give up and leave, Harry Kirby stepped out into the early afternoon sun. This time I didn't lose the turncoat; though the heavy traffic was a problem, I was able to keep Kirby's gray Fiat no more than two or three cars in front of me. We crossed the Seine, and drove along the boulevard St.Germain. As we approached the Café Deux Magots, Kirby turned right onto the rue des Saints-Pères. After about half a block, Kirby stopped to park his car. I parked further down the street and watched Kirby through my rearview mirror. He entered a white cement building through a pair of green wooden doors. I locked my car and walked back toward the building.

Across the street from the building was the Hôtel du Pas-de-Calais, whose lobby had a window that overlooked the street. I went into the hotel and sat in an armchair next to that window. I could see the pair of green doors across the way. An hour went by without anyone entering or leaving through those doors. I debated crossing the street, entering the building, finding Kirby, and killing him. But what about Slasky? What if he wasn't there? I couldn't kill just one—I had specific orders to get both. In any case, entering the building was a stupid thought. I hadn't the slightest idea what might be in store for me on the other side of those green doors.

Why, I wondered, weren't these missions thought out more precisely? At Langley, they had told us that assassination attempts would all start with at least six to eight surveillance teams. They spoke of hit squads consisting of a leader and several followers. There would be dress rehearsals, practice runs with timing charts, contingency plans, and emergency backup groups. We were promised that getaways would be meticulously planned; that as little as possible would be left to chance. But in actuality, *everything* was left to chance. You were given a packet of pictures and some skimpy vital statistics, perhaps a few additional scraps of information from the local stringer, a few code

words, and a round-trip airline ticket and hotel reservations courtesy
of the Uncle. From that point on, you were on your own. No one even
said "Good luck." It was as if all the talk of teamwork was a come-on
so that neophyte agents wouldn't chicken out and quit the service. So
why did I do it? Because it was thrilling? Was it my subliminal fascina-
tion with death? Or did I actually think it was patriotic? I guess I really
didn't know.

Sitting in the lobby of the Hôtel du Pas-de-Calais began to get on
my nerves. My heart was pounding ferociously; it always did when I
was stalking prey. Sometimes my heart beat so fast that I would become
alarmed. Never have I experienced anything as intense and visceral as
anticipating the taking of another's life.

* * *

"Is it more exciting than an incredible orgasm?" another agent once
asked Jim Byrd.

"Certainly," replied Byrd without hesitation. "Killing someone is
much more exciting than fucking someone. It's more tingling, more
stimulating, more electrifying, more meaningful, more indelible, more
everything. Actually, the act of assassination is indescribable."

"There is no such word as 'indescribable,' " the other agent had
said. "Everything is describable."

"Describe an incredible orgasm," challenged Byrd.

The other agent thought for a moment, and then said, "An incredible orgasm is more exciting than brushing your teeth, but less exciting
than being ejected from a supersonic jet at thirty thousand feet."

"In that case, killing someone," Byrd had said, "is more exciting
than being ejected from a supersonic jet."

"But less exciting than what?" insisted the other agent.

"Less exciting," Byrd had replied, "than being killed?"

* * *

I left the hotel lobby and returned to the rue des Saints-Pères, pretending to window shop, but always keeping my eyes on the green wooden
doors. I saw windows filled with uncomfortable-looking Louis XIV
chairs, heavily framed oil paintings, and piles of twenty-four-karat gold
jewelry. I walked on. Kirby and Slasky *must* have KGB watchdogs, I
mused. The colonel wouldn't travel without them. So where were they?
I scoured the street but saw nothing resembling Soviet henchmen. They
probably weren't around because the colonel wasn't around. The act of
attempting to trap two individuals in one suitable place was a pain in
the ass. Perhaps impossible.

I turned back toward the white cement building, and instantly froze. Harry Kirby and Colonel Slasky had stepped out onto the rue des Saints-Pères. I watched the two men look up and down the street. They saw me, but I apparently meant nothing to them. Three women shoppers jostled the two men as they passed them on the narrow pavement. I watched the shoppers say "Excuse me," and Kirby smile. Slasky turned his back to me. He was looking toward the boulevard St.Germain. For what? A car? His henchmen? The women continued down the pavement toward me.

I moved quickly through the shoppers, drawing my silencer-equipped automatic out of my belt as I walked. I bumped into Colonel Slasky, spun him around, and shot him three times in the left side of his chest. I turned and shot Harry Kirby once in the face and twice in the chest. Slasky had fallen on his side on the pavement. I bent over and put a bullet through his temple. Kirby was on his knees. I placed the end of the silencer in his ear and pulled the trigger. A small truck screeched to a stop. I crossed the street and ran toward the boulevard St.Germain. If there were screams and shouts and horns blowing, I didn't hear them.

I returned to my hotel room, locked and bolted the door, and positioned an armchair so that I could see the entire room. I checked the Ruger .22-caliber automatic and silencer that I had used on the rue des Saints-Pères. It was a funny-looking gun. Most of its barrel was the silencer. The boys at the Company called it an "assassination gun." I ejected the old magazine, oiled the automatic lightly, wiped it clean with a rag, popped in a full magazine, and rested the gun on my lap. I sat that way until dawn.

At sunrise, the telephone rang. I was expecting the call. It was Paul Picard, an agent with the French intelligence service, the SDECE. His responsibility was to get me out of the country and on my way home, alive.

I met Picard downstairs, and the two of us walked through the lobby and out the revolving doors to the pavement in front of the hotel. There was hardly any traffic on the boulevard. I had no idea where we were going; I simply followed Picard as he walked straight ahead.

Picard's Mercedes was double-parked on the far side of a line of idle taxicabs. Across the boulevard, directly opposite us, was a small tan Fiat. Seated in the Fiat were four men. Paul and I saw the Fiat and its passengers at almost the same moment, and realized who the four men were. Anyone with even a modest knowledge of the business would have known they were KGB agents. "Be calm," Paul said.

Two of the Soviet agents in the tan Fiat were sharpshooters. They were seated in the car's backseat, their high-powered .22-caliber sniper rifles resting on their laps. The rifles were equipped with electronic sights, allowing the sharpshooters to keep both eyes open while taking aim. Other than the circle of cabbies, the boulevard was empty. The gunmen waited, knowing there would soon be other opportunities.

I remained standing by the protected passenger side of Paul's Mercedes while he walked around to the driver's door. There was nothing but empty street between Paul Picard and the sniper rifles. Paul unlocked the car, and the two of us stepped inside the Mercedes. "*Bon,*" said Paul, smiling.

We drove off.

The Fiat followed.

Picard drove through the streets of Paris casually, not concerned in the least about the trailing Fiat. His manner of driving almost suggested that he preferred that the Fiat stay close behind us. I became frightened. I began to wonder if Paul Picard was in fact KGB, and if the two automobiles were in the process of spiriting me out of the country. I was horribly aware of the strong possibility that I could be heading for Russia and *not* the United States.

And then we swerved left onto a particularly narrow street. Suddenly, two large black Citroens appeared out of nowhere and slipped between our car and the Fiat. A third black Citroen materialized just as suddenly behind the Fiat, and the four cars stopped. As we continued driving, I saw the men in the three Citroens get out of their automobiles and surround the Fiat.

"Who are the guys who just bagged the Russians?" I asked.

"Friends of mine," said Paul Picard. He shot out of the narrow street and began driving like a madman. We went to neither Orly nor Le Bourget airport, arriving instead at a small airfield in total disrepair. The landing strip was overrun with weeds and rocks. A handful of private planes were tethered to the field. The tower was empty: one took off and landed at one's own risk. Across the way were several rusty old hangars and a boarded-up Quonset hut. There was, however, a shiny new Mystère-20 jet aircraft at the far end of the field. Paul drove directly to that plane.

Before I climbed aboard the Mystère, Paul and I hugged. The previous hour—the hair-raising danger to both of us on the streets of Paris, and his rescue—was the kind that instantly made strangers into lifelong comrades.

"Good luck, my friend," said Paul, smiling.

"Thank you," I said, climbing the small ladder and waving to Paul. A crewman pulled the cabin door shut.

An hour later I landed at London's Heathrow Airport, where I transferred to a commercial airliner bound for New York. I never entered the main terminal or passed through customs. I was simply driven from one airplane to the other, all the details prearranged. I felt mysterious, proud, patriotic; as though someone really cared.

*   *   *

As my plane was taxiing to its gate at Heathrow, a Major Valarie Kasilov, of KGB Wet Operations, was reporting the loss of Kirby and Slasky to his superiors. Slasky had been Kasilov's closest personal friend. "I will have my revenge," he said, upon completing his report. "I will personally kill the American executioner. I will find out who he is, and *where* he is, and I will kill him myself."

Kasilov appealed to his superiors. He explained that, regardless of his own personal motives, the killer was a cold-blooded professional who had apparently been operating successfully—too successfully—for years in the European theater, and that it would be best for all concerned if this particular assassin was eliminated. Major Kasilov said he was certain the killer was American—a CIA operative—who had entered Europe under various covers to do his dirty work. He agreed with his generals that isolating and locating the killer—under normal conditions—might be an extended and perhaps futile mission, but this wasn't a normal situation. Kasilov explained that there was a KGB mole in place, high up in the CIA's Clandestine Affairs Division, and that the mole would be a valuable source of information on the assassin. "We even know," said Kasilov, "that the assassin's code name is Sunny Sixkiller." The major asked permission from his KGB superiors to at least be allowed to attempt to find the murderer of his friend, and countless others, even if it meant traveling to the United States.

Permission was granted.

All of what I have just related was told to me later, much later, by CIA officials. They had learned about Major Valarie Kasilov's conversations with his superiors from a KGB agent who was present at those meetings. The Russian agent subsequently fled the Soviet Union and requested asylum in Canada. It was during the turncoat agent's debriefing in Toronto that the CIA was told the details of Kasilov's Moscow meeting, and his determination to eliminate the American who called himself Sunny Sixkiller.

*   *   *

Two days later, on April 24, 1975, I was seated on a bench in Central Park. New York was unusually hot. It was lunch hour, and bench space was hard to find. Pale, tense office workers had left their little cubicles in the tall corporate buildings of the East Fifties and Sixties for an hour of sunshine and peace. Some sat in silence, eating lunches out of brown paper bags, heads tilted up toward the warmth. Others preferred the shady side of the walkway. They all shared the benches with the elderly, the unemployed, the retired, and the loony. My bench, painted a dismal green and liberally stained with pigeon shit, was in a row of benches along a path that led to the zoo. Sitting beside me was Jim Byrd. Next to him was an ancient lady with a bag of groceries on her lap, eating a cream cheese and olive sandwich.

"The KGB knew exactly what you were planning to do," said Jim Byrd, staring straight ahead. He spoke in a stage whisper out of the left side of his mouth. He appeared listless, almost bored. Jim held last Sunday's thick *New York Times* on his lap, unopened. "All of your movements were known," he continued, "from the time you left your house in Los Angeles until the time you came home from London."

I felt that familiar stab of fear shoot through my bones. "You're sure?" I asked.

"I'm sure," answered Jim. "And you still accomplished your mission, and got away in one piece! Fucking amazing. Probably because, luckily, you did it where they least expected it."

"And if I hadn't done it there?"

"Any other place," answered Byrd, staring at the bench across the way, "and you'd probably be dead."

"Am I in danger now?"

"Probably."

My stomach knotted. "Will they be watching me?"

"Probably."

"Jesus Christ, Jim, is that all you can say? Probably. Probably. Probably. Shit."

"Easy," said Byrd, still staring straight ahead. "Take it easy."

I felt like doing anything but taking it easy. I wanted to lash out, do something about the situation, or at least run away and hide. Taking it easy seemed the least preferable option. We sat in silence for a few minutes.

"Is it good?" I asked. "I mean my being seen with you?"

"I guess not," said Byrd lackadaisically. "But most likely it's all academic. If your movements are so well known, then my relationship to you must be too. They may even know who our superiors are. Look, it's obvious. Someone has switched sides. We have a mole on our hands."

"A mole! Shit." And then I added with a flash of panic, "So what do we do now?"

"Bow out," answered Byrd.

"Bow out? What do you mean, bow out?"

"Take a leave of absence. Or maybe resign."

"Both of us?"

"Yep."

"Resign!"

"For a while."

"Why?"

"To get everybody off our backs," replied Byrd. "Maybe we're just too good. Or too stupid. Whatever we are, we're annoying the hell out of Moscow Center. And if we want to live a little while longer, we've got to lie low."

"That doesn't make sense, Jim. If that's the reward you get for becoming good at what you do, then half the CIA should be lying low. And that's no fucking way to operate, Jim."

"Maybe so," said Byrd simply.

The elderly woman sitting on the other side of Jim gathered up her grocery bag and walked away. A raggedy bag lady wandered by carrying junk in torn shopping bags from Bendel's and Bonwit Teller's.

We sat in silence for a long time. The Angel of Death was definitely hanging around Central Park.

I asked Jim what he was going to do.

"Go sailing," he said, "but don't tell anyone." He smiled a mirthless smile.

"Where?"

"The Med," Jim answered without enthusiasm. "I have a friend who has a forty-foot sailer. He keeps it docked at Antibes. Maybe we'll get as far as the Greek Islands. Who knows?"

"What about money?" I asked. "What are you going to do about money?"

"I've got some saved up," Jim said. "I can hang out for a while. If it runs out, and I still can't come back to the Company, maybe I'll free-lance. A lot of ex-agents are making a lot of money free-lancing."

"Yeah?" I said, thinking other thoughts.

Byrd said, "You remember Leonard Brill, don't you? Christ, he's cleaning up in Libya. He must have made millions by now."

I wasn't interested in Leonard Brill. "What the fuck am I going to do?" I whined.

"What do you mean, what are you going to do? You'll go back to Hollywood and create television shows. Control says so."

"He does?"

"Yep. You're too hot to handle. Remember?"

"I never thought he cared," I said.

A tramp rummaged through a large metal trash can. A black drunk a few benches down the path shouted at passing dogs. "Now there's a *good* dog. You're a good dog because you're a *black* dog." The park benches began to empty as lunch hour came to a close.

"I'll be seeing you," said Jim Byrd, sort of sadly. He stood up.

"Yeah," I said. "I'll just sit here a little while longer. I want to think about things."

"Okay."

"Hey, Jim, are we in any kind of danger? I mean *real* danger?"

"Yep," answered Byrd. He started to walk away, but returned to say, "You see, in the movies they always get the bad guys in the end. In real life, the bad guys are still out there. Real life sucks." Byrd stepped closer to me. "Be careful," he said softly. "Don't develop any patterns. If you follow certain patterns now, get rid of them in a hurry. Change the time you go for breakfast, or when you pick up your morning newspaper. Drive to your office in Hollywood down different streets, and leave your building by a different door. Keep your eyes open. Study faces. You may see someone who's not supposed to be there. Be careful. But don't be scared. Dogs bite people who are scared."

Jim stood up at attention, checked to see that his necktie was tightly knotted, and buttoned the middle button of his sport coat. Byrd had aged since the last time I saw him. His red hair was thinning, and his freckles were being replaced by liver spots. Byrd had always appeared younger than his years, but not anymore. He would be forty soon, and looked it. "By the way," he said, "Paul Picard's dead."

"Paul Picard?"

"Your driver in Paris. They found his body yesterday morning."

I felt it again: that stab of fear. The stab was becoming an everyday occurrence, a deformity; something I would have to learn to live with, like a nervous tic or a game leg. "How did he die?" I asked.

"He was shot. I guess those KGB sharpshooters you mentioned had to nail him sooner or later. Just to satisfy their frustrations."

"Jesus," I whispered. Paul, waving good-bye, flashed through my head. I could see him clearly, standing on that dilapidated airfield outside of Paris.

Byrd and I looked at each other without saying a word. A thin salesman wearing a porkpie hat and a plump girl in a print dress two sizes too small sat down on the other half of our bench.

"Oh, well," were the last words I heard Jim Byrd say. He turned and walked away. Suddenly, I felt very alone.

And someone who wanted me dead was only a few city blocks away.

"Not really."

"Christ, you're pissed. Are you ever going to stop being pissed at me?"

"Probably not."

* * *

One night in Boston, I had stood up Patricia Watson. I was flying in from the West Coast to spend the weekend with her. But I had ditched Treesh for an impressionable Boston College co-ed I had met on the plane from Los Angeles. It would have been impossible for me to leave the ripe and seductive co-ed without knowing how our evening would have ended. Besides, she was something new; a challenging novelty. Add to that the possibility of getting into her pants: scoring would bolster my always insecure ego.

I telephoned Watson from the airport, mumbled something about a sudden attack of stomach flu, and told her that I'd phone in the morning. I took the young co-ed to the bar of the Ritz-Carlton Hotel. I bumped into Patricia Watson there. Treesh was with a girl friend. I stammered some tongue-tied bullshit to Treesh that made about as much sense as my being with the co-ed in the first place. I may even have winked. Watson looked at me with a chilling fury I'll never forget.

After that night, my relationship with Watson was purely business. I tried to get Watson back into bed; God knows, I tried. I must have called Treesh asking for a date at least a hundred times after that disastrous night in the Ritz-Carlton bar. She always refused. She was a pretty but extremely poor loser.

Obviously, Treesh was competitive. According to her, she had been that way all her life: from grammar school, through Radcliffe, and into the Company. As a Cliffie, she had been president of her senior class and captain of the debating team. She was an expert equestrian, competing nationally in the steeplechase event. She had published a book of short stories and could have been a tournament bridge player. She joined the Central Intelligence Agency because it was a challenge. She wanted to see how well she could do in a predominantly male organization, and her competitiveness had pushed her to the highest position a female had ever reached in the Company. When I had asked her what drove her, she had replied, "I'm not a good loser."

* * *

I looked at her sitting across from me in the Friar's Club bar. She was a beautiful, intelligent woman. I may have made a terrible mistake. "I

Thirteen

There I was, sitting in Central Park, at the end of the Thursday afternoon lunch hour, with hundreds of people roaming around, and I still felt alone. With absolutely no one to turn to. And if I *could* turn to someone, what good would it do? After I told the person my troubles, how could he help? If a hit man wanted to kill me, he would kill me. I could carry a Thompson submachine gun under my overcoat, but he'd kill me anyway. Change my patterns. Look at faces. What did it mean? It wouldn't stop an assassin from murdering me. Not if the assassin set his mind to do it. If anyone knew that, I certainly did. Didn't I kill, regardless of bodyguards or patterns? Didn't Kirby and Slasky look at me when I was standing on the rue des Saints-Pères? Did seeing my face save their lives?

What a fucking way to live.

What kind of life was I living anyway? A pointless one, with little reward and a lot of risk. And no one giving two shits about the risk, or the patriotism, or my successes or failures. Nobody except the Russians, and they were the last ones I wanted to impress.

And then I thought of someone I could talk to. Patricia Watson. She was in New York; I knew because I had received a message from her at my hotel. I decided to find a telephone booth and call Patricia.

* * *

We agreed to meet early that evening at the Friar's Club. "I didn't know you were a Friar," Patricia said when she arrived at the bar. She sat down and snapped her long brunette hair back as if she were a swimmer stepping out of a pool.

I called a waiter over, and we ordered drinks. I was shocked to hear Treesh ask for a double bourbon and ginger ale. I ordered a Scotch on the rocks. "Hey, Treesh, did I ever tell you you're very pretty?"

"You tell me that all the time."

"Does it mean anything to you?"

got your message at the Plaza," I said. "How come you called at three in the morning?"

"That's when I got in," she answered.

"Where are you staying?"

"I'm not telling you."

"Jesus."

"How's your love life?" Patricia Watson asked abruptly. I was visibly surprised. It was not her kind of question.

"Not bad. My love life's not bad."

"Are you spoken for?"

"That's an interesting expression," I said. "Almost Elizabethan."

"Well, are you?"

"No, I'm not spoken for. But I *am* in the process of falling in love with an ex-cocktail waitress who works for me."

"How interesting," said Patricia Watson, who didn't sound interested in the least.

We ordered refills; another Scotch on the rocks for me, and a second double bourbon and ginger ale for Treesh. It was very strange to see her drinking like a fish. Maybe she would get drunk. Then I could take advantage of her.

"Don't get any smart ideas," Watson said. "I've learned to hold my liquor fairly well."

"How come everybody can read my mind?"

"You have very graphic expressions. You'd make a lousy poker player. How did it go?"

"How did *what* go?"

"Your trip to Paris."

"Fine. I got the job done. And got away in one piece. But my driver didn't. Paul Picard didn't."

"I know that."

"If you knew everything, why the hell did you ask me how it went?"

"I thought you might add something I *didn't* know."

"Did you know we have a mole prowling around the Company?"

"Yes."

"And that Moscow Center is watching me, and others—like Jim Byrd and maybe even you—and that maybe all our lives are in danger?"

"Yes."

"Aren't you afraid?" I asked.

"No. Are you?"

"Yes," I answered. "Very."

"Scaredy-cat."

"How did you hear about our little mole?"

"Control told me."

"What else did Control tell you?"

"I was told that you are to be 'retired.' "

"Retired?"

"Dropped. Dropped from my assignment book."

"How 'bout that? I'll bet Asshole Oliver is delighted. For how long?"

"Until you hear from me," answered Watson. "Or Jim Byrd."

"Jim Byrd's going sailing," I said. "He's chartering a boat and going to the Greek Islands."

"When?"

"I don't know." And then I remembered that Jim had told me not to tell anyone.

"Well, good for him," said Patricia.

"Listen," I said, returning to more important matters, "will the KGB know I'm retired?"

"Yes, but it probably won't matter. They'll still want to kill you."

"Then what the fuck good is my retiring going to accomplish?"

"It cuts your chances of being killed in half."

"How do you figure that?" I asked, finishing my second drink.

"Now you can only be killed in the United States, instead of the United States and Europe."

I could only sigh. She was getting even for all sorts of things.

"At least you won't be walking the halls of Langley, hung up to dry, like the other grounded agents," said Patricia Watson. "At least you have an office in Hollywood you can go to. At least you can go on working at *some*thing."

"When does my retirement start?"

"Now," Patricia said.

* * *

I spent the next three months in Hollywood mulling over a new talent show. I was convinced there were tons of exciting entertainers roaming the streets with no place to go; with no outlet for their crafts. There had been several successful talent programs in the past—Major Bows', Arthur Godfrey's, Ted Mack's, et cetera—so why not one now? Something with an up-to-date look and a flair to it.

I presented my idea to the boys at ABC. I explained that I would like to do a daily half-hour TV program with five or six good, entertaining acts, and one or two awful ones for laughs. A panel of judges would rate the acts, and the winning act would win a couple of hundred dollars. I told the boys that the money wasn't the important factor— the program was. All the acts—the winner *and* the losers—would love the show because they would be getting what they wanted more than money: exposure. As far as I was concerned, an entertaining talent program was a natural. New talent would flock to our auditions, happy to be given the chance to be seen. The public would be entertained by these acts, and the network would get what it wanted most—a hit television program.

The ABC-TV boys liked what I said, and they agreed to put up the money for a pilot. I went right to work auditioning everybody I could find. After several weeks of tryouts, I became painfully convinced that I was wrong. There weren't tons of exceptionally talented people roaming the streets. What were roaming the streets were tons of exceptionally *un*talented people: kooks, loons, horrible singers singing dreadful versions of "Feelings," atrocious comedians, embarrassing acrobats. I returned the pilot money to the American Broadcasting Company and dropped the project.

And then one night, while tossing and turning in an attempt to fall asleep, it dawned on me. If I couldn't do a talent show that had more good acts than bad, I could certainly do a talent show that had more bad acts than good.

And that's what I did.

I returned to the television networks and sold "The Gong Show" to NBC.

Part Three

The sole cause of man's unhappiness is that he does not know how to stay quietly in his room.
                                                                    —Pascal

UNKNOWN COMIC: What do you call a Mexican with a vasectomy?

CHUCK BARRIS: What?

UNKNOWN COMIC: A dry Martinez! *Wild laughter from the studio audience.*

UNKNOWN COMIC: Do you like sex?

CHUCK BARRIS: Yes.

UNKNOWN COMIC: Do you like sports?

CHUCK BARRIS: Yes.

UNKNOWN COMIC: Then take a fucking hike.

CHUCK BARRIS: You can't say that on television. *Barris pushes the Unknown Comic off the stage.*

* * *

February 4, 1976.

"The Gong Show" was a smash, if somewhat controversial, hit on coast-to-coast television. Everybody either loved the show or hated it, but it seemed that in either case everyone was watching "The Gong Show." That's all that seemed to matter. Soon, there would be a series of "Gong Show" prime-time television specials, a "Gong Show" movie, "Gong Show" editorials in many of the country's newspapers, "Gong Show" books, gongs for the house (to "gong" your wife or friends), "Gong Show" games for kids, gong shows for charity in churches and synagogues, gong shows to entertain the passengers on cruise ships or the customers in bars and cafés. There were gong shows being performed on the stages of grammar schools, high schools, and colleges. "Gong him!" became synonymous with "Throw him out!" or "Get rid of him!" When someone or something was "gonged," that person or object was deemed too awful to exist any longer.

"There is no way," said Clifton Fadiman, "of reconciling the vision offered by Shakespeare or Newton with the vision of life offered by 'The Gong Show.'"

" 'The Gong Show,' " said a show-business trade paper, "is the first TV variety show to feature the lunatic fringe."

Both were relatively true statements. The program certainly had its share of oddballs. The weirdest of the weird, the worst of the worst. And only the very worst would be gonged. To be gonged on "The Gong Show" was the lowest, the lamest; a pronouncement of despicable and indelible personal consequence. Something like a concentration-camp tattoo. To some, maybe even more demeaning than that.

Of course, every now and then, there was a good act—sometimes a *very* good act. The good act was there to keep the program in its proper perspective. If every act was dreadful, how would one be able to differentiate the bad from the *really* bad?

Hence the good act.

Followed by a three-hundred-pound lady in a string bikini, singing "Your Cheating Heart."

Followed by a pair of boys disguised as a vagina and an umbilical cord, bellowing "Having My Baby."

Followed by the Unknown Comic in his seedy brown-and-tan checkered sport coat held together by a large safety pin, and his scuffed black-and-white golf shoes with the scalloped tongues, shouting: "Chuckie baby! Hey, Chuckie, Chuckie, Chuckie!"

CHUCK BARRIS: Yes? What do you want?
UNKNOWN COMIC: Is my fly open?
CHUCK BARRIS: No, it isn't.
UNKNOWN COMIC: Well, it should be. I'm peein'.

* * *

The half-hour "Gong Show" consisted of seven or eight acts, a host, and three celebrity judges. The act would perform, and would either be gonged by one or all of the judges (literally by having a judge smash a mallet against an immense Korean gong) and dismissed posthaste, or else be allowed to finish. If the act *did* finish, it would then be rated by each of the three judges on a zero-to-ten basis, with zero being extraordinarily unpleasant. The act, standing beside the program's host, would listen to the score, along with the inevitable slander and derogatory epitaphs that were sure to come from the unmannerly studio audience, the rowdy studio orchestra, the obscene studio stagehands, sometimes even the celebrity judges and my playful show staff. The act with the highest score at the end of the show would win a few dollars and a gold-plated gong. And as for the other acts? Their memories of show biz—with all its glamorous and narcissistic trappings—were ample reward.

"The Gong Show": The Christians (the act and host) versus the lions (everybody else), right there on the boob tube for everyone to watch. "The Gong Show" gave the little person his or her moment in the spotlight—and the consequences thereof. The rest of the world was given the opportunity to be jealous and kick shit in the little person's face. (A microcosm of life?)

Someone—Andy Warhol, I think—predicted that one day soon everybody would be a celebrity for fifteen minutes. I thought fifteen minutes might be thirteen minutes too many. On "The Gong Show," everybody was a star for the first forty-five seconds of their act. At least. For the last forty-five seconds, they were gongable.

And when they were gonged, who would the performers turn to, astonished, eyes brimming with tears? The program's host, that's who. And who would they kiss or bear hug when they weren't gonged? The program's host, that's who. And who would be left on an empty stage if the performer walked off in a huff? The program's host, that's who. And who was the program's host?

Me.

* * *

"Why you?" Lucy Sue Glopp had asked while spreading Borden's canned whipped cream on my pecker. "Why do *you* want to host 'The Gong Show'?"

We were lying naked atop my massive four-poster bed. "Greed," I answered, my arms clasped behind my head. "Pure and simple greed."

I told Lucy Sue that I had known that the show would be a big hit (and that I would make a lot of money) *if*—and it was a big *if*— the program's host knew what the show was all about. The show was make-believe, camp, a put-on. It was a caricature of all the amateur hours that had come before, and as such had to be played tongue-in-cheek. It was supposed to be amusing, not serious. But if the host thought "The Gong Show" was a legitimate talent hunt, a serious stairway-to-the-stars type of thing, we were dead.

The NBC daytime television network had selected a host who was convinced we were doing exactly that. The clod considered himself David Merrick, Alexander Cohen, and Sol Hurok rolled up in one, discovering new stars for the show-biz firmament. And there was nothing I could do to make him understand my vision of the show.

Lucy Sue Glopp mumbled something indistinguishable from somewhere deep in my crotch.

"What did you say?" I asked.

She raised her chin and said, "What did you do?"

"About what?"

"About the dumb host."

"I killed the fucker."

"Which fucker?" she asked, dabbing a fresh supply of whipped cream on my tool.

"What do you mean, which fucker? The *host!*" Sometimes I wondered if Lucy Sue was in the same city that I was.

"Yadina," she mumbled.

"What? Take that out of your mouth so I can understand you."

"I said you did not."

She was right. I didn't kill the fucker. But I had to get rid of him, one way or another. If I let the putz continue as the NBC daytime host, the entire project would have—as they say in Hollywood—gone right down the toilet. The agony of seeing a format come together and display signs of becoming a highly entertaining, spontaneous, and identifiable television show—and then see a misguided host turn it into something it was never meant to be, something that would surely fail—was unbearable.

"Shit! Piss! Fuck!" I would wail.

It was awful.

I would watch a celebrity gong a dreadful singer. The host would ask why the celebrity had done it, and the celebrity would say something like, "Because his socks don't match." (A perfect "Gong Show" reason for gonging someone.)

The putz-host would stand back aghast. And then, when he regained his composure, he would more often than not chastise the celebrity, greatly confusing the audience.

"But this is 'The Gong Show,' " the celebrity judge might say, "not the Van Cliburn eliminations."

"This," the host would counter, glaring at the flippant celebrity judge, "is a human being with aspirations."

"Oh, fuck off," I would say, which the clod never heard because I was standing yards away in the wings of the stage. I could have killed the guy. But I didn't. Instead, I appealed to Madeline David.

Madeline David was the vice-president of daytime television programs for NBC. She was also a friend. Madeline agreed to replace the man on one condition: that I host the show.

"*Me!*"

"You," she said.

"Jesus."

"You know the show best," she added logically. "You helped create it. You know better than anyone else what the show's all about. Besides, you're as bad as the acts—maybe worse. The performers will be able to identify with you. It's either you or (as you call him) the 'putz.' You have to decide before you tape again. I don't want to do another week's worth of shows and have to scrap them. I'll scrap this past week's, and that's all. If you won't do it, then we go with the putz, and we go with the putz for the rest of the first thirteen weeks."

"If we go with the putz for the first thirteen weeks," I moaned, "there won't be a second thirteen weeks."

"Then do it yourself," Madeline snapped.

I panicked. "We start taping the next week's shows tomorrow at noon."

"Then call me and let me know your decision no later than eight o'clock tomorrow morning. Remember, hosting the show will radically change your life. So think about it carefully."

"Eight o'clock tomorrow is just twelve hours away!"

Madeline shrugged. I left her suite at the Beverly Hills Hotel and returned to my production company in Hollyweird to think about it.

It was a little after eight-thirty when I arrived at our building at 1313 Vine Street. Everyone had gone home, and the building was dark and gloomy. I turned on a few lights in the corridors, unlocked my office, lit some lamps, and sat down behind my desk.

There were some definite pros to hosting "The Gong Show." I would become a national (maybe even an international) celebrity. Airline stewardesses would attend to me more than to other passengers, and airline public-relations personnel would meet me at airports and whisk me to my baggage on little go-carts. Movie theaters would let me in for nothing, and legitimate theaters would supply me with free house seats on the aisle. I would be invited to political rallies, TV talk shows, motion-picture premiers, and charity balls. I would drive around in limousines and read about myself in *Time* and *Newsweek.* Paparazzi would chase me with their cameras, and fans would want my autograph and articles of clothing. Girls would want parts of my body. Cute, juicy girls, I imagined. It would be exciting and fun.

I never considered the possibility that paparazzi could be a fucking pain in the ass, or that the juicy girls who would be offering themselves to me would not be juicy girls—why would juicy girls *need* to offer themselves to anybody?—but rather, horrendous, pea-brained things, either dried-up or obese. It never entered my mind that I would be unable to have breakfast unmolested at a coffee-shop counter, or unable to stand in a movie line again in peace and quiet. Or wait for a hot dog at a football game. In fact, there wouldn't be any more football games at all—or any other sporting events, for that matter. And all because of the "beer factor": the time it took the other spectators to get soused and courageous and seek me out, screaming, "Gong! Gong! Hey, Chuckie baby! Gong!" and yell all sorts of things, some of them not very pleasant. (Exactly when the beer factor went into effect would vary with the sport. It would be the second period in hockey, the third period in football, and the seventh inning in baseball.) How was I to know that I would always be at the mercy of the asshole beside me in a restaurant or on a street corner, who would laugh, and point, and shout, "Chuck Barris! Hey, fellas, look who's standing over there. It's the guy from the TV show!"

"Big deal," another would say.

"Hey, look," still another would say, "he's carrying a newspaper. He reads! Hey, you guys, he can read!"

"Who cares? I never watch his program anyway."

And then they would all laugh.

Who could foretell that one morning I would be waiting in my car for a red light to change, and that I would see a pretty girl sitting on the passenger side of the car next to me smile and wave? She would roll her window down, and signal me to do the same. I would roll mine down cheerfully, curious to know what was on her mind; what she would say. You know what she would say? She would say, "I think your program stinks, and I think you stink." Then she, and her girl friend, the driver, would laugh in my face. And me without my morning coffee. Who could prophesy that in the not-too-distant future, I would shy away from airports, arenas, stadiums, early evening walks, and parties that included strangers? That I would find myself staying home more and more until I hardly ever went out? That one day I would wake up and realize I had become a quasi-hermit?

Not me. I never considered stuff like that when I thought about being a celebrity.

So I sat in my empty office and weighed all those pros and cons. It was very quiet. A wall clock chimed, startlingly loud in the still of midnight.

While the clock was tolling the hour, someone tried to kill me.

Maybe the assassin's shot missed me because I moved. Out of the corner of my right eye I had thought I had seen something in my office doorway. The door was behind me, about six feet to my right. I moved my head back ever so slightly to turn to look at what had caught my eye, and saw a brilliant fireflash. Then I heard the thunderous noise of a pistol exploding at relatively close range.

The report from the shot deafened my right ear. I was intact, but paralyzed with fear; nobody had ever shot at me before. I stared at the doorway, stunned and helpless, like a deer in the presence of a tiger. The assassin could have approached my desk and shot me from point-blank range. But he didn't. He had probably panicked at the sound of his gun, and fled. A rank amateur; a wasted contract. That assassin (I thought much later) should have been drummed out of whatever service he belonged to.

Ultimately, I rose from my chair, my legs almost too rubbery to use. I slowly began to comprehend that my life had been threatened. Then it dawned on me that the hit man might still be near by. I raced to my desk, pulled open a bottom drawer, and grabbed a Colt .45 automatic. I spent the next twenty minutes checking every nook and cranny of our offices, but the assassin had obviously left the building.

I returned to my office doorway, traced the path of the bullet, and found the spot where it had entered the opposite wall. The size of the bullet hole was rather frightening, considering it might have been on the right side of my head.

Just then, the telephone rang. It scared the shit out of me. Phones had a way of doing that to me even on the best of occasions. Whoever was calling was using my private number; its little light was blinking. Not many people knew my private number.

"Chuck?" said the party on the other end. "Chuck? Is that you?"

"Yes. Who's this?"

"Patricia. This is Patricia."

"Treesh!" I yelled, thrilled to hear her voice. "Treesh, someone just tried to kill me! Someone just took a shot at me right here in my goddamn office! Jesus Christ, Treesh, I can hardly stand up. My legs feel like jelly, and I'm deaf in one ear. Whoever it was just shot once and ran away."

"You should be happy he ran away," replied Patricia Watson rather calmly.

"I am. You're right. I'm *glad* he ran away."

"Maybe whoever it was was just trying to scare you."

"Well, he did. He goddamn fucking scared the shit out of me."

"Are you okay?" she asked.

"Yes," I answered, deflated and exhausted, "I'm okay."

"Good," she replied. "I'm calling to tell you that Jim Byrd's dead."

* * *

" 'I did not realize how motley are the qualities that go to make up a human being.' You know who said that?" I asked.

"No, and I don't give a shit who said it," replied an inebriated Lucy Sue Glopp.

"Somerset Maugham said it."

"Good for Somerset," slurred Glopp.

It was the next night, and we were at Chasen's. Lucy and I had guzzled four Scotch and sodas before ordering dinner, and two after finishing. The thought of drinking all those Scotches bothered me. I never used to have more than one drink before dinner. Now, I was up to four. Or five. And, of course, Lucy Sue wanted wine with the meal, and liqueur with dessert. Needless to say, I was drunk. It seemed I was getting drunk more and more, especially when I was with Lucy Sue Glopp, and I was with Lucy Sue almost every night. And she was always drunk as well. That night, Lucy Sue was very drunk and exceptionally loud. She sat in an ill-mannered slouch in her section of the booth, arms folded across her chest, a smirk on her face. I didn't notice the smirk. I was thinking about Jim Byrd and how I loved the son of a bitch. He taught me all the good stuff I knew. He was my best friend. He was the only person I could laugh with in the entire Company. "Shit. Piss. Fuck," I muttered.

"What?" asked Glopp.

How had he died? I wondered. *Where* had he died? Who had killed him? Was it the mole? Was it the KGB? In my shock, I had forgotten to ask.

I listened to Lucy Sue laughing her periodic shrill laugh, and felt the shoeless pad of her foot rubbing my crotch. "Your time is up," she said.

"My time is up?"

"Our blood tests," she replied. She was referring to the blood tests the city required one to take when applying for a marriage license. "Tomorrow is the last day they're valid."

"Right," I said with the exaggerated authority of the soused.

"So what are you going to do about it?"

"Do about what?"

Lucy Sue's smirk left her face. It was replaced with a mean scowl. "Are we getting married tomorrow or not?"

I giggled. I was definitely drunk.

"If not tomorrow, then *when?*" she asked. "How about tomorrow night in Las Vegas? We don't even need any blood tests there."

"If we don't need blood tests there, then we don't have to get married tomorrow night," I said proudly. "We can get married anytime we want to."

"If not tomorrow, then when?" hissed Lucy Sue Glopp.

I shrugged an inebriated shrug.

"Tomorrow?" she asked.

I told her I couldn't go anywhere tomorrow.

"Then when *can* you go somewhere?"

I drank the rest of my cappuccino. Was I next? I wondered. Was whoever killed Jim planning to kill me next? Was the person who took a shot at me in my office from the same group that killed Byrd?

"You're not listening to me."

"I'm sorry."

"Remember when I told you that if you didn't marry me within the thirty days the blood tests were good for, I would leave you? Do you remember my saying that?"

"Yes," I answered.

"Good-bye," said Lucy Sue Glopp. She gathered up her belongings and left.

* * *

UNKNOWN COMIC: How do you keep an idiot in suspense?

CHUCK BARRIS: I don't know.

UNKNOWN COMIC: I'll tell you tomorrow. *Wild laughter from the studio audience.*

UNKNOWN COMIC: What's the difference between a shower curtain and a piece of toilet paper?

CHUCK BARRIS: I don't know.

UNKNOWN COMIC *(pointing at Barris):* Here's the guy!

CHUCK BARRIS: Get off the stage!

* * *

That weekend, paranoia really set in. We were taping "The Gong Show," and I was panic-stricken from the moment I walked onstage. Was the man who killed Jim Byrd sitting somewhere out there in the "Gong Show" studio audience? Was he pleased with the knowledge that this would be my last performance? Would he be waiting for me when I left the theater? Then the band began to play, and the audience started cheering.

"And now," said the announcer, "here is the host and star of our show, Chuck Barris!"

The curtain went up, and I made my entrance. I was wearing a tuxedo coat, a blue denim work shirt open at the neck, jeans, and cowboy boots. And a hat. Always a hat. Its brim, pulled down over my eyes, prevented me from seeing the audience. Like an ostrich sticking his head in the sand, I always hid beneath my hat.

When the applause subsided, I said, "Welcome to 'The Gong Show.' Here's an esoteric act if ever there was one. Ephemeral. It's an ephemeral act. One that should get us our Emmy. Do we have an Emmy? We don't? Well, this should get us one. Anyway, ladies and gentlemen . . . Big Nose!"

Big Nose, a bone-thin weirdo in a flowered shirt and sarong, leaped onto the stage. He was in his early twenties, ugly as cat shit, with an act worthy of someone suffering from some form of advanced mental disease. He proceeded to play a toy flute while doing a dance in ladies' platform shoes. Then suddenly, Big Nose dropped his flute and ripped off his sarong. Bare-chested, he proceeded to jump hither and yon, dressed in white shorts with red polka dots worn over a bright yellow leotard. He rushed to a battered steamer trunk, opened it, and began pulling out endless amounts of old newspapers with wild abandon. I was standing backstage watching the loon, mesmerized by the utter stupidity of it all. What, pray tell, could have been running through his deranged mind when he created this mishmash? Was there a message in this lunatic act? Was Big Nose a genius transcending our ability to understand what he was attempting to say? Or was he just a jerkoff?

Big Nose was gonged. I joined him onstage.

"Why?" groaned Big Nose. "Why? Why?"

"I don't know. I don't understand," I said, sweating profusely, attempting to spot a killer in the audience. Why did I think there was a killer in the audience? Nobody said there would be. "Win a few, lose a few," I told Big Nose, and then to the audience, "We'll be back with more *stuff* . . . right after this message."

Commercial.

There was a mechanical failure. The taping of "The Gong Show" was temporarily halted. I was standing on my mark in the center of the studio floor. As I stood there, I saw everything more distinctly than I have ever seen anything before: the lights, the people, the scenery, the floor, the band's instruments—as if everything had been Windexed. I turned my body very slowly in a circle. I saw the stagehands behind me joking and laughing on the stage, their laughter almost deafening. I saw the three celebrity judges sitting behind their console, wisecracking and cavorting. I turned some more and saw the audience in front of me, yelling at me: "Chuckie baby! Chuckie baby!" I continued turning and saw the band on the far side of the stage, ribbing each other. Their shouts sounded like shrieks. I turned once again and found myself back where I had started. I had come full circle. Everyone was having a good time—everyone except me. My heart beat furiously. I was suffocating. "Chuckie baby! Chuckie baby!" The din grew louder and louder and louder, and my breath shorter and shorter.

And then, suddenly, it was quiet.

* * *

"What do you mean, you collapsed?"

"It wasn't really serious," I said. "I passed out during a 'Gong Show' taping. The doctor said it was overwork."

"Sure," said Lucy Sue Glopp.

"Sure what?" I asked, switching the telephone from one ear to the other.

"Sure you're overworked. You tape how many days a week? Two days a week. That's real overwork."

"I want to see you."

"No way."

"Please."

"No way."

"I was shot at a couple of nights ago. In my office."

"You were *what?*"

"I was shot at. Someone tried to kill me."

I heard Lucy Sue's shrill laughter. "I'll bet."

"And a good friend of mine died. I need to see you."

"Come on, Chuck, get off it."

"Can't I come over?"

"Nope."

* * *

During the next week, I telephoned Lucy Sue Glopp constantly. She spoke curtly and hung up as soon as possible. I would stare at the dead phone, place the receiver back in its cradle, and then run to my car and drive directly to Lucy Sue's apartment. But the effort was just as disappointing. She never released the chain on her front door. She would speak to me through the small opening between the door and door frame. She would say the two of us were finished; that this time she wasn't kidding, and that I should respect her privacy. On one occasion she told me to leave before she called the police. I couldn't believe she would actually call the police, but she swore she would. She said the bad publicity would serve me right. "You'll freak," she said.

It didn't make any sense: my standing at her front door begging, my obsession with Lucy Sue Glopp. Who needs her? I would ask myself, and promptly discover that *I* needed her. Lucy Sue Glopp had burrowed her way under my skin—a grasping, blood-sucking parasite, a low-life leech who might have been a bitch, but was never a bore. I missed not being with her. I missed Lucy Sue's crude, racist humor, her vile mouth, her sullen good looks, her sexual perversions, my delight in being satisfied and satisfying her in bed. "You make me feel ten feet tall," I would tell her, over and over again, and she did. I walked around with the air of a lover, a stud, a goddamn Don Juan.

When it became obvious that Lucy Sue was serious about not seeing me, I thought it best that I force myself to forget her. "Screw her," I told myself in my bathroom mirror. "I'll date others."

The dates were agonizingly dull. Even Penny Pacino made me antsy. And, to make matters worse, I would hear about Lucy Sue wherever I went. She had a new actor boyfriend who was reputed to be the best-looking twenty-year-old dude in town. One morning, an 8" × 10" photograph of the adonis appeared on my office desk. I suspected Lucy Sue had arranged to have it put there.

"What is this fucking picture?" I shouted one night in her doorway, waving the hunk's glossy 8" × 10" in the air.

"Will you please keep your voice down?" Lucy Sue said through the chained front door, enjoying my pain. "You'll wake the neighbors."

"Fuck the neighbors," I shouted.

I was sure her neighbors heard my blasphemy, and I was glad. They had taken to peering at me through their windows. They saw me beg; listened to my supplications; watched me grovel and squirm. "Don't you have anything better to do?" I shouted at the curtained windows. I waved the upright index finger of my right hand admonishingly at the invisible neighbors.

"That's enough," snapped Lucy Sue. "Now go away. I have guests."

"How many?" I asked. "More than one? Did I interrupt a gang bang?"

She slammed the door shut.

* * *

I began spying on her. I spent hours in my parked car outside Lucy Sue's apartment, watching her come or go. Occasionally, I would race up the street to a garage and pee, then hurry back, worried that I might have missed her. Missed what? What was I looking for? Was I trying to discover who Lucy Sue was sleeping with? Or was I trying to discover if she was lying and there wasn't really any lover at all?

And then I would wonder if I was losing my mind. What profit was there in my pussyfooting around her block? Did I delight in heaving back and forth in bed at night, waking the next morning exhausted and ill-tempered? Come now, I would say to myself, all this anguish for that piece of shit? All this torment for an ex-cocktail waitress, a two-faced cunt who wants my money, house, name, and peace of mind? Did I really want to become half of a completely insane, self-destructive, self-defeating union?

Yes! I screamed. Yes! Yes!

I returned once again to the chained apartment door. I stood in the cool evening air, rehearsing what I would say. I wanted to be sure it was perfect before I knocked.

I have come, I would announce joyfully, to ask for your hand in marriage. I want to marry you. I want to go now, this minute, to Las Vegas and get married. No blood tests, no nothing. We'll just go out to the airport and get on the first plane for Vegas. We'll be married before the night is over.

And when Lucy Sue Glopp accepted, I would turn to the court-yard—to the curtained windows that hid those busybody, smug, holier-than-thou fuckhead voyeurs—and shout: "We're getting married! The party's over, folks. Back to your boring bottles of beer and sitcoms. You won't have me to laugh at anymore." And then I would kiss Lucy Sue, in the center of the courtyard, so that everyone could see.

I took a deep breath and knocked.

She wasn't there.

The next morning, I left for New York. I had to get away; from Hollywood; from Lucy Sue; from my memories; from everything.

I went to Paris, and the Hôtel Raphael. I spent a month there, sitting, thinking, and in general trying to figure out just what the hell I was doing with myself.

During my first week at the Hôtel Raphael, I telephoned my office in Hollywood and told key parties where I was. Some of my associates were worried to the point of despair. Others were furious. "He's off on another one of his foolish escapades," one was supposed to have groused, "without any concern for any of us." My repeated disclosures that I had no immediate plans to return home only verified my detractors' worst assumptions: the production company was doomed.

Because of my being out of the country, Chuck Barris Productions was unable to tape "The Gong Show." I had already cost the company thousands of dollars in studio penalties, crew payments, celebrity fees, and other related expenses. Those expenses would continue to escalate the longer I stayed away. Eventually, we would run out of backup shows entirely, along with our flimsy excuses for using reruns. We would then be subjected to network and station lawsuits. Our reputation as a conscientious and responsible TV program supplier would be critically compromised, and all of my employees would pay the consequences.

"So when are you coming home?" they would ask.

"Soon," I would reply. "Soon." By the second week, I didn't telephone at all.

I might have stayed in the Hôtel Raphael forever, had it not been for a telephone call from Lucy Sue Glopp.

"I'm in London," she said, "on my way to Hong Kong. I'm getting married."

"Are you serious?" I asked.

She told me she was absolutely serious. She was meeting her husband-to-be in Hong Kong, at the Peninsular Hotel, the next afternoon. They were to be married the following evening in the hotel's main ballroom. "The man I'm going to marry is very rich," she said. "He's in the electronics business."

I asked her how she had found me.

Lucy Sue said she had called my office. "Your secretary told me where you were. She said you've been in Paris for weeks. Found a little trollop, have you? I'll bet you're teaching her all my old tricks. Well, anyway, I wanted to tell you all about my marriage plans myself. I didn't want you to hear it from anyone else."

"Why?" I asked.

"So I could hear your surprise and disappointment with my own ears. You *are* disappointed, aren't you?"

"In all honesty, I think I'm sick about it."

"Good. Aren't you going to wish me luck?"

"No. What time are you leaving tonight?"

"My flight leaves at midnight."

I checked my wristwatch. It was exactly two forty-five in the afternoon. "You can't get married," I blurted out. "Can I see you before you leave? Can I meet you at the airport?"

"If you can get there in time," she giggled.

I dropped everything and dashed for Le Bourget airport. I forgot about how rotten and low and mean she was; all I could think about was that she was about to get married—to somebody else—and that I had to see her. We had agreed to meet at Heathrow Airport's departure gate for Air France Flight 728 at eleven P.M. I made it only by the narrowest of margins.

When I reached the departure gate, I saw Lucy Sue sitting by herself at the end of a row of waiting-room seats. Two bags (both familiar) were at her toes, a trashy novel on her lap. "They're great for traveling," she used to say, though she also read trashy novels when she wasn't traveling.

I made a speech that I had rehearsed on the flight from Paris to London. In essence: This time I'm serious. Take me to the nearest justice of the peace, and I'll be more than happy to say "I do."

"I don't believe you," she replied when I had finished. And she was right.

I guess there was a duplicity in my voice that was hard to hide. Even I noticed it. I hadn't sounded convincing at all, and I knew why. Something about Lucy Sue Glopp was different. I suppose that over the last few months I had made Lucy Sue Glopp into a legend, something larger than life; and now, seeing her once again, I realized that she wasn't a legend at all. Lucy was just a desperate girl trying her best to get married—trying to cash in while she still had some chips. Obviously, she had always been that way. I just hadn't noticed before. The myth I had constructed in my mind during the past weeks and months —the idea that Lucy Sue Glopp was an excitingly perverted and thrilling creature that I had to have—was just that, a myth. Something that wasn't real. What *was* real was the woman sitting beside me in the airport lounge: a mean woman, not too cunning, not too bright, not overly warm or affectionate. Just a hustler whose street smarts told her that the electronics genius in Hong Kong would make it to the altar, and that, no matter how many times I *said* I would, I *never* would.

"You don't believe me?" I said, suddenly not caring so much if she did or didn't.

"No."

"So what are you going to do?" I asked, officially throwing in the towel.

"I'm going to Hong Kong as planned, to get married." Her face was drawn and dejected. She had accepted my towel.

Her plane was boarding. I walked Lucy Sue as far as I could, kissed her cheek, and said good-bye.

She smiled, turned, and disappeared into a crowd of passengers. Though there was a deeply etched expression of melancholy on her face, it was the prettiest I had ever seen her look.

I sat in the Air France terminal all night, smoking cigarettes and drinking Scotch. At eight o'clock the next morning, I boarded a plane for New York. I heard a cabin door close, and didn't hear another sound until we landed seven hours later. Walking into the terminal at Kennedy International Airport, I thought of Lucy Sue. I wondered if she was having a pleasant trip.

She wasn't. She was dead.

Fifteen

Lucy Sue Glopp's plane never made it to Hong Kong. It hit a Greek military training plane over Athens International Airport, and all one hundred and sixty-three people on board perished in the resulting crash. There was a picture of the stricken Air France jetliner on the front page of the next day's *New York Times*. I saw the newspaper on a newsstand when I arrived inside the terminal.

It never ceases to amaze me that there is always someone present with a camera when a disaster takes place, and that the camera is always loaded and ready, and that the photographer has the presence of mind to calmly lift the camera, focus, and snap the kind of picture that appeared that day on the front page of the *Times*. The photograph showed the huge airliner aflame and careening toward the earth. The plane was falling sideways, a lower engine smoking heavily. Only one long row of little oval windows was visible. Was that the side where Lucy Sue Glopp was sitting? Was she still holding the trashy novel in her hands? Was she looking out one of those little oval windows and wondering what was happening? Did she realize that the aircraft was going down, that she had only seconds to live? Was she screaming? Shitting herself? Too petrified to do either? How long did she suffer the horrible sensation of dropping to her death? Forever?

For an instant?

In the months and years that followed, I thought of Lucy Sue every time I passed her apartment. Every single goddamn time.

* * *

It was the morning of July 10, 1976, when I saw the picture of the doomed plane on the newsstand at Kennedy. It seemed as though I had been away from America for years instead of five weeks. I spent my first night in New York alone, in a massive Plaza Hotel suite, watching television.

Watching me.

A "Gong Show" that I had taped months before was being broadcast. I was cavorting on the stage like a wild man; sweating, shouting, giggling, wearing an Indian headdress, tuxedo jacket, white shirt, black tie, and basketball shorts. I was throwing a big multicolored rubber ball to Gene Gene the Dancing Machine, a large, fat stagehand who was attempting to dance to our closing theme. Gene was throwing the ball back to me while dancing. Jaye P. Morgan was wrestling with somebody on the floor behind the celebrity console. All of the evening's "Gong Show" acts filled the stage behind Gene Gene the Dancing Machine. The freaky collection of performers were leaping and screaming and gyrating like maniacs. (At least half of them *were* maniacs.) It was bizarre, grotesque; the "lunatic fringe" on coast-to-coast television. And there I was, more hyper than ever, dancing, and grimacing, and falling down on the floor in mock exhaustion. I felt uneasy watching myself that way.

I turned the channel.

I found a debate on a Public Broadcasting station. The discussion was taking place in a hall on the campus of Princeton University, and a half-dozen serious executives from the three broadcasting networks —complete with gray flannel suits, sincere ties, and high black socks —were defending commercial television against the nasty accusations of a cocky, verbose, and extremely intelligent critic of the arts. The critic was dressed in a sport coat over a turtleneck sweater, and bell-bottom slacks. He wore sunglasses.

"And what have you given us, the viewing audience?" the critic was saying to the network television executives. "I'll tell you what you've given us. You've given us Chuck Barris, for Christ's sake! *That's* what you've given us. No pithy drama; no interesting innovations in comedy; very little ballet, theater, or controversial documentaries. Just Chuck Barris and his trash. As far as I'm concerned, Chuck Barris symbolizes everything that's wrong with television. His shows are drivel, and he's an embarrassment. If giving valuable air time and exposure to the Chuck Barrises of the world is the best you can do, then you've all failed, and failed miserably."

The audience gave the critic a standing ovation.

I slid down deep into my chair, hiding in an empty room.

* * *

I flew to Los Angeles the next morning.

It was good to be home. Apparently the entire Lucy Sue Glopp situation—the hurried flight from Paris to London, our scene at the airport, and her death—had shocked me out of my torpor. I guess I owed her for that. My associates at the production company were delighted to see me, and I them. We all went back to work with a feeling of relief. It was business as usual, and I was (or professed to be) happy. With one rather bothersome exception.

The televised debate from Princeton University gnawed relentlessly at me. I tried to ignore the hurt it had inflicted by working harder on the stage. But then, I wasn't sure if my "working harder" was helping or hurting what I was trying to do.

"What *are* you trying to do?" Buddy Granoff asked me. Buddy was a business associate—head of Barris Industries television sales—and a friend. Buddy was a feisty, no-nonsense, self-made man. He loathed bullshit, and loved the truth. He was always making creative suggestions, and asking pointed questions about our shows. Lately, his questions had begun to sound more and more like accusations. "You seem to be acting wilder and wilder."

"I'm trying to entertain," I answered. "Make people laugh."

"I see," he replied—but I wasn't sure he did. Buddy had taken to looking at me as though I was slipping away to some strange place and he was the only one who knew it. One night, as I was leaving the studio, I saw Buddy standing on stage, staring out at the dark, empty seats. I watched him for a bit. He was getting older—he would be sixty soon —and he looked it. "Did you hear that audience tonight?" I said to him enthusiastically, springing out of the shadows. "Did you hear them cheering? They really loved us tonight."

"Which only goes to prove you can't trust a studio audience," growled Buddy.

"What do you mean?" I asked, suddenly deflated. I hated to hear Buddy talk that way. I hated it because what he said was usually true.

"Studio audiences don't mean a thing," he went on, seemingly fascinated by the dark, empty auditorium. "A studio audience doesn't know if you're doing a good job or a bad job. They're just happy to be there. They're having fun participating in everything. Anyway, most of the audiences that come down to watch this show are your fans. They're college kids who love the way you're fucking with the establishment. College kids love that. But you're playing *to* the establishment, not to the college kids. So don't go by the reaction you're getting here in the studio. It doesn't mean a damn thing in Davenport, Iowa."

* * *

Another time, during a commercial break in a "Gong Show" taping, I made the mistake of asking Buddy how I was doing.

"You're fucking with the formula," he answered.

"Aw, come on, Buddy," I moaned, annoyed. "Give me a break." A hairdresser was attempting to comb my hair while a makeup man waited to touch up my face. I was far more interested in what was happening to the reflection in the hand mirror I held than in what Buddy was trying to tell me.

"You're fucking with the formula," Buddy repeated, "because you're bored. You don't fuck with a formula just because you're bored. You've always told the hosts of your other shows not to fuck with the formula when they're bored. You've explained it to them, time and time again: they might get bored with the repetition of a daily program, but they shouldn't change things. You've told them to stick to the formula —the one that worked in the first place. So why not follow your own instructions? We *know* the original 'Gong Show' formula worked. We *don't* know if what you're doing now works at all."

"What am I doing now?"

"Acting like a damn fool, and making everyone on the show act like damn fools."

I ignored what Buddy said. I did worse than that. I put the Popsicle Twins on "The Gong Show."

The Popsicle Twins weren't really twins. They were just girl friends. One was fifteen years old, the other seventeen. Both were adorable. The fifteen-year-old wore her hair in a ponytail, and had a face full of freckles. The older girl had bangs, dimples, and enormous blue eyes. Both had fresh, full, succulent bodies. Both had glowing peaches-and-cream complexions. Both wore T-shirts and short shorts. Both were a lecherous old man's delight; post-pubescent Lolitas who would have more than satisfied all the Humbert Humberts of the world. They called themselves the Popsicle Twins because they each held an orange Popsicle.

The girls skipped onto the stage barefoot, sat down on the floor side by side, crossed their legs Indian-style, and began to lick their Popsicles. That's all they did. They just licked their Popsicles. But the *way* they licked their Popsicles was something else. It was extraordinary, is what it was. The girls tongued the sides of the Popsicles, ran their full lips across the Popsicles and around them. They slid the Popsicles into their mouths slowly, sensually, in and out, in and out, and then ran their lips softly down the shaft of the cone-shaped Popsicles to their bases, and then back up again.

They were obviously giving the Popsicles a blow job. The two teenagers were teaching the nation the proper way to perfc m exquisite head. Every eye in that theater was glued to the Popsicle Twins' mouths and their Popsicles. Anyone who couldn't see the girls in person watched TV monitors hypnotically. Every stagehand had a hard-on. The celebrity judges were in a state of acute shock. Not one of them was capable of looking away, let alone leaving their seats to gong the act. "The Gong Show" band gave the Popsicle Twins a standing ovation. Jaye P. Morgan said, "That's the way I started. I give the girls a ten!"

When the show aired, the telephone switchboard at the National Broadcasting Company in New York lit up like a Christmas tree. The East Coast was appalled. The wife of a United States senator had her husband paged on the Senate floor and demanded he make an immediate motion to ban "The Gong Show" from television. Two New York City police demolition instructors had to interrupt their lesson on defusing explosives because the eyes of the class were glued to the silent television set suspended from the ceiling behind them. At first the police demolition instructors were angry. Then they noticed what the other cops were watching, and what the Popsicle Twins were doing, and called a five-minute break.

Executives at NBC snapped into action. They immediately terminated the "Gong Show" feed to the rest of the country. The Popsicle Twins were never seen in the Central or Pacific time zones. The president of NBC made a personal telephone call to me in Hollywood. He said, "You do something like that again and you're off the air! Forever! I want fucking ratings, not fucking cocksuckers!"

I apologized to the president. It was a mistake to allow the Popsicle Twins to perform on "The Gong Show," and I admitted it. "I thought they were funny," I told Buddy Granoff, "but what do I know? I don't know anything, I guess."

"I don't know many things, either," replied Buddy, upset and disgusted, "but one thing I *do* know. I know you can't thumb your nose at propriety and expect to be a long-running winner. What you've been doing lately isn't in very good taste, and bad taste never works for long. You can't fuck with taste."

You can't fuck with taste. It seemed I'd heard that before somewhere.

The commercial break was over. It was time to go back onstage. I moved, stopped, turned, and hollered, "Hey, Buddy, do you think I symbolize everything that's wrong with television?"

"Probably," he answered.

I think from that moment on, I never wanted to see the inside of a studio again. But it would take a while before I would make it happen.

* * *

On October 2, 1978, I received a telegram instructing me to come to Washington, D.C. The boys at the Company had a surprise for me.

During the flight from Los Angeles, I read an article in *Saturday Review* magazine that shocked and depressed me more than anything I had ever read before. I was shocked because I didn't expect to read about myself in that prestigious magazine. I was depressed because of what the article's author, Peter Andrews, had to say about me. The article was entitled "The Hating Game." It was a devastating annihilation of every one of my shows—and of me.

Among other things, Andrews wrote: "Without exception, they are unremittingly witless, tasteless, illiterate, and stupid—I'm not being obscure here, am I? Additionally, all five Chuck Barris programs display what seems to be his almost psychotic hatred of women. No opportunity is ever missed to show a woman as some sort of Daffy Duck who doubles as the town moron and the community punchboard. Barris's shows amount to a systematic assassination of women, and that his victims skip to the executioner's block fairly squealing with delight at the prospect is no defense."

Included with the article was a picture of me jumping in the air. The caption read: "Barris reveals his passion for self-debasement."

I stared at the magazine in my lap. Reading the article, I felt a surge of nausea. I began rereading until I came to the part that turned my stomach.

Psychotic hatred of women. Systematic assassination of women. Victims skip to the executioner's block.

I ran to the airliner's toilet. I had a violent case of diarrhea.

* * *

"For outstanding service" was the simple statement from my CIA superior. He handed me a medal and a presidential citation. The medal was placed around my neck. It was round and bronze, and dangled from a wide gold ribbon. The president's signature was at the bottom of an 8″ × 10″ parchment commendation. The parchment was inscribed with the words "heroic" and "meritorious." It had been placed in a leather-bound cover. "Particularly for your work in Paris," added my superior.

"The Central Intelligence Agency is proud of you," said someone else.

A third gentleman made a short speech about my being a patriot in our country's first line of defense, and something about a war that had already begun. I wasn't paying much attention to him. My mind was wandering. I was thinking about the strange dichotomy of being crucified by my peers for attempting to entertain people and lauded by my peers for killing them.

* * *

I returned to Los Angeles on October 4, 1978.

On the same day, Anton Gurnek arrived in Manhattan. Gurnek was a businessman, his port of embarkation Rome. In fact, Anton Gurnek wasn't the businessman's real name. "Business" had nothing to do with his real profession. Gurnek was really Valarie Kasilov. The purpose of Kasilov's trip was to locate and kill me.

* * *

A few days later, in an apartment tucked away in a corner of Beverly Hills, a pretty redhead in her late twenties (who was never able to comprehend that she was a pretty redhead) stood in the center of her living room. She drank black coffee from a china cup and saucer. The pretty redhead's hair fell to her shoulders. She had large green eyes, high cheekbones (when she was at her proper weight), and full, soft lips. Placing the cup of coffee on a small antique desk, she inserted a piece of paper into a portable typewriter, and typed the following letter.

Dear Shithead,

I hope that by the time we are in our golden years and sitting together in our rocking chairs, I will understand you just a little bit more. Just a little bit. I stood in front of the museum for over an hour. I don't think I've waited for anyone for more than ten minutes. And I waited, even though I knew you wouldn't be there. Still I waited, wondering why I was waiting. I wanted to yell out, "Hey, it's okay. You don't have to show up. I don't give a fuck anymore." But I couldn't.

What I also hope in our old age is that I will understand *me* a little more too. And the power you hold over me now, even after all this time and all that has happened. Mostly I am writing this letter to let you know

it's okay. You can keep standing me up for the next forty
years (you'll be eighty-eight and I'll be seventy-two) and I
guess I'll keep waiting on corners. God knows why, but I
guess I will.

I've decided to accept you as you are, the way I've
decided to accept a lot of people whom I love and who
don't behave the way I want them to. I would dearly love
to be able to say, "Fuck you, you went too far." Except you
went too far in 1968 when you stood me up at the Beverly
Hills Hotel, and in 1970 when you stood me up in front of
the Steuben Glass building in New York, and the dirty
tricks you played on me in Malibu in 1972, and in Carmel
in 1973, and in Philadelphia in 1974, and somewhere else in
1975 and 1976, and in Lisbon in 1977, and in front of the
museum in 1978.

Jesus, I love you, because you are tender even though
you growl, and you do nice things for people, even though
you hate to tell anyone about the nice things you do, and
you're more loving and sweet and funny than anyone I
know (when you want to be loving and sweet and funny),
and you make me happy, and I want to be happy, and I
want *you* to be happy, and I know that's a long shot. A *real*
long shot. And I know we are never going to get together,
so you don't have to be rotten to me anymore. We are
friends, whether you like it or not. We are stuck with each
other, we're a unit, you and me, and all I'm asking is that
you try in the future to treat me like a person.

And by the way, where the fuck were you while I was
standing out there in front of the museum? What an asshole
you are.

                                          Love,
                                          Penny

                         * * *

Two days later, I phoned Penny. "What kind of shit is this?" I
asked.

"What kind of shit is what? My letter?"

"Yes, your letter."

"It's self-explanatory."

"It's a lousy letter," I said, "and I'm not going to see you again
for the rest of my life."

"That's fine with me. You want to take me to a late lunch?"

"Absolutely."

We ate at the Beverly Hills Hotel, outside in the sunshine where it was warm and pretty. I told Penny she looked beautiful.

"Thank you," she said. She wore a simple white dress.

I said I was sorry about the museum. "My head was all messed up."

Penny nodded. She was smoking a cigarette. She only smoked cigarettes when she was angry.

"And I had to go away on business."

She nodded again.

"You don't believe me."

She nodded again.

"Are you ever going to speak?"

Penny blew cigarette smoke in my face, and said, "Was this like the time you had to go away on that business trip to Lisbon?"

"Here we go again," I moaned.

Penny was working herself into a rage. I could tell. Soon she would start cursing like a truck driver and saying "man" a lot.

"Probably trying to get in some little sleaze's pants," she growled. "You were, weren't you? Some bimbo you had the hots for."

"Listen, Penny . . ."

"Listen my ass. I know what happened. You were in Paris for a month banging a fucking bimbo, man, and the bimbo left you because of some asshole thing you did or said to her. And then you went chasing after the bimbo to London. Some fucking *business* trip, man."

I smacked the tabletop with my fist and shouted, "Will you please stop talking like a goddamn truck driver!" Others turned to glare. I glared back, and they turned away. I lowered my voice and said, "Look, Redhead. I know you're mad, and you talk like a truck driver when you're mad, but you've got to believe me when . . ."

"*Believe* you! *Me* believe *you*! Are you crazy? You are a liar. A congenial, pathological, habitual liar."

"Congenital. Not congenial. Congenial means . . ."

"Look, man, don't give me any of your fucking grammar lessons today. Anyway, as far as I'm concerned, you're sick. Really sick. But I must be just as sick. I love you. More today than yesterday, and all that kind of crap. So I must be just as sick as you, mustn't I?"

I didn't know what to say, so I just bobbed my head up and down.

"At least waiting for hours at the L.A. Museum wasn't as bad as going all the way to Lisbon just to take you home," mumbled Penny Pacino. "Talk about sick. *That* was sick."

* * *

It *was* sick.

I went to Lisbon on a dare.

I had been traveling across the United States on a promotional tour to publicize a new television show I had created and sold. The program was just about to begin airing all over the country, and I was on the road trying to drum up interest for the goddamn thing. On the very last day of the tour, I was in St. Louis airport's VIP lounge with my publicity coordinator and good friend, Jane Bulmer. Jane had just excused herself to go to the ladies room. As soon as she had left, I ran down to the main terminal to buy her a bunch of fresh flowers in gratitude for her help on the tour. When I returned to the VIP lounge, Jane was still gone. And that's when I noticed the girl.

She was sitting in a corner by herself, reading a magazine. I could see at a glance that she possessed the kind of beauty I adored: fresh, scrubbed, and wholesome. Right out of Vassar—or any of the Seven Sisters, for that matter.

She was about twenty-seven or twenty-eight. She had the ubiquitous straight blond hair and blue eyes seen at most New York debutante balls, Virginia fox hunts, and Smith alumni meetings. She was an All-American Beauty Rose. Or so it seemed.

Maybe it was the flowers. Holding them in my hand probably precipitated my atypical behavior. Without a second thought, I walked over to the girl, and, mindless as to who might be watching or listening, said, "I would like you to have these flowers."

She looked up from her magazine and replied, "What am I going to do with them?"

I was stunned, but, much to my amazement, I rallied. "Take them on the plane with you?" I asked rationally.

"I have enough baggage to take on board the plane as it is," she replied. "Thanks, but no thanks." She returned to her magazine, and I returned to my seat and sat down.

I was furious.

I jumped up, and, still clutching the bunch of flowers, walked briskly back to the girl. I said, "You are the goddamn least romantic person I have ever met in my entire goddamn life. I've met a lot of unromantic people. But you—*you* are the least romantic of all. And a girl, too!"

She looked up from her magazine and smiled (without parting her lips). She looked at me for what seemed like forever. Finally she said, "Well, if you're such a romantic, why don't you fly to Lisbon and meet me for dinner?"

I asked her as calmly as I could—though I was stunned down to the tips of my toes—when she was going to Lisbon.

"Now."

"Where will you be staying?"

"At the Ritz Hotel."

I went back to my seat without saying good-bye. I still had the goddamn bunch of flowers in my hand. When Jane returned from the ladies room, I gave her the bouquet. She kissed my cheek.

"Where are you going?" asked Penny Pacino, a week or so later.

"To Lisbon," I answered.

"Why?"

"Business problems."

"Take me?"

"I can't."

It was July, and Lisbon was hot. I was exhausted from a long plane ride and an early morning arrival. The Ritz Hotel was nothing to rave about. I waited endlessly in the empty lobby for a room clerk, and again for a bellboy. I left a note for the girl in her box and went to my room. The room was roasting, and the air conditioner was broken. I telephoned down to the desk and told them about my air conditioner. An hour later, an engineer arrived. I tried to tell him about the air conditioner, but he could understand neither words nor pantomime. I told the engineer to go fuck himself. He understood that, and glowered at me. I told him to go fuck himself again.

I dozed naked on top of the sheets. I woke at noon. The housemaid said there had been a revolution.

"While I slept?" I asked.

She nodded and smiled. She was missing four front teeth.

I dressed and hurried down to the message desk. The girl from the St. Louis airport had left a note in answer to mine.

"See you at five. Luv, Kate." The message clerk told me there was an epidemic of cholera in the city.

The day passed slowly. My eyes burned from lack of sleep. An American in the hotel lobby warned me that no one would be allowed

to leave the country with more than five hundred dollars. "The fucking
revolution," he said by way of explanation. I was carrying five thousand
dollars in cash and travelers' checks. What was I to do?

The day became hotter. That evening at five, it was more oppres-
sive than at noon. I carried my suit coat on my arm as I entered the
hotel bar. Kate was sitting on a bar stool. She waved and I approached
her, totally rejuvenated. As I walked toward her, I couldn't help thinking: this is just like a movie. Like a Doris Day-Rock Hudson movie.
No doubt I'll marry Kate, and no doubt we will bore our friends to
death with the story of how we met.

And then I saw it. She smiled and I saw it. Her tooth. The upper
right front one. One of the two big ones. It was completely black. Dead.
Almost comical-looking. As if she had covered the tooth with a small
piece of licorice, like we did when we were kids.

How could I have missed a black front tooth?

The All-American Beauty Rose had a black front tooth!

I was unable to concentrate on our conversation. I was distracted,
mesmerized by her decayed and decrepit fang. "I'm sorry," I said,
"what did you say?"

"I was talking about the revolution. Have you heard about it?"

Was the black tooth there in St. Louis? It couldn't have been. I
certainly would have noticed it. Or would I? Maybe she acquired it
while in Lisbon. Did she know she had a black tooth? Should I ask?

"Your mind seems to be elsewhere," she said, slightly annoyed.

"I'm afraid I'm very tired. I arrived early and wasn't able to nap.
I'm sorry if I'm such a clod."

"Did you hear about the cholera epidemic?" she asked, her black
tooth bobbing up and down.

I thought the evening would never end. But it did, which was
worse. I was forced to return to my hot and humid room with the faulty
air conditioner. I began drinking heavily. I wondered what to do about
the five thousand suddenly-illegal dollars in my suitcase, and the cholera buzzing around the halls. In due time, I panicked. And then I did
what I usually did when I panicked: I called Penny Pacino.

"Come to Lisbon," I begged. "Please. You've gotta come. You
gotta help me get out of here. You've gotta keep me company going
home. My office will get a plane ticket to you right away."

"What's the matter?"

"I think I'm having a small nervous breakdown."

"How small?"

"Not so small."

"Why?"

I wanted to say, "Because I came to Lisbon to meet the love of my life, except the love of my life had a black tooth, and that was the last thing I wanted in a love of my life. And not only was the girl a disaster, but there is also a revolution in progress, and a cholera epidemic, and I am going to have to stay in this lousy country for the rest of my life because I have over five thousand dollars in cash. And since I'm going to be confined to quarters in this overheated, cholera-infested hotel for a lifetime, you might as well be confined with me, because you're the only person in the world I could stand being in the same room with for the rest of my life." I wanted to say all of that. Instead, I said, "I don't want to come home alone. I don't think I'll make it."

"Why aren't you capable of coming home alone?"

I couldn't think of a sensible reason.

"You're as capable of coming home by yourself as anyone else," said Penny calmly, as if she were talking to a six-year-old on his first day at school.

"No, I'm not," I whined.

"Try."

"No."

Penny came to Lisbon to take me home.

The night she arrived we had dinner in a tiny restaurant on the waterfront. Penny Pacino asked if the business problem I had come to Lisbon to solve was what disturbed me so.

"Sort of," I replied, averting my eyes.

Penny said, "While you were out of the room, someone slipped a note under the door. The note read: 'Was it something I said? Good-bye, and take care of yourself. Luv, Kate.' Love was spelled L-U-V. Was *that* the business problem?"

"Since when did you begin reading my mail?"

"I couldn't help reading it. It came sliding in open under your room door. The words were staring me in the face!"

"That's no excuse."

"The hell it isn't."

There was silence at our table. I checked my wristwatch. It was twenty after one. The Angel of Cholera was passing overhead.

"*Was* it something she said?" asked Penny disgustedly.

"No. It was her black front tooth. She had a black fang in the front of her mouth. It turned me off."

"Makes sense."

I said, "I'm really glad you came, Penster."

* * *

That had been over a year before.

"Yeah," said Penny, lighting a cigarette, "time sure flies when you're having fun."

I left Penny Pacino on the patio of the Beverly Hills Hotel's Polo Lounge smoking her ninth cigarette. There seemed to be something I should say, and I was fairly certain I knew what it was—yet it was impossible for me to say it. And there was nothing I could do about it. I explained to Penny that I had to get back to the studio, that it was late. I kissed her cheek and walked away. I knew she was going to cry. It was a good thing I was leaving. I hated to see Penny cry.

* * *

Meanwhile, television was becoming a nightmare for me. After my talk with Buddy Granoff, I grew more and more disillusioned and insecure. I couldn't understand why the critics were painting me as such an archvillain for my productions—especially "The Gong Show"—when my only aim was to make people laugh.

One might think that, under such pressure from others and from myself, I would have toned down "The Gong Show"; that I might have exercised restraint. It would have been the normal thing to do. But that's not what I did. I overcompensated in reverse, becoming crazier than ever before. Consequently, the shows grew wilder and wilder.

It was only a matter of time.

We were taping ten "Gong Show"s every weekend, five on Saturday and five on Sunday. Rehearsals began at eight o'clock in the morning, and we finished the last show at midnight. A strange momentum would develop during those weekends as the hours went by. In the morning we drank coffee and ate doughnuts, and tried to wake up. By noon we were silly. By early evening, the atmosphere was usually hectic and growing crazier by the hour, often bordering on out-of-control. It was one of those nights—as we passed from slightly out-of-control to foolish abandon—that Jaye P. Morgan flashed her tits on coast-to-coast television.

The shows that evening were exceptionally bizarre. During the third show, just before the dinner break, someone resembling an ex-con took twenty minutes' worth of bows. (Considering that the entire program lasted half an hour, the bowing took up a disproportionate amount of time, to say the least.) It all began with his first bow. The ex-con had done a fairly good imitation of Elvis Presley. He had costumed himself in satin and rhinestones, and he had all of Presley's extroverted physical moves down pat. He sang "Hound Dog," ending with a groin-rending split at center stage. It was a rousing finish. Flushed with the joy of having gone all the way without being gonged, the ex-con treated himself to an exuberant bow. Our drummer, Mark Stevens, gave the man a respectful drumroll, adding a few strong whacks for good measure. The ex-con used the piercing rim shots as punctuation for deep dips and violent hip swivels. More whacks, more dips. More whacks, more swivels. It became apparent the ex-con was waiting for some sort of musical crescendo; a chord; something to signal that his act was over. Without it, he would obviously dip and swivel until the cows came home. We paused for two commercial breaks, but Mark never stopped whacking his drum. After the commercial was over, we simply rejoined the swiveling, dipping, twirling maniac who, after fourteen or fifteen minutes, was clearly staggering from exhaustion, his eyes glassy, his rhinestones drenched in sweat, his crotch undoubtedly racked with pain from the endless splits. At the twenty-minute mark, he dropped. The ex-con was carried offstage to a standing ovation.

After the dinner break, the first act on the fourth show of the evening was gonged for singing poorly. He was a perpetually scowling man in his early twenties, and apparently a pathologically sore loser. He glared at the celebrities, especially the one who wielded the mallet, and then glared at me. I told him I had nothing to do with his being gonged. He told me to go fuck myself. Unfortunately he said it into a microphone that was attached to my lapel. He then stomped offstage and out the stage door, leaping up to batter the red EXIT sign into bits and pieces with his fist as he went.

During the very next act, an elderly man's testicle dropped into view. It was a wizened testicle, to be sure, but a testicle nonetheless. It was the property of a septuagenarian ballet dancer who looked much older than he was. He "danced" to the music of *Swan Lake,* using a cane and wearing a loose-fitting black tutu. He wasn't very good. He pranced around, devoid of any plan. He kicked his legs high into the air. It was during one of these kicks that his nugget—a long, skinny one —flopped out from behind the tutu and hung like a marble in a sack of chicken skin. The damn fool didn't even notice, or else he didn't care, and he continued dancing and kicking in his indiscriminate fashion. It was disgusting. An ancient and desiccated male Rockette, bouncing around like a damn fool with his ball akimbo. Aggravated, I sent two stagehands to catch the geezer and drag him away to his dressing room.

Between the fourth and fifth shows that night, the stagehands notified me they were quitting the network. "If it's between you and them," said Father Ed Holland, "then, goddamn it, it's you." I told Father Ed and the rest of the boys they should all have their heads examined.

The reason the stagehands were going to quit was a long and involved story. It began with Gene Patton, known to television fans as Gene Gene the Dancing Machine. Gene, as I've already mentioned, was a mammoth stagehand who had various responsibilities at the studio. One day, during rehearsal, I saw Gene dancing by himself in a dark corner. The huge stagehand never moved his feet—just his body from the waist up. He was terrific. I asked him to dance on "The Gong Show." He accepted the invitation, and in due time became a national hero. The network—in a tersely worded memo stating that stagehands must remain stagehands, and not performers—ordered Gene Patton off the show. I ignored the memo. In fact, that's when I put another stagehand, Ed Holland, on the program as a pious, gregarious priest who never knew his ass from first base when it came to theological problems. Periodically, Father Ed made an appearance on "The Gong Show," asked a question—Is there life after death?—and then became lost, confused, and unable to talk properly. That was because I would have Father Ed's cue cards laced with twenty-five dollar words that weren't there in rehearsal, and some highly creative pornographic expressions (which he was petrified to say on television, and rightly so). As an added irritant, I would shuffle his cue cards so that they were horrendously out of order. The result was a stammering, stuttering, inept, sweating, blushing priest. As soon as Father Ed was off camera, he would race for his hidden bottle of Jack Daniel's.

NBC was horrified that I had used yet another stagehand, and that this particular one was portraying a bumbling, tongue-tied priest. An even terser memo was dashed off stating that I was to desist from using stagehands on any Barris shows, or *else.* Or else what? And why? The networks had always been the cause of a great deal of frustration and unnecessary pressure; the corporate bureaucracy at its worst. It wasn't fair. True, they paid me good money. But then, I provided them with a sizeable profit. And when they annoyed the shit out of me, I had to remain docile as a lamb. Well, fuck them. Why should they be immune

to sleepless nights? Let them swig Maalox, and get the runs, and see
how much fun *that* was. Aggravation seemed to be a one-way street.
It should be a two-way street; and if it wasn't, why wasn't it? From that
moment on, I vowed to harass the network as often as I could, and
ignoring terse corporate memos was a splendid way of beginning.

Consequently, I did not desist from using stagehands. To the
contrary, I conscripted a third stagehand, and then a fourth, and fifth. A
handsome electrician named Joe the Animal portrayed an Italian movie
star fallen on hard times. Joe—known on "The Gong Show" as Gian-
carlo Miweenie—would appear just before a commercial break; un-
shaven, clothes in tatters, his toes sticking out of his shoes, begging for
$460 so he could buy a Gucci attaché case. Another stagehand, Red
Rowe, played an inebriated construction worker who would unexpectedly appear on stage and drag off by the arm whomever was performing.

The more memos I received from NBC management, the more
stagehands I employed. I used stagehands as bumbling policemen, inept
jugglers, overweight tumblers, and drunken hecklers. One night, a
stagehand—*not* Red Rowe—staggered up to an act, grabbed him by the
scruff of the neck, and pulled him behind the curtains. The burly grip
told the startled ventriloquist that he would find his fucking puppet up
his ass if he ever showed his ugly, untalented face in our studio again.
Of course, the stagehand could have been brought up on charges, fired,
and dropped from the union. But he wasn't. Everyone thought it was
part of the show.

NBC raged, and I beamed. The network veeps in Programming
and Standards and Practices must be awash in Maalox, I thought
happily.

And then the edict came. The tersest of memos. The ultimatum.
If the stagehands perform on one more "Gong Show" they will be fired.
Hence the Father Ed speech in my dressing room: "If it's between you
and them, then, goddammit, it's you. We'll all quit the goddamn network and stay with you and the show."

I explained that, contrary to TV producers' and stars' convictions,
programs do not go on forever. There would be a day (sooner than they
might realize, I thought to myself) when "The Gong Show" wouldn't
be on television. But they, the stagehands, would still be at NBC
working on the *next* show. The boys caucused again, and I guess they
grudgingly agreed with me. They didn't quit.

On the last show of the evening, I blew the Unicycle Kid into the
audience. I didn't mean to; I just did.

The Unicycle Kid was coming down from Oregon to perform on "The Gong Show." He asked to bring an assistant. Not wanting to incur the extra expense, I said no to the assistant, explaining that, whatever the assistant did, we would provide someone from our staff to do the same. The assistant's responsibility came at the end of the act. He touched a burning torch to a gasoline-drenched hoop and then to the back of the Unicycle Kid's gasoline-drenched overalls as he went by, igniting the cyclist's garment and turning him into a rolling inferno. The Unicycle Kid, his back in flames and sitting atop his single wheel, would then peddle his contraption up a teeter-totter, through the flaming hoop, and down the teeter-totter; at which point the assistant would immediately douse the Unicycle Kid with liquid from a small fire extinguisher. We broke down the assistant's duties into two parts. Larry Spencer, one of our writers, would ignite the hoop and the Unicycle Kid, and I would extinguish him.

While the Unicycle Kid was doing his preliminary tricks—such as juggling three bottles of milk while balancing himself on his one-wheeler—I was informed by a stagehand that there wasn't a small fire extinguisher on the premises, only a very large one. I said it would have to do, so the very large fire extinguisher was dragged onto the stage by two stagehands. The fire extinguisher was more than very large. It was gigantic; the biggest fire extinguisher I had ever seen in my entire life. I couldn't lift it. I would only be able to aim it. Not having any idea how powerful the fire extinguisher's stream might be, and not wanting it to fall short of its mark, I had the stagehands haul the heavy metal cylinder as close to the flaming hoop as we could without blocking the Unicycle Kid's route.

Before I knew it, we were at the Moment of Truth. The music stopped. There was a drum roll. The audience sensed something atypical for "The Gong Show"; something professionally exciting about to take place. The Unicycle Kid pedaled hither and yon in preparation, eventually positioning himself in front of the teeter-totter. The drumroll heightened. The Unicycle Kid took off, whizzing up the teeter-totter. In his excitement, Larry Spencer failed to ignite either the hoop or the Unicycle Kid. Spencer ran out of time trying to set the hoop aflame, and missed the Unicycle Kid as he went by.

I was monumentally disappointed. Not because the Unicycle Kid's act had lost its boffo finale, but because I wouldn't have the opportunity to use the mammoth fire extinguisher. I had never manipulated a fire extinguisher before, and I had always wanted to. So I decided to dash off a blast anyway, even though the Unicycle Kid was flameless. My rationale was: better safe than sorry. I pushed down the lever and hit the Unicycle Kid at the base of his spine, just above the cycle seat. I was amazed at the force of the extinguisher's stream.

So was the Unicycle Kid.

The Unicycle Kid was malcontent as it was, peeved that Spencer and I had deprived him of his spectacular finish. He wore a horrid scowl, having gone through a barren hoop in a pair of harmless overalls. That was about the time I hit him with the awesome stream of water and chemicals from the mammoth fire extinguisher.

The Unicycle Kid's scowl disappeared in an instant, only to be replaced with a look of terrified wonder. He had suddenly become airborne. The powerful fire-extinguisher stream lifted the Unicycle Kid off his unicycle and thrust him up into the air in much the same way as a NASA rocket is launched. His flight was a sort of quasi-arch, his body still in the seated position as if his one-wheeler had remained beneath him. The Unicycle Kid landed on a cue-card girl. The poor girl sustained multiple rib injuries. The Unicycle Kid bruised his right buttock.

The end of the show was delayed for almost half an hour while we attempted to bring order out of chaos. I vaguely remember a nurse taping the cue-card girl's ribs, and the Unicycle Kid's mouth unable to close from the shock of his unrehearsed flight.

It was during the end of that fifth and final show of the night that Jaye P. Morgan flashed her tits.

I guess you might say we got carried away with things. It had been a long, hard weekend, and a particularly arduous day and night. We were all exhausted, but the shows had been good; one or two better than good. We knew we had two or three days off before the grind of auditioning and taping would begin again. Consequently, though we were drained, the cast, staff, and musicians drew on some mysterious reservoir of energy that propelled us to an almost inhuman level of hysteria.

The "Gong Show" acts were behaving like the world-class idiots they usually were at that time of the show, hamming it up on what was most likely their last appearance on television in this lifetime. They behaved as they always did; leaping and mugging and falling down and jumping up; your standard running amok. (I remember noticing that one performer had a rubber chicken head hanging out of the open fly of his trousers, but I was too tired to make him stuff it back in.)

And then, for some unfathomable reason, I ripped off my tuxedo jacket, whirled it over my head, and threw it into the audience. Seconds later, Ray Neopolitan, our bass player, ripped off his jacket, whirled it over his head a few times, and threw it into the audience. Our conductor, Milton De Lugg, did the same thing. Throwing jackets into the audience became contagious. Gene Gene the Dancing Machine did it, and so did Father Ed, and Joe the Animal. Jaye P. Morgan didn't have a jacket, so she simply ripped open her blouse, popping her tits out on coast-to-coast TV in the process. Realizing it wouldn't be wise to toss her blouse into the audience, Jaye P. closed it, notching one or two buttons for safekeeping. Although her tits were exposed to our studio audience for only seconds, and were edited out of the show before it aired, the incident caused us months of disquieting repercussions.

Immediate consequences occurred to several of the cast. Gene Gene was the first victim. Jaye P.'s tits caused the Machine to take his eyes off an incoming basketball. The pass caught him full force in the nose, making it bleed profusely. Our guitar player, Billy Neale, swallowed his chewing tobacco, and our pianist, Milton De Lugg, jammed a thumb into his B-flat key with enough force to require a piano tuner the next day and the growth of a new thumbnail.

During the weeks that followed, I attended dozens of network meetings. I was harangued, chastised, threatened, and warned. But the storm blew over, as storms do. When the smoke cleared, I had a folder full of reprimands, and orders to apologize to an appalling number of veeps, all of whom I dreaded apologizing to. But I did.

Jaye P. Morgan was banned from appearing on "The Gong Show" again.

We missed her.

As if my other problems with the individual shows themselves weren't enough, I had to put up with Honey Bun Miranda. Honey Bun Miranda was black as night and wide as a small Dodge van. One day, she left an infant on one of the chairs in our reception area, wrapped in a stained and torn blanket. Honey Bun Miranda said it was my baby. (It wasn't.) Honey Bun wouldn't take the baby back. It was my baby, and that's all there was to it.

"It really isn't, Ms. Miranda," said my secretary patiently on the telephone.

"Yes, it *is!*" she yelped. "An' if he don' bring that baby and hisself back home soon, I'm gonna *kill* him."

Every day at noon, Honey Bun Miranda telephoned the office and said that if I didn't come home with the baby, she was going to kill me.

Every day my secretary, sighing wearily, would explain to Honey Bun Miranda that the baby wasn't mine. Every day, Honey Bun Miranda would reiterate her claim that it was, and that she was going to kill me posthaste.

About a week into this diatribe, we began locking our office doors and stationing armed guards in the reception room. (We still lock our doors, and the guards are still there.) Everybody was on the alert for the arrival of Honey Bun Miranda. None of us were the least bit concerned with Harley Windsor.

Thus it was that Harley Windsor was able to saunter through our various security checks, past the secretaries, into the inner offices, and, not finding me, barricade himself in Larry Spencer's office, and place a bomb on his desk. Mr. Windsor demanded that his "Gong Show" be redone with new judges who would give him a perfect score—not the gong he received—thereby launching his career on its rightful course. (Mr. Windsor played the cello while whistling bird calls of North America.) As people from the thirty floors of our office building emptied into the streets, Larry Spencer, a mild-mannered creature more concerned with his balding pate than bird-call-whistling cello players, quietly peed in his pants.

The bomb never went off. Instead, Harley Windsor harangued the damp and frightened Spencer about the injustices of game-show scoring procedures, and threatened on several occasions to return and kill me. He concluded his visit by setting afire the trash in Spencer's wastebasket. The firemen later joined the policemen in the building's lobby. Both departments failed to notice Harley Windsor leaving the premises.

I left for Paris on a short business trip the next morning. While I was there, a pale, golden-haired young man came to my house and demanded to see me. He said I was his lover, that I had jilted him, and that he was going to kill me. I wondered if there was a prolonged full moon in Hollyweird or some other rampant hostile karma I wasn't aware of. I hoped fervently that when I returned from my three-day trip the threats, by some miracle, would have ceased.

But they didn't. And they haven't.

* * *

One evening, about two weeks after my lunch with Penny at the Beverly Hills Hotel, I was at home, sitting in front of the fire, thinking. I was thinking about my production company, and the CIA, and of how overwhelmingly sick I was of both. I wanted to do something new, something I had never done before—like painting, or writing, or making a movie. I was sick of television: sick of the obnoxious v.p.s, and the death threats, and the hostile critics. And I was even sicker of the CIA. I was glad I had been retired. Had I not been retired, I would have resigned. At least, that's what I told myself. The thrill I had once gotten from the Agency was gone—replaced by uncertainty, anxiety, and even self-loathing. The loss of my friend Jim Byrd—the waste of it all—tormented me. I sat there, trying to remember exactly what manner of pleasure I had derived from killing people. How had I rationalized it back then? How could I have?

Gradually, my mind turned toward Penny, and my thoughts grew more pleasant. We had had lunch together that afternoon, and Penny had looked adorable. I remembered thinking to myself: goddammit, the Penster is really pretty. Her red hair; her green eyes; her scowl; her slightly chipped front tooth. With a heart as big as I didn't know what, and all mush, and hugs, and kisses; and sexy as a son of a bitch, even when she's an itch. There was no doubt in my mind, as I mused, that someone could fall in love with the Penster. But she *is* an itch, I reminded myself, and I should never let myself forget that very important fact. She *is* an itch.

As I was musing in front of the fire, an automobile stopped at the foot of my driveway. The car and its four occupants had, unknown to me, driven by my house many times that day. The man sitting in the front passenger seat smiled. "His gates are wide open," he said smugly.

"I guess we won't need this," said the driver, putting an electronic genie away in the car's glove compartment.

The passenger in the front was pleased. The open gates were a good omen. He signaled to proceed, and Major Kasilov's automobile rolled up my driveway.

Sixteen

All four KGB agents were heavily armed. One of the agents seated in the rear held a high-powered rifle with an infrared sight. Kasilov ordered his driver to stop just short of the house. They would walk the rest of the way. Kasilov was nervous. He had come a long distance and waited a long time for this moment. He would avenge his friend's death, and the deaths of all the other comrade agents. Kasilov's emotional goal blinded his usually alert vision. He failed to see the three drab olive green U.S. government–issue Chevys driving out of the three-car garage in front of him. Or the two additional sedans coming up the driveway behind him.

Four of the government cars surrounded Kasilov's automobile. The fifth idled twenty-five feet away. A Soviet intelligence agent, sitting in the back of Kasilov's car, asked nervously, "What should we do, Comrade Major?"

"We will sit here and wait," Kasilov answered.

"For what?" asked another KGB agent from the rear of the automobile.

Kasilov didn't answer. For what? A good question. And there is an even better question, thought Kasilov to himself. How did we get caught?

Kasilov saw the window of the car alongside his roll down. A CIA veteran named Post signaled Kasilov, and the KGB major lowered his window. Kasilov and Post studied each other. The tired CIA agent flicked a cigarette butt away and said, "Major Valarie Kasilov, I want you to know there are twenty of us. I don't suggest you, or any of your friends, use your guns. I do suggest you allow us to take the four of you into custody. If you and your friends come peacefully, you will not be harmed. Come out with your arms in the air and you'll be on an airliner for Moscow in the morning. Cause any trouble, Kasilov, and you'll be dead in less than a minute. Think it over." Post rolled up his window.

Kasilov did not believe the American. "He is lying," he said to the others.

"What is he lying about?" asked one of the KGB agents.

"About the airliner to Moscow," answered Kasilov.

Watching from my living room window, I saw the KGB agents come out of their automobile with their hands above their heads. Post put one Soviet agent in each government car. An American climbed in the empty KGB automobile. There was a lot of backing up and turning around, and then all of the automobiles were gone. I pushed the button and watched my gate close. Then I returned to my armchair and stared at the fire. Post was a good man, and a good operative. He had alerted me, and we had planned the operation two days before (highly visible signs that I was at home, open gates, et cetera). It had all gone as Post had said it would.

But what if Post had not been on top of it? What if he had not learned of Kasilov's presence in the United States, and of its significance to me? And would he be on top of it the next time? "Shit, they'll get me sooner or later," I said aloud. I knew they would, if they really wanted to.

It was just a matter of time.

* * *

Toward the end of 1979 I decided to try something new. I wrote, directed, and starred in a motion picture. It was called *The Gong Show Movie*.

It was to be my last hurrah.

If the movie was a success, I would have something to do for the rest of my life: make motion pictures. If the movie failed, it would be one blunder too many. I would remove myself, one way or another, from the public eye. Not for any melodramatic reason. Just for peace and quiet.

It took me forty days and nights to shoot the movie, and five months to edit it. Then I had to tour the country to promote the goddamn thing. I traveled to thirty cities in thirty-two days in a grueling trip that ended disastrously.

It even began rather poorly, with the motion picture's early reviews. They were less than enthusiastic. The most succinct was the *Albuquerque Tribune*: "Life is cruel enough without Chuck Barris constantly around."

The publicity tour was exhausting. I was tired and cranky most of the time—especially the morning in Duluth. It was six o'clock, and I was standing outside the stage door entrance to one of the city's television stations, waiting for someone to open the door. I was watching the sun rise, and not really enjoying it.

Finally the stage door opened. "Hi!" said a girl with huge eyes opened to the max. "I'm Kathy! I'm the assistant production coordinator!" The girl spoke in exclamation points. I hated people who spoke in exclamation points. Particularly at six in the morning when I was exhausted from traveling, and sleeping on pillows with unfamiliar smells, and lumpy beds with mohair covers. And those motherfucking wake-up calls.

"Let me take you to our Green Room!" piped Kathy the a.p.c. She led me to a cramped oversized closet painted a puke green. Inside was a worn couch and five torturously uncomfortable bridge chairs. "Coffee!" yapped Kathy. Before I could answer, she handed me lukewarm mud in a Styrofoam cup. I took a sip and winced, and watched the other guests watching me. The other guests were sitting in all but one of the bridge chairs. The empty bridge chair was dented into an almost unusable position.

"Make yourself comfortable!" chirped Kathy, pointing to the deformed monstrosity.

"Up yours," I muttered to myself, and sat down.

A woman stormed into the room and walked directly to me. "Hello, I'm Monica Starr!" she boomed. (Did *everyone* in Duluth talk in exclamation points?)

I disliked Monica Starr immediately. For one thing, she was taller than I was; and for another, she had mean eyes. You can always tell if someone is nice or not by their eyes, and the cunt that was standing in front of me had a first-class pair of mean eyes. I also disliked her dress, her shoes, her teased blond hair set in an ancient hairdo, and her tone of voice. I wondered what function this aberration performed.

"I'm co-host of 'The Morning Show,'" she explained, and then corrected herself. "Co-hostess, I should say. Or is it co-hostperson? Hahahaha." (I didn't give a rusty fuck.) "Now tell me, Mr. Barris, are you as crazy and wild and obnoxious in real life as you are on television? Hahahaha."

I didn't believe she'd said that. "I don't believe you said that," I replied, but she didn't hear me. She wasn't listening.

"Never mind," said Monica, sighing. "I'm not interviewing you anyway. Chuck is. *We* have a Chuck, too. Chuck Dawn. Chuck's interviewing you. I'm interviewing Jessica, thank God."

Jessica Goldstein, one of the other guests in the Green Room, was surrounded by her friends and publicists. She flashed me an icy smile. I smiled back. God, you're ugly, I thought while smiling at Jessica. "Jessica is the author of the best-seller *Sex in the Executive Suite!*" exclaimed Monica proudly.

Mary, Mother of God, I moaned to myself, and watched the Green Room spin around me. I took a deep breath, and the room stopped spinning. I withdrew into my mutilated bridge chair and ruminated about my life. What warped configuration of circumstances had led me to this atrocious city? To this repugnant Green Room? Why was I here, I mused, when I could have been, if I so desired, basking in the sun on the French Riviera? Or walking along a rocky coast in Maine?

Greed had led me to the uncomfortable bridge chair. Pure, unadulterated greed. So I could promote *The Gong Show Movie,* and hopefully help it succeed. And make more money. And what would I do with more money? Take another trip to Lisbon? I was about to wail, *"Shit! Piss! Fuck!"* when someone said something to me.

"Pardon?"

"I said hello!" repeated a wholesome-looking chap, sending my thoughts scurrying for cover. "I'm Chuck Dawn!"

I don't recall much of what Chuck Dawn and I chatted about— only that he wore short white whoopee socks, and I detest a man who wears short whoopee socks of any color. Whoopee socks come up to the ankle, and any guy who dresses in a suit and tie and wears whoopee socks is a real Charlie B-Minor dork. I've always believed that a man who displays his ankles is evil at heart. Grown men who wear whoopee socks revolt me in much the same way as grown men who still wear their college class rings. Or grown men who wear their letter sweaters to class reunions. Or grown men who eat filet of sole for dinner. Or grown men who weigh the same as they did in high school. Or grown men who wear miniature campaign ribbons in their coat lapels. Or grown men who tuck their ties into the top of their slacks, or their shirttails into their underwear. They're all evil at heart. I thought about these things as they marched us to the studio that aired "The Morning Show."

Minutes later the program started, transmitted by wire and electron beams and projected against the screens of picture tubes in television sets throughout northern Minnesota and Canada. Duluth, International Falls, Cloquet, Hinckley, and even Toronto. Millions of people were watching Jessica Goldstein answer Monica Starr's questions. Jessica Goldstein was wowing them, stopping many an American and

Canadian spoon between cereal bowl and mouth with such old auto-matic spoon-stopping words as cunnilingus, fellatio, vaginal frustra-tion, penis envy, carpopedal spasms in males, multiple orgasmal expres-sions, clitoral manipulation, stuff like that.

Jessica Goldstein received an enthusiastic ovation from the studio audience, as enthusiastic as forty-three half-dead senior citizens could be at seven-thirty in the morning. Monica Starr clapped energetically at the camera, smiled, and said, "We'll be back with TV producer and personality—and more recently *motion picture* producer and *star*—Chuck Barris, right after these messages."

I thought I was next, but I wasn't. Matt Decker was next.

I wondered where Matt Decker had come from. I didn't see him in the Green Room. Maybe the station didn't allow blacks in the Green Room. Matt Decker and Chuck Dawn discussed the plight of the black ballet dancer in America. Black ballet dancers couldn't seem to get themselves hired by prominent repertory companies. I wondered if anyone gave a fuck about black ballet dancers' problems. Certainly not the slowly atrophying studio audience. Hardly any of the wrinkled octogenarians sitting there had ever seen a ballet, let alone a *spade* ballet dancer. The room began to spin again. I had to blink several times before I could make it stop.

Chuck Dawn feigned interest in Matt Decker's dilemma, but obvi-ously detested both his guest and the subject. Dawn's eyes gave him away. They were panicked, darting eyes; little brown buttons working themselves into angry creases. Dawn's instincts must have told him that if he didn't get rid of this nigger-pansy and get to Barris quickly, his contribution to "The Morning Show" would be less than thrilling. He'd end up making Monica Starr look good, and, shit, he hated that worse than rat poison. Later, Dawn would see who on the show's staff booked the boring jig in the first place, and have the one responsible fired.

"It's not so much that very few blacks are in ballet," continued Decker. "There are, in fact, few dancers of *any* minority in ballet. Few Mexicans, few Orientals. Why? Because it's the nature of the beast."

The dancer's concern was apparent, his approach intelligent, his voice warm but firm. Decker's red and white striped, open-necked sport shirt and tan pleated slacks suggested a comfortable, calm demeanor. He was undoubtedly a bright and creative man, and I grew to like Decker more and more as I listened to him. But how many others liked him, or cared about his problems? How many people in the TV studio? In the city of Duluth? In the state of Minnesota? It seemed to me that as we spread further and further out, less and less people would care about Decker, or any of his thoughts. If you added Wisconsin, Michigan, Indiana, and Ohio, the interest in the situation would be almost infinitesimal. Considering the billions of people on earth, the concern with Decker, and Decker's world, became—on a one-to-ten scale—a statistical cipher. A motherfucking zero. Decker disappeared in the sample, like rain down a rain spout. And if you applied the old transitive property: if $a=b$, and $b=c$, then $a=c$ . . . nobody cared about me either.

"You're next, Mr. Barris," said a stage manager.

I was led onstage, and to a settee. The settee was covered with a horrendous floral print, and trimmed with tufts and scallops. I sat opposite Chuck Dawn. His settee appeared newer than mine. Dawn sat smiling at me, with his legs crossed. I could see his white whoopee socks and exposed ankles.

There was a lot of fussing as to where I should pin my microphone. Did I mind it here? Or how about here? Maybe here is better? Kathy, the a.p.c., kept asking me if I was comfortable. Was my cushion all right? Was there anything I wanted? Coffee? A glass of water?

And then we were on the air, and Chuck Dawn said, "And now let's welcome Chuck Barris!" Dawn applauded politely, encouraging the audience to do the same. "Well, hello, Chuck. It's nice to have you on 'The Morning Show.' "

"Thank you. It's nice to be here," I replied softly.

Dawn smiled and said, "Tell me, Chuck, how does it feel to be known as the 'King of Schlock'?"

"Pardon?" I answered, unable to believe my ears for the second time that morning.

"I said how does it feel to be known as the 'King of Schlock'?"

The room began to spin again. Suddenly, I was covered with sweat. My upper lip twitched ever so slightly. A rage, familiar and violent, battled with my attempts to remain composed. My thoughts were in disarray. I laughed an idiotic, nervous laugh to camouflage my anger. I was sure it didn't fool anyone. And my fury grew, stoked by the smile on the face of the malevolent young man sitting opposite me. Dawn wasn't the least bit displeased with my inability to reply. On the contrary, he took pleasure in the dramatic pause, my obvious display of discomfort, the hushed quiet in the studio while everyone watched me flailing about like a fish out of water.

"Wow," I finally said, "that's a hell of a welcome. And I haven't even had my second cup of coffee yet."

"You haven't answered my question," said the ever-smiling Dawn. "How do you feel about being called the 'King of Schlock'?"

"How would *you* feel?"

"That's not an answer," said Dawn the prober. Dawn the tenacious television journalist. Dawn the media bully, ambushing a guest and then clubbing him to death with his microphone. "I'll ask the question again. How does it feel to be known as the 'King of Schlock'?"

"I have never found the word *schlock* to be flattering," I answered nervously.

"Is that all you're going to say about it?"

"Yes."

"Okay," said Dawn. He shifted his ass on his settee and tossed a conspiratorial glance sideways at the audience. "Let's move on. Nationally syndicated television critic Stanford Arnold wrote, and I quote, 'Even more than loud talk on TV, I hate shows by Chuck Barris. I confess I have never watched a Barris show all the way through, being allergic to slop and degradation.' Unquote. Do you consider your television shows slop and degradation?"

"I thought we were going to talk about my new motion picture."

Dawn smiled, turned to the camera, and said, "Yes, we'll talk about that, and lots more, right after this message."

During the commercial break, Chuck Dawn fussed with the pillows on his settee, and said, "I hope you don't mind these questions," and without waiting for an answer, added, "Don't worry, we'll get to the movie. By the way, what's the movie called?"

"I *do* mind the questions."

"Excuse me?" said Dawn, concentrating on readjusting his microphone.

"I said I *do* mind your stupid fucking insensitive questions."

Chuck Dawn looked up from his lapel and glared at me. "Just a second . . ."

"Just a second my ass, you little white bread cocksucker. I'll just a second you. What's with all this bullshit about being the King of Schlock? You said it four times in less than a minute. And slop and degradation. What kind of crap is that? I was promised that we would talk about my movie, and *not* my television shows." My anger was out of control, on its own. No matter what Dawn would say, it wouldn't be good enough. He was in deep trouble. He had out-of-control rage sitting just a few feet away from his pearly white ankles.

"Look here," said Chuck Dawn, sensing danger and looking for help with his eyes, "I don't know anything about not asking you . . ."

"You don't know anything about anything, you little prick."

"Hold it right there," hissed Dawn. "You may feel put down—I can appreciate that. But my viewers want to know the answers to these questions, and it's tough shit if you feel put down. If you don't like the heat, you shouldn't go out on tours. Besides, it's mighty tough to feel sorry for a rich and supposedly successful person like yourself."

"Yeah?" I said.

"Yeah," said Dawn.

* * *

As far as my last hurrah was concerned, it couldn't have been more embarrassing. *The Gong Show Movie* was a flop. It opened in theaters across the country on a Friday and closed three days later.

We did make it to the premiere. It was a typical Hollywood premiere, with lots of bands, and cheerleaders, and bleachers across the street so that thousands of spectators could watch the stars enter Grauman's Chinese Theatre. There was a red carpet, television cameras, newspaper photographers, and gossip columnists interviewing whomever they could get their hands on.

It was during that premiere, with me standing in the back, my chin resting on the shoulder-high wall behind the last row of seats, that I realized *The Gong Show Movie* was bound to fail. The first third was good. It was zany and wild. If at that point the movie didn't appeal to the intelligentsia, it certainly would entertain the "Gong Show" faithful and a lot of their friends. But unfortunately, just about a third of the way through, I couldn't resist trying to make a serious motion picture. A film that said something. It was a disastrous mistake. Now, not even the "Gong Show" faithful would come. Nobody would come. I had promised myself I would never do television again, and now I couldn't make movies. None of the motion picture studios would want me to. I was left with my only other alternative: disappearing off the face of the earth.

I became a recluse.

I sold my home in Bel Air, most of my furniture, and my cars, and moved into a small apartment in south Beverly Hills. I readjusted to apartment living quickly; the only annoyances being the public, and my dog, Albert. I put up with Albert as best I could, but found coping with people a major problem. I was constantly cornered by idiots who wanted to be on "The Gong Show," and taunted wherever I went by strangers shouting, "Gong!" As I mentioned earlier, I took to wearing sunglasses, a fake beard, and a Phillies baseball hat wherever I went. It didn't help.

So I went out of business.

I shut down all of our television production, dismissed most of my employees, and vacated my office building in Hollyweird. I retained my controller, my secretary, and a receptionist, and moved them to a small suite of offices in Beverly Hills. I completed all of the above by the spring of 1980.

In June, I flew East.

The Duck drove me to the airport. He told me I was going to kill a wop named Moretti. He accused me of being a "burn-out," and wasn't sure I would be able to pull it off. I told the Duck to go fuck himself. What I didn't tell the Duck was that I had vowed never to kill again after the Moretti job.

"This is it," I had told Simon Oliver, my senior CIA control officer, when he proposed the hit. "I'll do this assignment, but from now on you'll have to give your dirty work to some other guy. You've already retired me, and I plan to stay that way."

"My, my, I think you're serious," said Oliver, working a clinched grin around his pipe stem. "Have you forgotten that the reason you were placed in *temporary* retirement has now been removed?"

"I know about Kasilov," I said. "But retirement agrees with me. Besides, I doubt if the KGB has forgotten about Sunny Sixkiller—and there are a ton of Soviet hit men where Kasilov came from."

That meeting had taken place a week earlier in Los Angeles. Now I was back in New York, arriving at the Plaza Hotel in the middle of a heat wave.

"Can I help you?" asked a hotel reservations clerk.

"Sixkiller. Sunny Sixkiller."

"Ah, yes, Mr. Sixkiller. You're pre-registered. You can pick up your room key across the lobby at the message desk."

A cheerful clerk gave me my room key and a message. I walked to a corner of the lobby and opened the envelope. Inside was a key to another room—room 1632—and a note. The note read:

> Go there now. He will be back
> between 7:00 and 8:00 P.M. You
> must accomplish everything tonight.
> Tomorrow is too late.

My skin prickled with a rush of anxiety. It was now ten minutes to six. I crossed the lobby and boarded a crowded elevator. By the time the elevator reached the sixteenth floor I was its only passenger. I wandered through the halls, searching for room 1632. I found it at the end of a long, empty corridor. Noting where it was, I retraced my steps until I came to a men's room. I pushed the door open and walked in.

I entered a stall, closed the door, and threw the latch. I placed my valise on top of the toilet seat and pulled its zipper open. I rummaged through its contents until I found my automatic and silencer. I fitted the silencer to the gun and slid a full cartridge clip up the automatic's handle. I cocked a cartridge into the chamber and flicked off the safety catch. I placed the gun between my jeans and shirt, at the small of my back. I put the two extra cartridge clips in the right hand pocket of my sport coat. I dug around the bag until I found a pair of pigskin gloves at the bottom of my valise. I put on the gloves and readjusted my corduroy sport coat. I walked out of the stall and looked at myself in the mirrors above the wash basins. I checked for unusual bulges or bumps in my sport coat. There were none. My mustache and beard were still in place. I had everything I needed. I was all set to go.

But I didn't go.

I continued staring at myself in the mirror.

I was looking at my eyes, trying to see the fear in them. Trying to determine if I appeared as frightened as I felt. Could someone else look at me and know that I was scared shitless? I had always been scared before a hit—usually for a good reason. But what was my reason that evening? Was it what the Duck had said? That I was a burn-out, and burn-outs fuck up? Did he put a hex on me? Did that motherfucker jinx my last job? I studied the mirror for answers and all I saw were my eyes. Worried eyes. I closed my valise and left the men's room.

I glanced up and down the hallway. It was empty. I returned to room 1632. I checked the hallway again. Still empty. I quietly placed the valise on the floor. I pulled my gun out from behind my back, put it into my sport coat pocket, and slipped the room key into the door lock. I wondered if he was in there already. What if he was? What if there were others with him? Why wasn't I briefed more thoroughly for this assignment? And why didn't I think of these fucking questions earlier? Why did I always think of a hundred questions when the key was in the lock?

I pulled the key quietly out of the door and wiped the sweat off my forehead with the sleeve of my sport jacket. I put the key back in the lock and said to myself: just remember, this is your last job.

I twisted the key slowly and pushed, waiting for someone to say, "Who's that?" The door opened to reveal a small, dark room. I removed the key from the lock, picked up my valise, and stepped inside. I shut the door slowly, trying to forestall committing myself. I wanted to be as certain as I could that I was the only one in the room. Eventually I closed the door with my back and leaned against it, attempting to catch my breath. My heart was thumping against my rib cage and my sport shirt was stained with dark blotches of perspiration. How could I ever have enjoyed such terror?

As my eyes adjusted to the darkness, I began to pick out the details of the room. An unused queen-size bed. A bureau with nothing on it but hotel advertisements and directories. An armchair and a television set on a portable stand.

The bastard's only five feet tall. Remember that, I said to myself. He's only five feet tall.

I noticed two windows in the far wall opposite the door. The window on the right had an air-conditioning unit bolted into it and probably couldn't be opened. I walked across the room to the windows, measuring my steps as I went. The window with the air conditioner was sealed shut, as expected, and I tried the other window. It opened wide; city noise and the muggy evening heat rushed in. Across the way was a windowless brick wall. I leaned out the open window and looked down at the alley sixteen floors below, then walked away from the window without shutting it.

The room's closet was empty. I placed my valise and sport coat on its floor, closed the closet door, put my gun under my belt in the front of my jeans, walked over to the bed, and lay down on my back. I placed my hands behind my head and listened to the sounds of the city: taxicab horns, sirens, clopping horses pulling carriages through Central Park. Everyone oblivious to my little drama in room 1632, just as I was oblivious to theirs. Fears and worries jammed my head, but I refused to pay attention to them. *He's a little bastard. He's a little bastard.*

I'm not sure how long I lay on that bed, or how many times I ran to the door when I heard footsteps and voices in the hallway. But it seemed that no one would ever stop at room 1632.

And then someone did.

I jumped quickly to my feet, and in two steps was against the wall on the blind side of the hall door. I kept my automatic under my belt, my right hand on the grip. I listened to the key turn in the door slot, the door handle twist, and the door open.

I watched him step into the room.

I couldn't see his face. Just his back. He wore a dark brown leather jacket and black gabardine slacks. The hair on the top of his head was sparse, but like Benjamin Franklin's it grew long and curly down the nape of his neck and over his ears. And he *was* a little bastard. Just about five feet tall. Maybe a hundred and ten pounds. He stared at the open window. He apparently didn't remember opening it.

I hit him from behind with the full force of a running start and all of my one hundred and fifty-five pounds. The momentum carried the two of us forward together, my chest up against his back. I grabbed the neck of his leather jacket in my left hand and the back of his belt with my right, and still moving, pushed Mario Moretti across the room, and out the open window.

* * *

The next night, at an outdoor table at Ferrara's Restaurant, on Grand Street in the section of Manhattan known as Little Italy, I briefed Simon Oliver on the job, and then handed him my Company credentials and a letter of resignation.

"You're making a mistake, Barris," Oliver said, cool despite the heat, tamping his fucking Dunhill pipe bowl with a solid gold Dunhill doohickey. "But I'm not overly concerned. You know why?"

"Why?"

"Because you'll come back into the fold."

"Really?"

"Without a doubt," he said, crossing his arms and legs at the same time. "Mark my words."

After leaving Ferrara's, I returned to a small suite I had taken at the Parker Hotel on West Fifty-sixth Street. I intended to stay for three or four days—just enough time to think a few things over; to think about what to do with myself next.

I stayed for over a year.

Seventeen

August 4, 1981. New York.

In the year that had drifted by, I had become very attached to suite 711 of the Parker Hotel. I was convinced the suite would be lucky for me: Seven/eleven.

The suite was in a rear corner of the hotel's seventh floor; quiet, dark, with no view except for a building across the alley. Various businesses occupied the floors of that building, and various pigeons nested on its windowsills. And my windowsills, too. I spent most of my time writing *Confessions of a Dangerous Mind* and staring out of the suite windows. Consequently, I became an expert on the life-styles of the employees toiling on the other side of the alley, and the pigeons. I knew when certain workers took their lunch breaks and when specific pigeons took their naps. During the hot and humid summer, I could pinpoint almost to the minute when the air conditioners would buzz on in the offices and small factory lofts across the way: 11:15 for the dress manufacturer, 11:40 for the two architects, between 12:05 and 12:10 for the drapery firm. I also knew when the pigeons wanted to hump. The birds' horny cooing would wake me up in the morning, sometimes as early as five or six o'clock. I would fling a book at the window and listen to the pigeons flap in panic as they left the sill. I would yell, "Go fuck some other place," but the pigeons never listened. They would return the next morning and hump their little asses off.

My three rooms—the bedroom and living room, plus a small kitchenette—were quickly overrun with the necessities of New York living as well as the usual accoutrements of life. But Gracie, my maid, kept things relatively neat with her fierce determination. Gracie was a lifesaver. When I would periodically give up smoking my pipe and throw away my tobacco in anger, Gracie would quietly retrieve the pouch from the wastebasket and hold it until my next nicotine fit, which would promptly occur not more than two hours later. Gracie took care of me when I had the flu, lacing my tea with whiskey smuggled from the hotel bar, and she would steal flowers from other rooms and arrange them in bowls on my windowsills.

"Watch out for the pigeon shit!" I would tell Gracie. There was lots of pigeon shit on the windowsills.

The elevator operators, Nick, John, Al, and Mohammed, ran errands for me, and the hotel's switchboard operators, Sally and Rose, screened my telephone calls—the few I had—with the wary tenacity of White House appointment secretaries. And the General—the wise and philosophical hotel maintenance man—rushed to fix every mishap in my suite as if I were a kindly paraplegic. Everyone—the switchboard girls, the elevator operators, Gracie, the General, and the night clerks —watched carefully to see that no one went directly to my room. I was loved and protected, comfortable and cozy, and happy—very happy— in Suite 711.

On the few occasions I ventured outside those guarded little rooms, I did so cautiously, wearing the beard and sunglasses. I only visited a few places, and generally when they weren't very busy. Like the Oyster Bar of the Plaza, or Rumpelmayer's. Occasionally, I slipped into a movie or concert at Carnegie Hall, but not much else. It was a simple existence, pleasing and relatively carefree. So when Sally rang my room to tell me there was a visitor in the lobby, I panicked. I had received telephone calls before, but never a visitor.

"He claims he's your friend," she said.

"Who is he?" I asked. I was frightened.

Sally told me who he was.

"What the hell does he want to see *me* for?" I told Sally to send him up.

* * *

"Puxton's my name, and spying's my game."

That was the first sentence Robert Lawrence Puxton III (I shall call him that) said when I opened my door.

Robert Lawrence Puxton III thought saying phrases like "Puxton's my name, and spying's my game" was cute. And that he was cute. Even, at times, downright funny. Robert Lawrence Puxton III said cute things like "Puxton's my name, and getting laid's my game" at Dartmouth, where he played football, and was first team All-Ivy League. While in college, Pux was the classic hail-fellow-well-met backslapping member of the Sigma Chi fraternity—maybe the hailest fellow of them all. His was the voice you heard the loudest whenever the boys would get together and run through a few choruses of "Dartmouth's in Town Again, Run, Girls, Run." Pux was an all-around good guy, and one of the most popular men on campus for the four years he dwelt in Hanover, New Hampshire.

At some point during graduation week, however, Pux contracted a strange (but not uncommon) malady. He stopped maturing and remained a college boy for the rest of his life. It was an illness Puxton understood. He realized his college years were the best he would ever experience, so in a fashion he never left them. That's why he still wore his Dartmouth College class ring and thought saying things like "Puxton's my name, and spying's my game" was cute. And he was a year older than I, the simple fuck.

I knew all about Puxton because we grew up together in Philadelphia. We were schoolmates at Lower Merion Senior High School. Puxton was a great-looking guy, the tallest one in the crowd; blond hair, decent athlete, and the first of our bunch to "go steady." I didn't see much of Pux after high school, but we all heard about his exploits in the hills of Hanover. He had become somewhat of a legend; his collegiate drinking, barroom brawling, womanizing, shit like that. And then our lives crossed once more. In Camp Peary, Virginia. Pux and I ended up in the CIA together. We came by different routes, but got there just the same.

When Pux and I met, we hugged, and Pux yelled "Wow!" a lot. Puxton had lost some of his good looks, and he was pudgier than I had remembered him. His blond hair had thinned, which didn't help his jowly face. But he was still the hailest fellow you'd ever want to meet, and continued to slap backs with the gusto of a muscle-bound imbecile.

When we finished our CIA training, Pux and I went our separate ways again. We stayed in touch over the years, but I avoided seeing him whenever I could. He had become too gung ho for me. Puxton was applying the same college-boy enthusiasm to the Company as he had at Dartmouth, and that was a little hard to take. And now there he was, standing in my hotel doorway, towering over me, bloated and red-faced; still immaculately dressed, still smiling from ear to ear, still one of the world's most lovable assholes.

I wasn't the least bit pleased to see him. Puxton represented the Central Intelligence Agency, and I hated the Central Intelligence Agency. "What the fuck do *you* want?" I said, noticeably less than cordial.

"How ya doin', Chuckie baby?"

"I'm fine. What the fuck do you want, Puxton?"

"You look great. You really do."

"I feel good."

"I'm glad to hear that. May I come in?"

Without waiting for an answer, Puxton walked through the door, slapping me on the back as he went by. I saw stars. Pux sat down on the couch, gave his trousers a little tug at the knees to preserve their creases, and smiled.

What an immature fuckhead you are, Puxton, I thought to myself.

If Robert Lawrence Puxton III had matured at all, it was in his manner of dress. Pux had progressed from tweed sport coats with elbow patches and black and white saddle shoes to banker's gray three-piece suits and polished black leather cordovans. There was an ostentatious white carnation pinned to his suit-coat lapel. A gold chain swung through a buttonhole on his vest and disappeared into a vest pocket. There, it became attached to a thin gold pocket watch. I appraised the watch as an expensive family heirloom while Puxton studied it. "I can only stay an hour," he said. "Actually, I have *less* than an hour."

"Are you going to tell me why you came, Puxton, or not, because if you're not, I'm going to throw your fucking ass the hell out of here."

"Easy, partner, easy. I can understand your being annoyed about me barging in on you. I can respect that. But just give me a chance to unwind. Just let me take a minute to look at your happy face. I've *missed* you, Chuckie baby."

I didn't say anything. I just stood there with my arms crossed over my chest, extremely pissed off. What the fuck was going on? Puxton wouldn't visit me for social reasons. So why *was* he visiting me? And why wouldn't he get to the fucking point?

"I just got here," Puxton said, reading my mind. "If you give me a second to cool off, I'll get on with it, Chuckie baby. I'll tell you one thing, though. You're not going to win the host-of-the-year award, you little bastard. Got anything to drink?"

"No."

"Right," said Puxton. "By the way, I never saw so many pretty twats as I did walking down Fifth Avenue. Hubba hubba, Goodrich rubba. Nothing like that in Washington, I'll tell you. And each one was prettier than the next. I guess you're used to all the pretty New York snatch by now. Bet it must drive you nuts walking up and down Fifth Avenue. Ever hit on any of that cooze, Chuckie baby? You're a famous man. You must . . ."

"What is it you wanted to see me about, Puxton?"

"*Gong!*" yelled Puxton.

I groaned.

"You know," said Puxton, tightening the knot of his tie, "I loved 'The Gong Show.' I really did. Did it get an Oscar?"

"Oscars are for movies."

"What's for television?"

"Emmys."

"Did 'The Gong Show' get an Emmy?"

"No."

"Well," said Puxton, pulling his shoulders back dramatically, "it sure as shit should have."

"Awards are like hemorrhoids, Puxton. Sooner or later every asshole gets one."

Puxton collapsed into his lap laughing hysterically and moaning, "That's terrific! That's terrific!" When he could catch his breath, he said, "What a mind you have."

"I didn't make that up. William Wyler did."

"You know what I got a kick out of most of all?" asked Puxton, ignoring what I had just said. "You! The show was okay, but *you* were terrific!"

"Thanks, Pux."

Puxton shouted, "Hey, Chuckie baby, Chuckie baby, Chuckie baby!" and then he jumped up and slapped my back during a fit of uncontrolled hysterics. "I just loved it when that guy used to yell that at you," said Puxton, still laughing like a jackass. "Yeah, you were great, Chuckie baby. I just wanted to tell you that."

"Thanks, Pux."

"And all the time you were doing hit jobs for the Company."

"That's right."

"Amazing."

"What the fuck do you want, Puxton?"

"You feelin' okay?" he asked, sitting down again.

"Yes. I'm feeling fine."

"You sleeping and eating all right, and everything?"

"Yeah, Pux, I'm sleeping and eating all right, and everything."

"So you're fit?" he asked with a note of concern.

"Yes, I'm fit. Don't I look fit?"

"Yeah, as a matter of fact, you do."

"I should be. I run three consecutive eight-minute miles every morning before breakfast." Which was a lie.

"Good," said Puxton. "Did you hear about the Polish jailbreak?"

Chuck Barris

"No."

"It was yesterday. Pass it on." Puxton wheezed at his little joke.

"See you around, Pux." I said, walking toward the door.

"Where're you going?" asked a startled Puxton, his brow all furrowed.

"Since you're not going to tell me why you came, I'm throwing you the fuck out of my room."

"The Company wants you to kill someone," he said hurriedly.

"I thought so. Get the fuck out of here, Puxton."

"I've gotta explain the job to you."

"I've resigned from the CIA," I said, still standing by the open door. "For good!"

"I know," replied Puxton. "Everybody knows you resigned. That's one of the main reasons Control wants you for this particular job." Puxton seemed worried. I hadn't returned to the living room, and I didn't appear as though I was going to. "Look," Puxton said, moving to the edge of the couch, "you gotta let me explain this job to you, Chuckie baby, you really do. It won't take long. At least give me a chance. I was sent here by the boss to lay it out, and if you don't let me, Control'll give me a new ass when I get back. So just let me lay it out for you. Please. For old times' sake?"

I said nothing.

"And by the way," added Puxton, "Oliver wants you to know that if, after hearing all the details, you want to turn it down, you're obviously free to do so."

"Thanks a lot."

"And no hard feelings, buddy boy. Absolutely no hard feelings," said Robert Lawrence Puxton III cheerfully. I'm sure it was the same tone of voice old Pux used as an undergraduate, as he told Dartmouth freshmen they weren't going to be accepted as pledges for his beloved fraternity. "And no hard feelings, buddy boy. Absolutely no hard feelings."

I walked to a small chair near Puxton and sat down. "Okay, Pux," I said. "Lay it out."

Eighteen

The Company had located the mole—the CIA agent who was leaking information to Moscow Center. This particular mole was deep inside the Agency's deployment division.

"Very deep inside," said Puxton. "The information this mole's been transmitting has caused incredible havoc internally and externally. The mole's plotting is responsible for the deaths of some of the Company's best men. Your pal Jim Byrd, for one."

"Jim Byrd! This is the mole that got Jim?"

"Yep. Byrd, and the Frenchman—I forget his name—the one that got you out of Paris one step ahead of the Ruskies."

"Paul Picard."

"Yeah, Picard. That's the guy. And there were others. Oh, and hear this, buddy boy. It's the same mole that set *you* up in your office in Hollywood. That was a pretty close one, wasn't it, Chuckie baby? The whole thing turned to garbage because the hit man was jumpy. Isn't that so? But as I understand it, a good gun would have had you dead to rights, am I right?"

"You're right."

"And that's not the only time this mole has had you pegged."

"Really?" I said, both scared and excited.

"Yes, really," said Puxton, warming to my guarded interest. "Remember your Paris job, when you were . . . hey, this place isn't wired, is it, Chuck? You wouldn't do that to me, would you?"

I told Puxton that my apartment wasn't wired.

"You're writing a book, and I hear it's inside stuff about the CIA," said Puxton, suddenly full of righteousness and indignation. "I don't want anything I say to . . ."

"Who told you that I was writing a book?"

"I heard."

"You heard right."

"Am I in it?" asked Puxton.

"No."

"Good," said the holier-than-thou Puxton. "And you'd better watch just *who's* in it, if I make myself clear. Where was I?"

"My Paris job."

"Correct, the Paris job," said Puxton. "You were sent to eliminate a CIA turncoat named Kirby, right? Well, that mission was a trap, Chuckie baby—a goddamn fucking trap."

"A trap?"

"You bet your ass it was. You were set up, buddy boy. And it almost worked, except you screwed it up by hitting them where they least expected it."

"I still don't understand, Puxton," I said irritably. "What trap?"

"Let's see if I can explain it to you. You weren't really supposed to get Kirby and Slasky. They were supposed to get you. That was the mole's plan. Didn't your pal Byrd tell you afterward that the KGB had been on to you all along? Of course, Byrd didn't know the details. He didn't know it was the mole that set you up by feeding information to that big shot KGB agent . . . what's his name? . . . Kasilov. Major Kasilov. Caught in Los Angeles, in your back yard, I believe. Then snuffed somewhere else. Wasn't that Post's mission? Yeah, I think it was. Mind if I smoke? It's a cigar. It might stink up the place."

I told Puxton I didn't mind if he smoked a cigar.

"Yeah," Puxton continued, spitting the end of the cigar toward a wastebasket and missing, "when Control sent you to kill Slasky and the turncoat Kirby, it was a legitimate mission. But our mole found out about it, told Kasilov, and they figured out how to turn it against you. The mole and Kasilov were going to make sure that *you* were the one who ended up getting shot in Paris. Only their plan got messed up. You beat them to the punch somehow. And some assholes in the Company were calling you a burn-out." Puxton laughed at the irony of it all.

Thinking back on it, everything Puxton said made sense. "I see," I murmured. And I did. It had all been a trap. I had gotten lucky, tailed Kirby to Slasky, and shot them first. If I hadn't been lucky that day, I would now have been dead for over three years.

"Anyway," said Puxton, puffing contentedly, "this mole's damage has been so close to your ass—what with your buddy Byrd, and the Frenchman, and yourself as targets—Control thought you might have a personal interest in plugging this leak once and for all. And there's another reason why Control wants you to do this job—probably the most important reason of all."

"Yeah? Why?"

"Because there's a good chance you're the last person the target might suspect."

"How come?"

"Simple. You resigned from the Company a year ago. You made it perfectly clear to everybody that you weren't interested in the spy business anymore. And everybody believed you. And they still do. Add to that your holing up in this hotel like a . . . like a . . ."

"Recluse."

". . . recluse, and letting everybody know you're a recluse, and . . ."

"I didn't tell anybody anything."

"Well, everybody at the Company knew. And by now everybody at the Company's forgotten about you. And if they haven't forgotten about you, they think—and I'm not speaking for myself, now, I'm speaking for everyone else—they think you're some kind of fruitcake."

"Fruitcake?"

"You know what I mean. Nutty. Mentally confused. A burn-out. A guy who's more interested in sitting by himself in a couple of dark rooms . . ."

"Now, come on, Pux, do these rooms look dark?"

". . . than looking for hit jobs. Mind you, all of that's perfect for the mission. This mole has access to the whereabouts of all CIA agents, and might suspect someone on the active list just sort of showing up in the neighborhood. You're different. You could show up and not throw a scare into an already jumpy mole."

"And then again, I could," I said, watching for telltale signs on Puxton's face.

"Yeah, I guess you could," Puxton confessed, his voice drifting off. We sat silently for a few minutes. Then Puxton said, "Well, let me put it this way. The Company thinks you might be able to get away with it. But I gotta be honest with you, Chuckie baby. It's a hairy one. Really dangerous—simply because the mole may not think your killing days are over. Or, for some reason or other, the mole may still want you dead. In either case, when you're spotted, the mole may make immediate plans to blow you away. I really don't know what to tell you." Puxton looked genuinely distressed.

I was going to ask how the Company finally located the target— the turncoat mole—but I figured it didn't really matter.

"What do you think?" asked Puxton.

"I think Control, and everybody in the fucking CIA, is full of shit, that's what I think. What kind of a sucker do you take me for? You say I wouldn't throw a scare into an already jumpy mole. That's all shit, and you know it as well as I do. If Control, if Simon Oliver, wants a mole killed, all he has to do is pick out one of his fair-haired hit men and have him do it. Or put together a squad of killers, ambush the fucking mole, and get it over with. Or arrest the bastard, toss him in jail, and throw away the key. The reasons you've mentioned for me doing this job are bullshit, Puxton. *Pure, unadulterated bullshit!*"

"Why are you so mad all of a sudden?" asked a bewildered Puxton.

"Because I *know* why Simon Oliver sent you here to talk me into doing this job. It's because Simon Oliver's a prick. A first-class prick. He sent you here to make the offer because he knows I can't refuse it. He knows I'll come out of retirement and kill this son of a bitch, or get killed trying—because this mole fingered my friends, and had a number on me. And still might, for all I know!"

"So what's wrong with that?" asked an uncomfortable Puxton.

"What's wrong with that? I'll tell you what's wrong with that. Oliver hates my guts, that's what's wrong with it. Ever since we first met, Oliver's hated my guts, and he's never changed his mind. If anything, he's hated me more. And I know he must have been really pissed when I told him I was resigning. You know why, Puxton? Because by resigning, I deprived the piss-ant the satisfaction of seeing me get killed. I took away his anticipated joy at hearing I had fucked up an assignment and been blown away. I quit undefeated, Puxton, and that really pissed Oliver off. You see, Pux, it's no big loss to Oliver if I'm killed. On the contrary, it would please the cocksucker no end. Besides, if I fuck up this assignment and get dusted, Oliver won't be losing an ass-kissing agent he *does* like. And if I *do* kill the mole, so much the better. It's a no-lose situation for Simon. That's why he sent you here to get me to agree to do this asshole job. Sure, he's hoping you succeed, because if you do, I'll either end up with my balls in my mouth, or make Simon Oliver a hero. And I'll tell you something, Puxton. You're just as big a prick as Oliver because you already knew everything I'm telling you. You know Oliver as well as I do, Pux. You know how he thinks, what's in the back of his devious mind, how he feels about me; you know it all. You also knew why he sent you, Puxton, and you came."

"So?"

"So *you* gotta live with that one, Puxton. Not me."

* * *

That day after Puxton's visit, I had another guest.

"Redhead!" I yelled, welcoming Penny Pacino with hugs and kisses, "what the hell are you doing in New York?"

"I came to see you."

"Don't you think you should have called first?"

"I was afraid if I did you wouldn't let me come."

"You mean you came all the way from Los Angeles on the pure chance that you *might* see me?"

"Well, not exactly. I'm on my way to London to see the tennis matches at Wimpletin."

"Wimbledon," I corrected.

"What?"

The pigeons hooted on the windowsill.

"A friend of mine is playing there," continued Penny. "I thought I would spend the tournament with her, and then sail back to the States on the QE-2."

"Come sit down." I led Penny Pacino to the couch that Puxton had occupied . . . the piss-ant. I was really happy to see Penny. I had often wondered why she hadn't barged in on me months ago. "Why didn't you try to see me months ago?" I asked.

"I thought you wanted to be alone. At least, that's the impression I got when I spoke to you on the phone. So I vowed to give you a year. Well, the year's up. Why didn't you call me?"

"I was afraid to."

We hugged before we sat down on the couch, and hugged again after we sat down. "It's really good to see you," I said, and then I asked Penny to tell me everything that had happened to her since I had last seen her.

"Well," she began, "I . . ."

I interrupted and said, "You look beautiful."

"Oh, my," she said, primping her hair and blushing. "I do *not* look beautiful. I look awful. But *you*. You look . . . mellow."

"Yeah, you're right. I think I have mellowed a bit. But come on, Penny, talk to me. What's new?"

"Well, Hollywood sucks. It's so pretentious and phony. You can't have a decent conversation with anyone. Everybody talks in résumés. 'How ya doin'?' 'Fine. I just finished a pilot for Twentieth Century-Fox, and I'm about to start a feature for Metro. How about you?' 'Oh, I have a score that's up for an Oscar, and I have two sides on the new

Sinatra album, and I'm just starting a new TV series for NBC.' Christ, it's enough to turn your stomach inside out."

"How's your love life?" I asked.

"None of your business. How's yours?"

"Nonexistent. You know, it's really amazing."

"What's amazing?"

"That you're not married."

"I *know*," said Penny Pacino. "And I'm thirty-five!"

"I'm not married, and I'm fifty-one."

"So let's hurry up and get married before we're so old we have to sit in wheelchairs during the ceremony."

I changed the subject.

We talked for over an hour. Most of our conversation was forced and useless. I thanked Penny for her phone calls over the past year. She said it was no big deal and told me about the weather in Los Angeles. (It had been exceptionally rainy.) I described my chambermaid, Gracie, the hotel elevator operators, and the telephone switchboard girls. Penny spoke at length about an exercise class she was taking in Hollywood. I went into a long and uneventful dissertation regarding the hardships of writing a book, and Penny gave a detailed account of the numerous new high-rise apartment houses along Wilshire Boulevard.

It was awful.

We were boring ourselves, and each other, to death. I knew I would much rather have admitted that I had grown tired of the hotel; that I was sick of staring at the four walls of my suite; and that I wanted very much to go home to Los Angeles. "I want to tell you I love you," I imagined myself saying, "but I'm too scared." And I imagined her saying, "Don't be scared. Tell me." And then I would have said, "I can't. What good would it do? If I ever leave here I could be killed. We'd live like a couple of convicts. What kind of life would that be for you?" But I said none of that. All I did was squander precious time.

And then, just when it all seemed hopeless, we began talking from somewhere down in our souls. For a brief moment Penny and I reached out to each other. At least we tried—and at least it wasn't boring. It began when I admitted what an emotional basket case I was.

"In what respect?" asked Penny.

"In every respect. But mostly when it comes to affairs of the heart."

"Ah, there's that old 'affairs of the heart' again," she said.

"Not my specialty," I admitted.

"That's not true. Way down deep you're a big fat romantic."

"A cynical romantic."

"What's that?"

"A cynical romantic? Oh, that's someone who doesn't believe romance exists but is willing to be proven wrong. Like an agnostic." What I would have preferred to say was that I might be a cynical romantic, but deep down I wished Penny would rehabilitate me and make me the pure romantic I once was. I was convinced she could do it.

"Well, I like you just the way you are," said Penny Pacino. "Cynical romantic or not."

I shook my head disgustedly. "Honestly, Redhead," I said, hating to say what I was about to say, "you wouldn't want any part of me. I'm so set in my ways, it's sickening. I'm moody and irritable. Jesus Christ, I've even got hemorrhoids! And I'll tell you something else. I'm not sure I can get it up anymore."

"You're lying through your teeth," said Penny.

"The *hell* I am. And one thing I *know* I don't want, and that's the pressure of going to bed with a girl half my age and an inch taller than I am, and having to get it up every night."

"Who says you have to get it up *every* night?"

"I don't want the pressure of every *other* night. Or once a week, for that matter."

"I don't know what the hell you're so worried about," Penny said. "You never had any trouble posting in the past. And I'm sure they have all sorts of new ointments and wonder creams . . ."

"To help you get a hard-on?"

"No. For getting rid of hemorrhoids. You give me a month and I'll bet I can cure 'em."

"It's humiliating to even talk about it," I said. "And even if I *could* cure my hemorrhoids, something else—some other debilitating embarrassment—will take their place. I can see myself ten years from now, sitting in a fucking rocking chair with a blanket around my legs, and you wiping the drool away from my mouth every five minutes."

"I wouldn't mind wiping your drool away."

"And I don't think I'm the faithful type at all," I said, hardly believing my ears. "I get tired of everything in six months. Listen, Pen, I'm too old to change my ways, even if I wanted to. And I don't even want to," which was the biggest, baddest lie of all.

"I don't care," she said. "I love you."

I told Penny she was crazier than I was. That's about when she
began to cry. I hated it when Penny cried, but that morning in the
Parker Hotel I felt worse than ever. It was a strange new agony—a hurt
that I had never experienced before with anyone. Watching her sob on
the couch beside me caused a wrenching pain that went right to the
marrow of my bones. Maybe I was tormented so profoundly because
I knew I was going to lose her once and for all . . . that this might be
our last hour together.

Penny must have noticed my anguish. She said she was leaving.
I told Penny I would accompany her down to the lobby. On the way
out of my room we stopped for a moment while she fixed her eyes and
put on a pair of sunglasses. At the elevators, Penny started to say
something, then stopped.

"What were you going to say?"

"Nothing," she answered. "Just this: why don't you leave here and
come back to California with me?"

I couldn't think of a legitimate answer so I said nothing.

Penny took a deep breath, and said, "You know what? I think I'll
forget about England. I think I'll just go out to the airport and go home.
I saw you. That's all I really wanted to do—that and go to F.A.O.
Schwarz. I went to F.A.O. Schwarz first thing this morning. I've done
what I wanted to do, so I think I'll just go home."

I said nothing. I just felt miserable.

In the lobby, Penny asked, "Are you *ever* coming home?"

"No, I don't think so," I said, putting my arm around her shoulders and walking her to the door. "I've tried to leave. I've gotten up
in the morning determined it would be my last day in the Parker Hotel.
I've gone so far as *telling* everyone that it was my last day, and asking
for my bill, and making moving arrangements, and even saying my
good-byes. All that shit. And then I don't do a goddamn thing. I just
stay. And keep staying. Now it's become a joke when I tell anybody it's
my last day. I have a hunch that in some retarded way, I'm happy here.
There's no production company to worry about, or trade papers in
every drugstore and supermarket to make me envious, or critics to read
and get nauseous over, or nitwits yelling, 'Gong!' everywhere I walk.
There's no Polo Lounge, or Schwab's, or Nate and Al's, or Rodeo Drive
to avoid because you'll see someone you know who will ask you what
you're doing these days. 'So what're you up to, Chuck? Got any new
shows comin' out?' The streets of New York seem safer to me than the
streets of Beverly Hills. There's something to be said for that, you

know. Besides, how many patty melts can you eat? How can you live in a place that's always eight-five degrees and fair?" I laughed, but nothing seemed particularly funny.

"Oh!" said Penny suddenly. "I almost forgot. I have something for you. I know you love quotations, and I found one about a week ago in a book I was reading. When I read it I thought of you." Penny pushed around the things in her shoulder bag until she located the scrap of paper she was looking for. "Listen to this: 'Which is a better world, the cocksucking, cunt-lapping, asshole-licking, fornicating, Happyland U.S.A. or the Roman Legion under Marcus Aurelius Antonius? Which is worse, to die with T. J. Jackson at Chancellorsville or live with Johnny Carson in Burbank?' I really like that, don't you?" Penny gave me the scrap of paper.

"It *is* good. Who wrote it?"

"Walker Percy."

"You know," I said, "it's funny. I've been carrying around a quotation for you, too." I pulled a piece of paper out of my pants pocket. "I must have been carrying this note in my pants for months, hoping you would arrive. See how crumpled and worn the paper is? It says, 'In affairs of the heart, I think I would rather suffer the emotional lows, the slings and arrows of defeat, the self-pity, the loneliness and discontent that comes with not knowing what's next, to the boredom and lethargy of a happy, secure household, knowing quite well what the next sentence, hour, and day will bring.' "

"Who wrote that?" sniffed Penny.

"I did."

"Is that how you really feel?"

"I think so."

Three mornings later, at dawn, I checked out of the Parker Hotel.

Nineteen

Friday, August 7, 1981. Boston was just as hot and humid as New York.

I was staying at the Ritz-Carlton Hotel. My room was small, but cool, the air conditioners were ancient, and hummed loudly, but they worked. I sat on the edge of my bed staring at the telephone for what seemed like hours. Finally, I lifted the receiver and called Patricia Watson.

"What are *you* doing in town?" she asked.

"I couldn't stand the four walls of my hotel suite for another minute. So I decided to go home to L.A. by way of Boston."

"Why by way of Boston?"

"So I could see you."

"You could have telephoned."

"I *am* telephoning. You see, Treesh, the way I look at it, it's fate. The Big Matchmaker in the sky can't stand our being apart for more than twelve months at a time, so He arranged for me to come to Boston tonight to see you. It's bigger than both of us, Patricia. Besides, you're the only friend I know of in the entire world that I can talk to these days without feeling like a deranged fool."

"You *are* a deranged fool."

"That's beside the point."

"I can't have dinner with you. I'm going to Wompsockett for the weekend. I promised my brother I'd come."

"You can't. I came all the way from West Fifty-sixth Street in Manhattan just to see you. You can't forsake me after I've done that."

"Oh, for God's sake, cut it out."

"Come on, Patricia, I've got to be more fun than your brother."

"It's a toss-up."

"Like hell it is. Make some excuse and get out of it. Please."

"How long are you going to be in town?"

"Until tomorrow morning."

"*Honestly,* Chuck," moaned Watson.

"Please. You can *always* see your brother."

"I'll call you right back," Treesh said.

She called back in five minutes. "I'm all yours," she said.

"Great! I'll pick you up at eight. Tell me where you want to go and I'll make a reservation."

"Can we eat at the Union Oyster House?" she asked. "I haven't been there in months."

"Absolutely."

"Wonderful. You don't have to pick me up. Let's meet there."

"Fine."

"I'm glad you called," said Patricia Watson.

* * *

There was over an hour wait at the Union Oyster House.

"So much for reservations," I said.

"If you'll just tell the hostess who you are, I'll bet she'll seat us right away," Patricia whispered in my ear.

Who was I? I brooded. I asked Patricia who I should say I was.

"Tell the hostess you're Chuck Barris."

"She won't care. Fame, thank goodness, is fleeting."

"She'll care. She looks like the type who never missed 'The Gong Show.' "

I approached the senescent hostess. She held a clipboard. "May I tell you who I am?" I said.

The elderly lady looked at me as if I were quite odd. "If you want to."

"I'm Sunny Sixkiller."

"I'm Maude," she said.

I stood near Maude, with my hands in my pants pockets, eavesdropping on a swinging-singles couple. They were leaning against a nearby wall. He was saying, "You were with him from Friday until Monday, for Chrissake! How am I supposed to feel about that?" "Don't feel bad, Lew," she replied. "I didn't come *all* weekend."

I returned to Patricia.

"Did you tell the hostess who you are?" she asked.

"Yes."

"What did she say?"

"She said it would be about an hour."

We left the restaurant and window-shopped through Quincy Mar-

ket. Later, we sat outside on a bench in the marketplace a few blocks
from the restaurant and talked about old times.

"Do you miss your job?" Patricia asked.

"Which one?"

"The Company," she replied.

"Which company?" I asked, slipping out of my sport jacket.

"Oh, come off it. The CIA."

"No." I bent down, hiked up my slacks and tied my shoelaces
tighter.

"How about the television company?" asked Treesh.

"Not at all. You know what I *do* miss?"

"What?"

"Being with you."

Patricia Watson was thirty-one. She was about my height, with
brownish blond hair that she wore in bangs. She had great tits and a
superb ass which she always kept hidden behind the same conservative
clothes she had worn as a Radcliffe student.

"I remember you when you were a Cliffie," I said.

"I know. You don't have to remind me. Do you know I'll be
thirty-eight next month?"

"Jesus, I thought you were thirty-one."

"Thirty-one! Don't I wish it." Watson giggled. "That would have
made me fourteen when you interviewed me."

I had interviewed Patricia Watson when she applied for a position
with the CIA back in 1964. I was one of many she had been required
to talk to. She came to the interview wearing a blue blazer, a tailored
white button-down oxford shirt, and a charcoal-gray pleated skirt. She
was wearing the same outfit now. Once a Cliffie, always a Cliffie.

"What?"

"I just mumbled, once a Cliffie, always a Cliffie."

"Brilliant."

Patricia Watson was a bright, aggressive girl, and loved working
for the Company. She had found her way through the maze of CIA
bureaucracy with ease, being promoted from one position to another.

"I'm sorry, Treesh, what did you say?"

"I'm not *that* boring, am I?"

"Of course not. I was just thinking about something else."

"About what?"

"About you."

* * *

We dated occasionally. Then we became lovers—when time allowed. We had wonderful moments. And awful fights. I started most of them. I wanted to know why she wouldn't marry me.

"Because," she would answer, "if I said yes you'd run for the hills. You just like the chase. You're like a child. You want what you can't have."

"That's not true," I would reply, wondering if it was.

"Besides, I'm not ready yet. I'm not ready to quit the Company."

"But you don't have to quit the Company."

"When I'm ready to get married, I'll quit the Company," she would always say.

And I would become livid, and itch for a fight. I'd usually get one. And then I'd pay her back by standing her up. Something less than adult behavior on my part, to say the least. Eventually, we stopped seeing each other. More accurately, Patricia stopped seeing me. She always had an excuse: sorry, not tonight. Sorry, not this weekend. I'm sorry, Chuck, but I'm really busy.

And so it went. We stayed in touch.

She *did* call me more than anyone else while I was hiding in the Parker Hotel. They were usually quickies. She'd just ask me how I was, and then hang up.

* * *

Another couple joined us on the bench outside the Union Oyster House.

Patricia Watson lowered her voice, and said, "Tell me how you've changed."

"Changed?"

"Over the last year. Since I saw you last. Since you've been a recluse."

"My johnson tends to drip more after I've finished peeing. I get these huge stains on my slacks. I have to wear dark suits now."

"Come on. Be serious."

"Okay, you want to know how I've changed? I'll tell you. I look at every day like it's my last."

"What do you mean?"

"Well, during the past few months I've been haunted by this feeling that I'm—I don't know how to explain it—running out of time. Consequently I find myself looking at things more intently than before. It's not a frightening phobia, or anything like that. It doesn't bother me, you know; give me sleepless nights, or anything like that. It's just something keen, something that's been with me for, like I say, months.

So when I look now, I *really* look. I study what I'm looking at as though I may never see it again. It's really funny. I stare at buildings, and paintings, and parades, and people, and store windows, and ice cream sodas, and they all look so much different than they used to look."

The other couple sitting on the bench beside us was listening. I glared at them and they looked away.

"Go on," ordered Patricia.

"All right. Another thing I've been doing lately is reading as much as I can. I've been reading a lot of the old classics. I never read them when I was a kid. I've been reading books like *The Mill on the Floss,* and *The Red Badge of Courage,* and lots of Faulkner and Hemingway."

"Is that why you left the Parker Hotel?" Patricia asked. "To get new books?" There was more than a touch of sarcasm in her voice.

"I left the Parker Hotel because I wanted to see old friends again, and whatever's left of my family. I want to go back to Los Angeles and see the people I worked with, and the places I hung out in over the last fifteen years. Dull as rat shit, isn't it?"

"Yep," said Patricia Watson, "it sure is."

We left the bench and walked back to the restaurant. On the way, Watson said, "This feeling that you're running out of time. It doesn't bother you? Is that true? It really doesn't bother you?"

"Not really. I discovered something Camus wrote. He said, 'One of our contemporaries is cured of his torment simply by contemplating a landscape.' I know what Camus meant, and he's right. That quote's helped me a lot."

"Ummmm," said Watson.

The Union Oyster House was noisy. It seemed everyone was talking at the same time, and as loudly as possible. The restaurant was crammed with people, and waitresses in T-shirts and jeans, and models of famous sailing ships, and large framed pictures of old Boston hanging on the walls. A Scott Joplin tape played in the background. The rush and excitement bothered me; my metamorphosis from Parker Hotel recluse to Oyster House patron had not gone quite as smoothly as I had anticipated.

We were seated at a small table. All of Boston had carved their initials on the tabletop. Our waitress approached us from behind my left shoulder and popped a cheery hello. It scared the hell out of me.

"Are we a little jumpy tonight?" asked Patricia Watson.

"A little," I replied.

We ordered tons of food. We had clam chowder, steamed clams, lobster, fried oysters and scallops, fresh corn on the cob, and coleslaw. The bread was freshly baked and oven warm. We drank beer and Coke, and finally hot coffee. I said, "I think my bladder's going to burst," and excused myself to go to the men's room.

When I returned, our waitress asked if we wanted dessert. I said, "No, thank you, we're way too full," but she brought it anyway. It was hot gingerbread with homemade whipped cream. We ate it. It was delicious.

After dinner we walked down Union Street. During the walk we put our arms around each others' waists. We discussed movies Treesh had seen, and books we both had read. "Do you want to come to my apartment?" Treesh eventually asked.

"Of course."

"Then fetch a cab."

It was a few minutes after midnight when we walked into Patricia Watson's apartment. She took my sport coat—I had been carrying it over my arm all evening—and hung it, along with her blue blazer, on a clothes tree in the hall. She turned on the air conditioner and started a recording of Beethoven's sonatas for violin and piano. We plopped down into two cozy love seats that faced each other. Treesh sat on the edge of her seat, leaning forward, her hands clasped together on top of her closed knees. Her folded hands kept her skirt in place. We studied each other.

Funny, I thought, how appearances can be so deceiving. I look disheveled and unorganized, Patricia upright and prim, when in truth I'm anything but unorganized, and Patricia is anything but prim. Far from it. I wouldn't exactly have accused her of being prim in Hawaii.

* * *

Maui, November 1969. It was three in the morning. We were in a hotel bungalow near the ocean. I had tied Patricia's hands behind her back with a pair of my high black socks, and was fucking her from one end of the bed to the other. And she was loving it. Later, I threw her naked body over my shoulder and started for the beach. I carried the nude Watson past other bungalows, the hotel swimming pool, and several lines of cabanas. We were probably the only two guests still awake. The hotel's lawns, pool, cabanas, and beaches were empty. I really didn't care if they were or not.

Patricia Watson kicked and wiggled. She hissed in my ear, "Put me *down!* What are you *doing?* Someone will see us. Put me *down!* Take me back to the room, for God's sake. Put me *down.*"

I didn't put her down. I took her to the ocean and threw her in. Her hands were still tied behind her back. She flopped naked in the shallow surf like a beached fish. She choked and coughed and gagged. I grabbed hold of her hair and pushed her head under the water. I said I would stop if she promised to suck my cock. Crying, she said she would. And she did. On her knees with her hands tied behind her back. In the moonlight. At four-thirty in the morning on a beach in Maui. I came in her mouth, pulled her out of the water, and untied her hands. We walked back to our bungalow. On the way she said, "That was great."

* * *

And now she sat opposite me in her pleasant, conservative clothes, her knees together, her hands folded above them. She smiled and said, "I'm ready to quit."

"Quit what?"

"The Company. I've had enough. I just want to settle down and find the same peace of mind you're looking for."

"Settle down?" I asked, nervously uncrossing and crossing my legs.

"Get married. Have kids. Do normal things."

"That's great."

"You don't believe me, do you?"

"No."

"Then why do you think I'm telling you all this?"

"A trial balloon. To hear how it sounds. You do that every so often, just to hear how it sounds. So the thought doesn't atrophy in your head."

Patricia Watson sat back in her love seat. "Honestly, Chuck, sometimes you can be rather annoying."

"Sorry."

Watson sighed and lit a cigarette. "Didn't I always say I would get married when I was fed up with the Company? I *always* said I would marry when I didn't want to work anymore. Well, I don't want to work anymore. I've had it with the Company."

"So who are you going to marry?"

"You."

"Sure," I said, breaking out in a cold sweat.

Patricia Watson noticed. She burst out laughing, kicking up her legs and throwing her arms above her head. "Wow!" she said, still laughing. "I've really thrown you for a loop, haven't I? Look at you. You're as pale as a ghost. And look at your face: it's dripping with sweat. You're the real marrying kind, aren't you? Just mention the word and you age ten years. Poor baby. Give me a kiss."

Patricia Watson pushed herself out of her love seat and walked toward me.

That's when I shot her.

* * *

I reached down and pulled up my right pants leg. Strapped in a holster just above my ankle was an AMT 380 "backup," a small stainless steel automatic whose bullet could drop a horse.

When Treesh saw the gun, she whispered, "Oh, my God."

The blast was deafening. It scared the hell out of me. Dazed and frightened, I watched Treesh lurch backward into her love seat, right herself, knock over an end table, and then trip over it and fall to the floor. She landed on her back with an expression of pure surprise on her face. Her mouth was open and she was probably moaning, but I couldn't hear her. My ears were ringing from the gun's blast. The room was filled with smoke that wouldn't disappear. I smelled the cordite, then tasted it.

I stood and looked down at Patricia Watson.

Watson the fucking mole. Watson the traitor, the plotter, the killer. Watson murdered Byrd, and Picard, and God knows who else —and tried to murder me. Then, horrified, I realized she was trying to stand up. I watched her hands clawing the air, searching for something to hold on to. The right side of her face, from scalp to chin, had suddenly vanished under a layer of thick, dark blood. I pulled the trigger a second time. The remains of Patricia Watson rose in the air, then came down to rest across the overturned end table. Her back was arched grotesquely, her arms and legs flung out to the sides.

I began to shake as I stood over Watson's body.

Why had she done it? I wondered. Why had she become a mole; a double agent—a traitor? Was it her fucking ambition? Could it have been that rising as high as she had in the CIA wasn't enough? Is that why she decided to play both sides—one team wasn't good enough for her? Did she have to make a name for herself on both teams, meet the challenge of playing both sides successfully? Or was it something else entirely?

I flopped into the seat Watson had been sitting in. I felt something hard when I landed. Tucked between the seat cushion and the chair's arm was an automatic, loaded and cocked.

* * *

An hour later, I met Robert Lawrence Puxton III in the bar of the Ritz-Carlton Hotel.

"Done?" he asked.

"Done."

"Atta boy!" he said. "Congratulations."

"Thanks."

"Here's to you," said Puxton. We tapped Scotch glasses and drank our drinks in one gulp. Puxton ordered refills. "How do you feel?" he asked.

"Rotten."

After a moment or two Puxton said, "Was there any trouble?"

"No. Actually, it was easier than I thought."

"Was she suspicious?"

"I don't know," I answered, "but I didn't take any chances. I used all the tricks. I carried my sport coat to let her know I didn't have a gun in my belt. I pulled up my pant legs and tied my shoelaces to show her I didn't have a gun strapped to either one of my ankles. Just for good measure, I let her put her arm around my waist. I even let her hang up my sport coat in her apartment. If she was suspicious, I think the tricks cooled her. By the time we made ourselves cozy, I guess she figured I was clean."

"She didn't suspect anything when you went to the men's room at the restaurant?"

"I guess not. She should have. It's not like her to be careless. I guess I got lucky. By the way, Pux, how old was that messenger boy? He looked like he just got out of high school."

"He's just out of Harvard," replied Puxton. "He's twenty-three. He's got a real baby face, doesn't he? But he's a good kid. Was the gun he passed you okay?"

"Yeah, I guess so. But I almost shit when your baby-faced messenger boy said he didn't have a silencer for me."

"How could you strap a silencer to your ankle?"

"Yeah, I know. But I hate the noise. It's just something else to worry about."

Puxton ordered two Scotches. He waited until he was served his, and then, while stirring his drink with a mixer, asked, "Do you think she had anything in mind for you?"

"I think so."

Puxton whipped his head up so that he could see my face, and said, "No shit. How do you know?"

"After I killed her I found a cocked automatic in her chair, tucked down between the cushion and the armrest. It was stashed in the only chair she sat in while we were together."

"No *shit!*"

"No shit, Puxton."

"Scary," said Puxton quietly, returning his eyes to his drink.

I noticed Puxton was acting rather subdued and unlike his usual boisterous self. Maybe my mood was contagious. "Pux," I said, "you gotta do me a favor."

"Anything, Chuck."

"You have to make sure Oliver doesn't go back on his word. He promised me peace of mind, and you have to make sure he keeps his promise."

"He will," said Puxton. "Oliver may be an asshole, but his word is good."

"I hope so," I replied. I explained to Puxton that I had told Oliver on the telephone that I would take the Watson job only if he made a deal with the Soviets to get their hit teams off my back. Trade if he had to. Return a couple of Russians in exchange for my life. Oliver had said he would think it over and get back to me. I told Simon I wouldn't leave the Parker Hotel unless I heard from him. He telephoned two days later and told me it was a deal. I had left for Boston the next morning.

"It's an important arrangement for me, Pux."

Puxton said, "I know."

"It's the arrangement that makes it possible for me to live happily ever after."

"I know," repeated Puxton.

"Just make sure Oliver doesn't forget."

"He won't," Pux replied. "I promise you he won't."

Three hours later, I telephoned Penny Pacino in California.

Twenty

We were married at the Beverly Hills Hotel.

The ceremony was in one of those ornate rooms off the main lobby. I forget the room's name. (They all have names.) To the left of the room's entrance is a jewelry shop that sells garish rings, made of large chunks of gold and diamonds, and ostentatious gold wristwatches. To the right, and around the corner from the room, is the Polo Lounge where men and women pretend to eat while they're talking deals. The deals run the gamut from major motion picture and television commitments to getting laid. Somewhere between the ostentatious jewelry and the sweet talk, Penny Pacino and I became man and wife.

I loved getting married, which shocked the hell out of Penny. I woke up at six that morning (the wedding was scheduled for noon) singing. The singing woke Penny up. She was immediately suspicious.

"Why are you singing?" she asked, half asleep, with slits for eyes and a furrowed brow.

"Because," I replied, "I'm happy."

She said I had something up my sleeve, and added, "You better show up."

My good mood actually alarmed her. I guess she had good reason to be concerned.

On the ride to the hotel, I had our driver Danny cue up a Beatles cassette to "All You Need Is Love" and play it over and over. Penny became seriously troubled. She said, "I think you really *are* happy! I think you really *do* want to get married."

"I do," I answered. "I do. I do."

Penny's confusion was dear.

The ceremony itself stank. It was hot in the ornate room (there were many excuses about the stuffed air-conditioning ducts), and the justice of the peace—a man Penny dug up—included a résumé of my shows in his prologue that really made me sick. "We have come here," he solemnly said, "to join together Penny Pacino and Chuck Barris. You all know Chuck Barris; the creator of "The Dating Game," "The Newlywed Game," "The Family Game," "The Game Game," "Dream Girl of 1968," "Operation Entertainment," "How's Your Mother-in-law?" and many others. Chuck Barris, who most recently brought us such hits as "The Rah-Rah Show," "Treasure Hunt," "Leave It to the Women," "The Dollar-Ninety-Eight Beauty Show," and "The Gong Show." *The* Chuck Barris, who I am sure will be back with new shows on television soon, to entertain and . . ."

I looked at Penny with an expression that implied I was about to either throw up or boot the idiot in his fucking nuts. Her eyes begged me to be patient.

After the ceremony was over, the justice of the peace shook my hand and told me how pleased he was to have become a part of our lives. I told the fuckhead I almost kicked his balls off. "The only reason I didn't," I growled, "is because I love my wife, and she would not have approved."

Of course, once the tasteless minister got into the heart of the sermon—the part about "in sickness and in health, until death do us part"—Penny and I sort of froze. Our four hands were joined in a knot in front of us, squeezing and sweating like crazy. But when the jerk-off justice of the peace said, "I now pronounce you man and wife," I knew I had just done the best thing I would ever do in my whole entire life.

There was a wild party following the ceremony. It lasted exactly one hour. Penny and I drank an enormous amount of champagne, which didn't seem to faze us, and we hugged and kissed a lot of people.

At three o'clock everybody filed outdoors and lined up on either side of the red carpet that ran from the hotel's entrance to the carport where our limousine was waiting. When Penny and I stepped through the entrance doors, we were startled. There was an unexpectedly large number of people yelling, and cheering, and waiting to throw rice and confetti: friends, family, fans, newspaper reporters and photographers, strangers, passersby, and the curious; perhaps a hundred people in each row. As we started down the red carpet, everyone began hollering good tidings and pummeling us with all sorts of debris. Halfway down the aisle, I saw the gun.

Twenty one

The gun was a Walther PKB. A perfect assassin's gun. The hand that held it was white, with a gold pinky ring on its little finger. Suddenly the cheers and good wishes dulled in my ears to a faraway sound. My face became numb to the rice and confetti.

I was terrified.

When would he shoot? Would it be too difficult to get off a shot? Too many people, crowded too closely together? I grabbed Penny's arm and pulled her toward the limousine, almost running the rest of the way. Our driver, Danny, was standing by the open rear door, smiling. His expression—the grin, the joy—was foolish. Who beams from ear to ear when someone is about to be shot to death?

I pushed Penny into the automobile, perhaps a bit too roughly. She plopped into the backseat, her legs splayed, her little straw hat tilted forward on her forehead like a drunk's. "Jesus Christ!" she boomed, pulling her skirt in place and fixing her hat. I sat down beside her, yanked the door out of Danny's hand, and slammed it shut. Our driver looked perplexed. I motioned with my head: let's get going! He seemed to take forever walking around the car to his seat. I shouted, "Leave, Danny! *Now!*"

Danny glanced at me through the rearview mirror. His eyes were confused, but he pulled away from the curb with a screech and shot off down the boulevard.

I turned to Penny. I could see that she was worried. She knew that I had become terribly anxious about something.

"You're white as a sheet," she said.

I didn't answer. I turned away and stared out my window.

"You can't let yourself get so upset," she continued. "It's going to be okay. It's going to be wonderful. We're going to be very happy together. Our marriage is going to be the best thing that ever happened to us."

My exact thoughts at the altar.

But now I said nothing. I was relieved that Penny was misled. Let her think I was in the throes of a bridegroom's remorse. If she wanted to believe I was pale and shaken because I had suddenly realized I was finally and unequivocally married, so be it. She obviously hadn't seen the gun. Fine. Her ignorance, considering the facts, was truly bliss.

And then Penny laughed. It was a loud, robust laugh. "Wow," she said, scratching the top of my head, "I knew some sort of aftershock was going to take place, but I didn't expect it to erupt so soon."

I said nothing. I just continued staring out my window, thinking. Thinking.

Who could it have been? Who was the killer? Was he CIA? Had they put a contract out on me because of my book? The Company knew I was writing *Confessions of a Dangerous Mind*. They had warned me not to write it. Even threatened me on one or two occasions. Veiled threats to be sure, like Puxton's, but threats none the less. And now that I had finished, had the time come to eliminate me before I handed over the manuscript to my publisher? I wondered if they would do such a thing. Why not? It had been done before.

"Look," said Penny. "Here, look at my nose. No warts, right? Not one damn wart since they pronounced us man and wife. Didn't you say as soon as they pronounced us man and wife, warts would start growing on my nose? Well, do you see a wart?"

"No warts," I said, without looking away from my window.

Maybe, I thought to myself—maybe it was someone from the KGB. It wouldn't have surprised me at all, knowing Simon Oliver as I did. Did I really expect Oliver to honor his half of the bargain? Of course not. I must have been nuts to think he would. Why would he? He hated me from the day he met me. I wouldn't be surprised if the anti-Semitic asshole told Moscow Center the exact time and place of my wedding. Him, trading Soviet spies to save *my* ass? Fat chance. The prick.

"Are we stopping at Winchells?" asked Danny. We usually stopped for doughnuts and coffee on the way to the airport.

I mumbled no.

"Am I allowed to ask where you two are going on your honeymoon?" he inquired.

"Yes, of course," answered Penny cheerfully, glad to be talking to *someone*. She leaned forward on the edge of the seat so she could be closer to Danny. My wife was so cute. I loved her so much. I heard her start our itinerary from the top, and then my mind wandered again.

Maybe it was some loon: an ex-"Gong Show" psycho. A Harley Windsor, or someone like that. It could have been any number of nitwits. My impending marriage was public knowledge. The newspapers had announced when and where it would take place. At least half my staff had come to me during the previous week, worried and complaining. They were concerned about how we were going to keep the creeps and weirdos away from the hotel, especially when Penny and I went out to the limousine. And there it was, that goddamn gun, at exactly the place they were all most troubled about.

So maybe Simon Oliver did keep his word. Jesus, I said to myself, wouldn't it be just like God to do something like that. He saves me from the Russians, but lets me get blasted by some son of a bitch lunatic I've never even thought about. Go know. Just when everything was getting to be perfect.

"SHIT! PISS! FUCK!" I hollered.

"What?" asked Penny, alarmed again.

"Nothing," I answered, returning to my window and my thoughts.

I wondered how I could find out who the killer was. My only clues were that he was white, and that he wore a gold pinky ring with a deep blue stone at its center. Also, that he carried a Walther PKB. This whole thing, I thought to myself, has the makings of a good game show. "Find the Killer." No, that's not a good title. "Man Hunt." Better. "Wanted!" Like the poster. That's good. That's *very* good. An hour drama. No, a half-hour. Once a week.

"WANTED!" I said aloud.

"What?" Penny asked again, showing signs of wear and tear.

"I think I've got a great idea for a game show, Redhead."

"Oh, no."

"I'm serious," I said, sitting up, pushing the thought of the last few harrowing minutes out of my mind, and moving closer to her. "I think I'm onto a great idea."

"Are you serious?"

"I just said I'm serious."

"Back to television?"

"Why not?" I asked. "I was always pretty good at it—and if the idea's fun to do, what's the problem? And this show *would* be fun to do." I moved around so that I was almost kneeling in front of Penny. "It's a half-hour program. Once a week. Each week we dramatize a crime: a murder, an embezzlement, a political assassination, a big-time jewel robbery, a . . . a . . . ."

"A spy case," said Penny, sitting up straight. "Someone steals some important government papers."

"Perfect! A spy story. Or a kidnapping. Or blackmail. You know, blackmail in Big Business. An important executive walks off with brand-new classified computer plans and threatens to sell them to a rival company. Or how about a mean and rotten guy, with the gift of gab, who makes millions of dollars by talking kind and gentle senior citizens into investing their pensions in bogus get-rich-quick schemes. The material is endless."

"So?" said Penny. "What's the point?"

"The point is to be the first person to recognize the thief—or the murderer, or the assassin—turn him in, and win a big prize. We'll take the key actor—the one who plays the killer, or the one who plays the cat burglar—send him out to some part of the country, and put a big reward on his head. The person who spots him first, and calls us, will get the reward! We'll freeze-frame the last shot of the show—the last close-up of the villain; the shot where he's running out the door, or jumping out a window, or jumping off the train, or whatever—focus on his face. Then we'll super a wanted poster over it—you know, the one that says WANTED on top, and the amount of the reward on the bottom—and give clues to what part of the country he'll be in."

"This man," Penny announced, full of enthusiasm, "was last seen in the Cincinnati–Columbus–Dayton area. The first person with any information leading to his capture will get a ten-thousand-dollar reward!"

"YOU GOT IT!" I shouted, standing up and hitting my head. I sat down again. "Only the reward will be a *hundred* thousand dollars. This show is prime time!"

"Calm down," said Penny, beaming. She really didn't want me to calm down.

I tried to calm down. I thought of the gun and the gold pinky ring for a few seconds, and decided there was nothing I could do about it. Not at that moment. "And if there's nothing you can do about it," Jim Byrd used to say, "learn to live with it." I would just have to learn to live with it.

"What are you thinking about?" asked Penny.

"I was thinking that if the fugitive wasn't caught during that week, we could bring him back for another episode, double the reward, and send him out again to another part of the country."

"Great!" said our driver, Danny, over his shoulder.

"Here we go again," said Penny. "From the frying pan into the grate."

"Into the fire," I laughed.

As the limousine passed through the entrance to the Los Angeles International Airport, the Beatles cassette began playing its last song. I turned up the volume and Danny, Penny, and I sang:

> *Ob-la-di ob-la-da life goes on bra*
> *La-la how the life goes on.*

> *Ob-la-di ob-la-da life goes on bra*
> *La-la how the life goes on.*